MW00475421

## Praise for *Friction*

With blinding insight, Roger Dooley conveys the wisdom of seeking attainment not by trying to climb over barriers but by removing them. Better than I've ever seen, *Friction* offers takeaways that allow us, systematically, to recognize and reduce obstacles to success.

—Robert B. Cialdini, *New York Times* and *Wall Street Journal* bestselling author of *Influence* and *Pre-Suasion*

For a decade I have been incessantly repeating the same phrase when I advise governments: "If you want to encourage people to do something, make it easy." The same advice works for firms. What do Amazon, Apple, Google, and Netflix have in common? They made life easier for their consumers by removing what Dooley calls "friction". Reading this book will arm any manager with a mental can of WD-40.

—Richard Thaler, Nobel Laureate and *New York Times* bestselling coauthor of *Nudge*

Friction, like entropy, is a fact of the universe—but friction, unlike entropy, can be reduced. Roger Dooley's new book is an important look at how to decrease the friction in your business, your marketing, and your life.

—Ryan Holiday, bestselling author of *The Obstacle Is the Way*

Every organization squanders time, money, and effort doing things wrong or doing the wrong things. Roger Dooley calls this nefarious force "friction." And in his smart and practical book, he shows you how to see friction and extinguish it. In a time when everyone has to do more with less, this book is an important read.

—Daniel H. Pink, *New York Times* bestselling author of *When* and *To Sell Is Human*

Friction is the enemy of success. It's hard enough to create something great. Don't make it hard to adopt it. Roger will show you the way.

—Guy Kawasaki, bestselling author of *The Art of The Start* and former chief evangelist of Apple Inc.

Understanding the enormous (and often hidden) costs of friction is enlightening. Making your business as frictionless as possible is what will make it both a lot less stressful, and a lot more profitable. After absorbing this magnificent teaching, you'll know how to do exactly that.

—Bob Burg, bestselling coauthor of *The Go-Giver* and *The Go-Giver Influencer*

Friction is everywhere. From what we buy to the fate of nations. And once you read Roger Dooley's *Friction*, you'll understand both its power and how you can harness it.

—Jonah Berger, Wharton professor and bestselling author of *Contagious* and *Invisible Influence*

Once you read *Friction*, there's no going back. You'll see friction everywhere, and you'll want to do something about it. The many case studies and anecdotes Dooley includes provide a road map for friction reduction.

—Nir Eyal, author of *Hooked*

Dooley's book will bring instant efficiency to any task you're tackling. An instant classic.

—Mike Michalowicz, author of *Profit First* and *Clockwork*

Roger Dooley's *Friction* is a must-read for any business leader who believes change should be the life blood for survival. It addresses the essence of transformation—and details of what it takes to convert theory into action.

—Martin Lindstrom, *New York Times* bestselling author of *Buyology* and *Small Data*

At WD-40 Company we know that physical friction is costly and damaging. In this book, Dooley shows that intangible friction can be even worse. He exposes the friction that surrounds us in our everyday lives as customers, employees, and citizens, and shows how understanding friction can lead to disruptive growth and personal success. Moving from friction to flow enables, encourages, and motivates, and understanding the power of flow will change the way you live and work.

—Garry Ridge, President and CEO of WD-40 Company

*Friction* is another great read from Roger Dooley. In a business world where companies spend lots of time and effort to make their own processes more efficient, few are paying attention to what makes the lives of the people they serve easier. In this comprehensive and highly readable book, Dooley demonstrates how devoting resources to easing the lives of clients and customers pays big dividends later. After you read *Friction*, you'll never see your own business (or anyone else's) the same way again.

—Art Markman, PhD, author of *Smart Thinking, Smart Change* and *Bring Your Brain to Work*

Roger Dooley's well-crafted and relentlessly useful book shows the power of putting on "friction goggles"—how organizations can become so much more effective, and so much less frustrating, when leaders focus on what ought to be easier to do and what ought to be harder.

—Robert Sutton, Stanford professor and coauthor of *Scaling Up Excellence*

Dooley shows how hidden frictions appear throughout organizations. The book contains practical actions to liberate employee effort, reduce bureaucracy, and heighten customer satisfaction. Its valuable takeaways make this a must-read for all managers.

—Paul J. Zak, PhD, author of *The Trust Factor*

Roger has written a practical and entertaining guide to the most overlooked driver of human behavior: friction. Those of us who spend our lives applying behavioral science research to real-world problems are well-acquainted with this powerful, yet subtle, force. However, up until now, there's never been a book that has comprehensively covered the topic. Whether you're a curious reader looking for a fun read or a business person looking for guidance, this book is for you. Highly recommended.

—Jason Hreha, Global Head of Behavioral Sciences of Walmart, Inc.

Roger Dooley nails it. An essential guide to winning in a consumer-driven economy.

—Mark Schaefer, author of *Marketing Rebellion*

Roger Dooley's new book *Friction* is exactly what your company needs to read before your next big strategic planning session. Dooley hits all the trends I'm seeing happen over the next few years and offers actionable insights. Put this book to work for you.

—Chris Brogan, *New York Times* bestselling author of *Trust Agents*

*Friction* is an instant classic. This profound book will open your eyes to the hidden friction points within your business as well as in your personal life and cause you to start asking the question: *How can you reduce these friction points to build a more profitable company and lead a more enjoyable life?*

—Ryan Levesque, #1 USA TODAY's Best-Selling Books author of *Choose* and *Ask*

*Friction* is one of the few books that not only enhances what you know, but changes how you see. A must-read if you want customers and prospects to stop pondering and start acting.

—Jay Baer, founder of Convince & Convert LLC and bestselling coauthor of *Talk Triggers*

For decades to come, the companies that will thrive will be those that relentlessly pursue an effortless customer experience. In *Friction,* Roger Dooley illustrates this new reality and shows how to achieve it.

—John Padgett, Chief Experience and Innovation Officer of Carnival Corp.

Friction burns and it opens the door for competitors to disrupt you simply by delivering a more intuitive, familiar, or modern experience. Here, Dooley opens the door for you to disrupt yourself.

—Brian Solis, digital analyst, anthropologist, and author of *X: The Experience When Business Meets Design*

Dooley's latest book shines a light on an important topic—friction. Too often, "how we work" creates bad, unnecessary friction resulting in frustration and lost potential. Conversely, good or necessary friction can make us change our habits and shake us from the complacency that plagues all too many organizations. Strong leaders recognize friction and ensure that they eliminate the bad kind and promote the good.

—Lisa Bodell, founder and CEO of FutureThink
and author of *Why Simple Wins*

History has shown that every industry is a ticking time bomb waiting for someone to disrupt by creating a better way. *Friction* will allow you to futureproof your business and see things as no one else in your industry does.

—John Jantsch, author of *Duct Tape Marketing*
and *The Referral Engine*

Many people know and talk about friction in experience but few do anything about it. Roger's book helps us see the friction that exists all around us, decide what is good and what is bad friction, and shows us what leading organizations do with their own friction. It's now up to us to do something about it. Our customers, clients, patients, and citizens are waiting.

—Adrian Swinscoe, *Forbes* contributor
and author of *How to Wow*

# FRICTION

# FRICTION

## THE UNTAPPED FORCE THAT CAN BE YOUR MOST POWERFUL ADVANTAGE

ROGER DOOLEY

NEW YORK CHICAGO SAN FRANCISCO ATHENS
LONDON MADRID MEXICO CITY MILAN
NEW DELHI SINGAPORE SYDNEY TORONTO

1 2 3 5 6 7 8 9 LCR 24 23 22 21 20 19

ISBN 978-1-260-13569-5
MHID 1-260-13569-1

e-ISBN 978-1-260-13570-1
e-MHID 1-260-13570-5

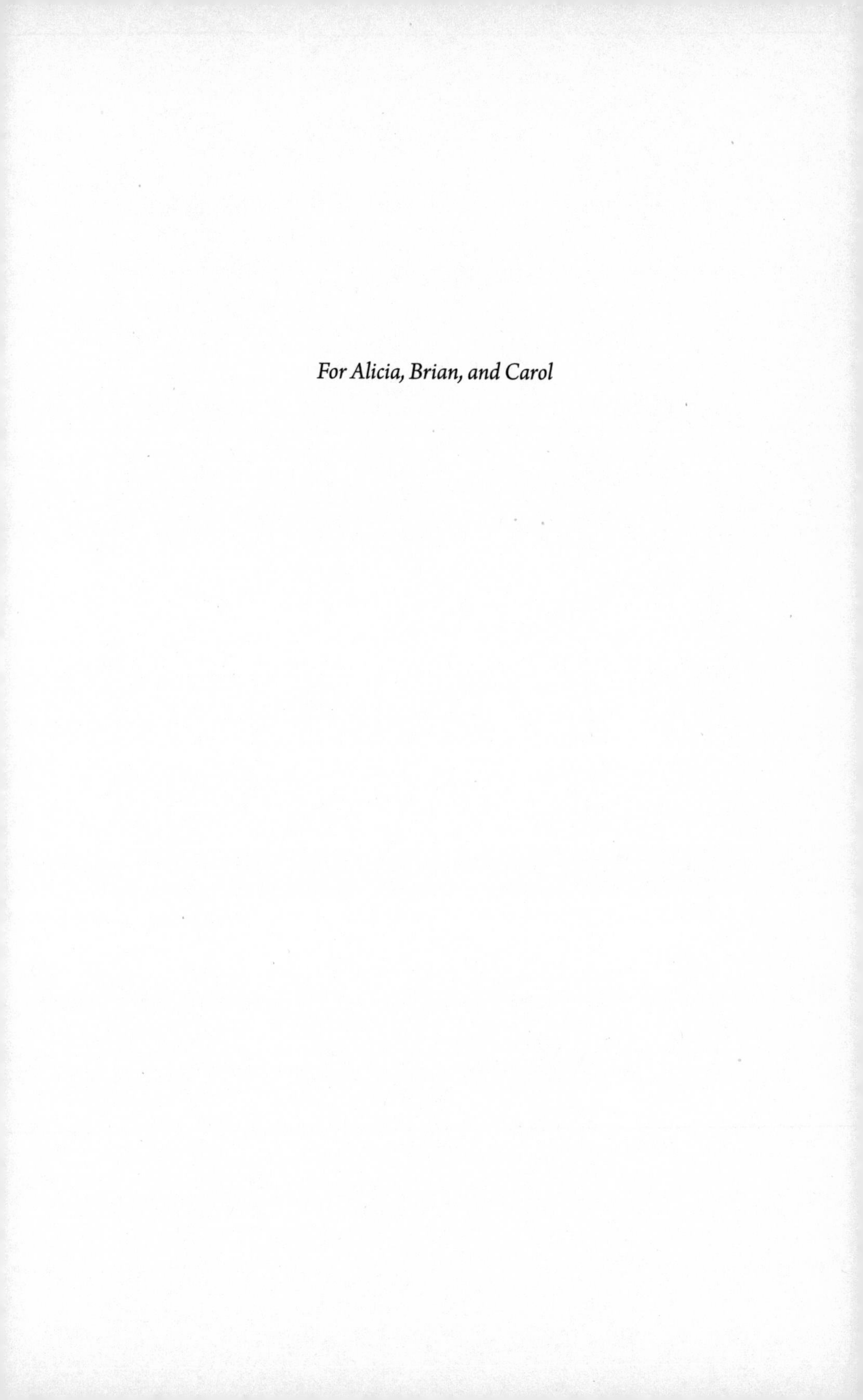

*For Alicia, Brian, and Carol*

# Contents

# Introduction

Do you read introductions?

I usually don't. At best, I skim them. Most authors use them to explain why they wrote the book. Then, the author summarizes the sections and chapters, telling you what lies ahead.

If you want to know what's coming, glance at the table of contents.

Instead, I'm going to start with a short fable . . . a modern-day fable, of course. If you aren't a fan of fables, don't worry, the rest of the book will be more traditional in style. If you *really* don't like fables, feel free to skip ahead to the first chapter.

## THE FRICTION GOGGLES—A MODERN FABLE

Evelyn and Aiden were senior managers at Packard Packaging, a midsize supplier of cardboard containers and other shipping materials. It was Saturday morning, and the office was empty. They were in the big conference room, hurrying to put the finishing touches on a presentation for the CEO Monday morning. The pair had been tasked with cutting costs by 10 percent in the Customer Service department.

"Sales are down, and the competition is brutal," the CEO had explained. "We have zero chance of hitting our year-end profit target if we don't get costs in line with sales right away." Evelyn and Aiden groaned inwardly when they heard that their target was 10 percent. This wasn't the first time cuts had to be made. In a previous round, they had installed an interactive voice menu system to process incoming calls. The CEO had been delighted when he saw that the new system reduced the calls handled by agents by 20 percent. A few open positions didn't have to be filled; one agent left to take a new job. Expenses were lower, and nobody had to be fired.

But this time, cutting an additional 10 percent was going to hurt. The agents taking the calls were already working at capacity. Evelyn had come up with some additional tasks that could be handled by the voice menu system. "We've got a list of the most common questions agents get asked, so we'll build a new question-and-answer menu. And, the IT department says they can fix it so if a customer wants to know the delivery status of an order, they can enter the order number right on their phone. No agent needed!"

Aiden agreed that this looked like the best solution. They analyzed the call volume and guessed that they could reduce the number of agents by the mandated 10 percent. Evelyn supervised the call center staff and didn't look forward to choosing which agents would have to go. And, she knew that scheduling problems would multiply. It was already hard enough to get agents to cover the extended hours the call center had to maintain.

• • •

The pair had worked out the details during the week and needed only a few hours Saturday morning to finish the presentation slides for Monday's meeting. "I can't believe we're the only ones in the office," Aiden said. Evelyn nodded, reaching for a donut. She had bought a dozen, thinking they could share them with anyone else working on Saturday. To her surprise, there was nobody else there. Then again, it was her first Saturday visit in months.

"I think everyone is working so hard after the last round of reductions that they can't wait to get out of the office for a couple of days. A few years ago, Saturday mornings were a lot busier in here," she said.

"And somehow I don't think the cuts we're proposing are going to make people feel better about the company," Aiden added glumly.

Evelyn was closing the donut box when a head peeked around the corner and said, "Hey, can I have one of those?" She and Aiden both jumped. When she saw who it was, she slid the box over. "Sure, take two, Sam. I bought way more than we needed."

Sam was the head of sales, and was the last person Evelyn expected to see on a Saturday. "I had to swing by to pick up some paperwork. I'm jumping on a plane first thing Monday," he explained. He inspected the donuts, grabbed one, and took a big bite. "Mmmm . . . apple filled, my favorite," Sam mumbled through a full mouth.

As he devoured the pastry, Sam leaned forward conspiratorially. "Hey, I noticed something on the way over here. Looks like Edna forgot to lock the safe. I thought about trying to close it up, but I didn't want to go near it. Edna scares me."

Sam stood. "Gotta run, tee time in an hour. Thanks for breakfast," he said, flashing the same smile he used to charm customers. He popped the last bite in his mouth and was gone.

• • •

"I sure didn't expect to see Sam in here," Evelyn said. "At least we unloaded one of the donuts. I should have given him another for the road." She looked at Aiden and asked quietly, "Do you think we should check out the safe? It's not supposed to be open."

The "safe" was actually a small room in the executive suite with a big sign that read: "Authorized Personnel Only." It was located behind Edna's desk. She was the CEO's assistant and had held that position for the past five CEOs. She wasn't the most pleasant person, but she guarded the CEO like a pit bull protecting a sirloin steak. She deflected almost every request to meet with the CEO, a service he and his predecessors apparently valued.

"I think we should leave the safe alone," Aiden replied. "What was Sam doing in the executive offices, anyway? Sneaking around?"

Evelyn quickly said, "I'm going. That safe shouldn't be open. Who knows what's in there?" She got up and began to walk briskly toward the executive offices. Aiden hesitated, and then jogged to catch up.

The executive offices were normally the quietest place in the building, and on Saturday the area was as silent as a tomb. Thick carpeting absorbed any sound from their steps. The doors to the executive offices were all closed. Glancing toward Edna's desk, the pair saw that Sam had been right. The safe door was slightly ajar.

"Can we just push it closed?" Aiden asked.

Evelyn replied, "I don't know if that will lock it." She confidently strode around Edna's desk and inspected the door.

"We should take a peek inside to be sure everything is OK," she said.

Aiden was horrified. "How would we even know if something was missing? We don't know what was in there to begin with. And what if there are cameras?"

Evelyn scoffed, "Cameras! Ha! No way. We didn't even get a parking lot camera until Tricia got her purse stolen on her way to her car."

"Besides," she continued with a sly smile, "haven't you ever wondered what's in there?"

"Not really. What are you expecting, jewels? Gold bullion? We're a packaging company. We don't do any cash business. It's probably a bunch of files."

"Well, we can make sure that nobody trashed whatever was in there before we lock up," Evelyn said, tugging the heavy door open. A bare bulb came on as the door opened, illuminating the small room. It seemed that Aiden's guess was correct. A bookcase on one wall held ledgers, some leather-bound. They had dates on their spines, and oldest went back to the earliest days of the company a century earlier.

"Wow, I bet there's some interesting stuff in those. Back then, the company made wooden crates," Aiden observed. Another wall had a row of file cabinets, presumably filled with more modern records.

He turned to go. "Everything looks shipshape, let's get out of here," he said. Evelyn turned too, then stopped.

"What's that?" She pointed to the bottom shelf of the bookcase. Barely visible in the dim light, there was a wooden box that looked as old as the antique ledgers. It was bound with brass, now badly tarnished.

"What do you think it is? A box of Spanish doubloons? Probably just more old stuff they didn't want to throw out," Aiden scoffed.

Evelyn ignored this, bent down, and picked up the box. "Damn, this is heavy," she said, placing it on a small table that was the room's only piece of furniture.

"Are you nuts? We're gonna get canned," Aiden blurted. "Put that back and maybe they won't notice anything."

"Where's your spirit of adventure, Aiden? We'll never get this chance again!"

They stared at the top of the box. A small drawing was etched into a brass plate. "Wow, nice work," Aiden said. It was a diagram showing a cylinder laying in a groove on a table. Something, maybe a weight, hung from one side of the cylinder.

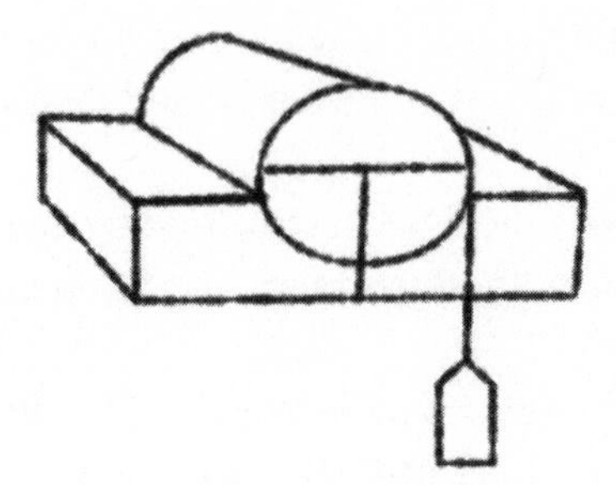

"Hey, I recognize that . . . give me a second," Evelyn said, studying the simple but elegant diagram. "Got it! It's from one of Leonardo da Vinci's notebooks. It's a friction experiment! Not many people know it, but da Vinci discovered the force of friction. You know, when two things rub against each other. He tried different materials and setups, and even calculated what physicists call the 'coefficient of friction.' He showed how things move when friction is low, and stop when it's too high."

"Is there anything da Vinci *didn't* do?" Aiden asked. "Anatomy, helicopter designs, the *Mona Lisa* . . . but I never heard about him in high school physics."

"That's because his work was lost for years. It took nearly two centuries before other scientists discovered the same laws of friction as da Vinci. Eventually, Leonardo's experiments were uncovered when people dug through his journals. And, I guarantee you, this picture is a lot like one of his friction sketches."

Aiden shrugged. "How do you even know this stuff? I definitely want to be on your team next Trivia Night. But what do you think this is?"

Evelyn didn't hesitate. The box was unlocked, and she lifted the heavy wooden lid. It was lined with red velvet, now faded and slightly threadbare. There was just one item in the box, a pair of goggles.

The goggles had round lenses and looked straight out of the Victorian era. Brass fittings and leather trim completed the effect. "Totally H. G. Wells," Evelyn commented.

"I was thinking more Jules Verne," Aiden retorted. "Now can we go?"

"Wait, I want to see how these look on you." Evelyn pulled the goggles out of the box. To Aiden's surprise, the leather didn't crumble into dust.

She thrust the goggles at Aiden. "Here, just look through them." Almost as an involuntary reflex, he took them. "You *are* nuts," he said, and held the goggles in front of his eyes. Two things happened almost simultaneously.

As he peered through the lenses, he became dizzy. The view of the little room took on rainbow hues that flickered. And then, a flash of bright light startled him.

"Sorry, did I scare you?" Evelyn said, holding up her phone. "I wanted to get a picture of you with those things on your face. Let's swap, and you get one of me."

Aiden was happy to get rid of the goggles. He still felt a bit disoriented as he took her phone. "Let's just get out of here. And don't break those things, they are probably valuable."

Evelyn held the goggles up to her eyes, holding just the ends. "Take my picture," she said, pasting on a selfie smile. As Aiden snapped the photo on her phone, she wobbled a little. "Whoa . . . I got dizzy there for a second. We need to go."

She carefully returned the goggles to the box, closed it, and returned the box to its original location. With one last glance around to be sure there was no evidence of their intrusion, the pair exited the safe. Evelyn pushed the heavy door, and it closed with a satisfying click.

"Let's wrap up our slides and go home," Evelyn said, looking slightly rattled.

• • •

The duo returned to the conference room where their laptops were open, and sat down. Aiden stared blankly at his screen. "I hate to say this," he said, "but I think the plan we just spent three days putting together is totally wrong."

Evelyn paused, and said glumly, "I know. You're right. We're going about this all wrong. If we add more options and paths to our automated phone menus, we're going to make our customers wait even longer to talk to an agent. We're already getting complaints about the system now. People want to know how to bypass the whole thing and get to an agent. We don't let them do that now because we thought too many customers would go straight for a human."

"Well, that should be telling us something," Aiden continued. "You are saying we designed the system to make our customers spend time and effort so we wouldn't need as many agents. I've listened to a few recordings from our system, and some customers get seriously frustrated. I heard one screaming, 'Representative! Agent! Operator!'—anything she could think of to break out of the menu. It didn't work."

"I agree, Aiden. I heard one customer call our system every nasty name he could think of. Then, he hung up. But what are we supposed to do? The CEO says we have to cut costs."

A few seconds of reflection caused them both to burst out, "That's the problem!"

"Making our customers work harder and waste their time to cut costs on our end is a death spiral," Evelyn proclaimed. "Sales will go down. Before long we'll be back in cost-cutting mode again. We need to make things *easier* for our customers if we want to grow sales."

They started batting around ideas that would let humans answer the phones more often. What if during peak periods supervisors took customer calls? "No time, they are always in meetings or working on reports for management," Aiden countered.

Almost as soon as he said those words, Aiden burst out, "What if we cut out a lot of that stuff? Half the people I see in meetings are on their phones or laptops, doing who knows what."

Evelyn chimed in, "And nobody looks at most of the reports we generate."

"So, you're saying we need to make things easier for our own people so they can make things easier for our customers? That actually makes sense," Aiden replied.

• • •

Soon, the duo was bubbling over with enthusiasm. Why had they not seen all this before? Everyone assumed things had to be done a certain way. Employees weren't happy because they were wasting time on red tape and bureaucracy. Customers weren't happy because they weren't getting personal attention. Instead, they were bogged down in outdated systems for placing orders and getting help. If someone was shipped the wrong product, getting a return authorization was a chore for the customer—even though it wasn't their fault! Just getting the return approved required a manager to sign off on it.

And what a mess things were internally. People spent way too much of their time in meetings and dealing with in-house e-mail. Getting the simplest thing done required multiple signatures. The budget was so tightly controlled that small expenses that would yield big results had to be postponed until the next accounting period. Even expense reports were time-consuming. A short trip to visit a customer had to be approved in advance and then ended with having to document everything, even a $2 coffee, with receipts.

Evelyn and Aiden fed off each other's energy. It seemed so obvious now. They discarded their original plan and started from scratch. Soon, they were finding ways to streamline customer interactions, often making things easier for their own staff at the same time. If the customer doesn't have to call to authorize a simple return, and the agent taking the call doesn't have to get a supervisor's approval, everyone wins.

They looked at how people were spending their time in the office and found lots of ways to save there, too. Meetings had proliferated like mushrooms. Most of them could involve fewer attendees, and some of them could be eliminated entirely. Dated rules and procedures could be dispensed with.

• • •

Evelyn ordered a pizza so they could keep working. As they ate, Aiden asked, "So what's with the box and goggles? Did da Vinci make them?"

"No, no way. They are old, but not 600 years old. They remind me a little of that steampunk stuff you see pictures of." Evelyn continued between bites, "I have to admit, I felt a bit woozy for a minute when I put them on."

"Me too," Aiden said. "Things looked different, but it's hard to explain. I sure hope nobody notices we were in there."

"Don't worry, nobody will know. But it was kind of exciting, right? And after—something sure got us fired up. I can't believe we were on the last slide or two and decided to toss the whole presentation and start over."

"Probably the adrenaline. I was sure that battle-ax Edna was going to jump out from behind a file cabinet and yell, 'Gotcha!'"

Evelyn chuckled at the image. "I guess it could have been the excitement; I was a little scared too. But I've been thinking. What if the picture on the box was a symbol? Think about it . . . that diagram is from the first experiment that discovered friction. And then, when we got back in here, we started seeing friction everywhere. It was right in front of us before, but now we're seeing it. And, we can't stop seeing it."

"Right . . . so those are magic friction goggles," Aiden teased her. He paused, and added, "But, I do feel like I was seeing things differently after our little adventure in the safe."

"Probably the adrenaline after all," Evelyn said. "Let's get back to work."

By the end of Saturday, they were exhausted but excited. Their plan was rough, and would require a lot of cooperation from other departments, but they thought it would make customers happy and energize employees. They hoped the CEO felt the same way on Monday.

• • •

The CEO leaned back in his chair as Evelyn and Aiden filed into his office Monday morning and fired up their presentation. "Show me what you've got," he ordered.

As they began to explain their new approach, the CEO looked puzzled at first. As they progressed, he leaned back and crossed his arms. His face reddened. He finally exploded, "You had one job—figure out how to cut costs in customer service by 10 percent! I was expecting a list of names, not a plan to redesign the company!

"Where did all this garbage come from? Last week, you had things under control. I've got a board meeting in less than a week, and you are the last department to submit your cost reductions!" he thundered. "I'm sure you've got some good ideas in there, but we don't have the time to do them or the money to pay for them."

Aiden argued, "But these changes won't really cost anything. Getting rid of old and ineffective rules, cutting down on meetings that nobody pays attention in, and eliminating reports nobody looks at. These will all save money and, more importantly, let our people do a better job for our customers!"

The CEO shook his head. "We already had a plan. What happened to you two?"

"It was the goggles," Evelyn blurted out. "We put them on and started seeing friction everywhere. Customers who couldn't get through to a real agent. Complicated procedures for orders and returns. Dumb rules that waste our people's time. Way too many meetings that don't get anything done."

"I have no idea what you are talking about. Have you both gone crazy?" The CEO looked even angrier, but then his face changed. "Goggles? Did you say *goggles*?"

"I know we shouldn't have touched them," Evelyn said. "It was my fault. Somebody left the safe door open, and when we went to close it we found the box. I made Aiden put them on and then tried them myself.

They changed everything for us." No point in mentioning Sam's role, she thought.

The CEO looked stricken. "My predecessor warned me not to even open that box. He didn't know who made them or where they came from, but they ended up with our founder, George Packard, a hundred years ago. He's the one who built the company, and back then customers loved us. A few of his successors supposedly used them, too, during the time the company grew like crazy.

"But my predecessor said they were dangerous. He ended up getting fired by the board because they couldn't agree on the company's focus. He wanted to put employees and customers first—he said profits would follow. The board wanted him to focus on the shareholders and the quarterly dividend. His only job, they said, was to keep profits growing at a steady pace and protect the payouts.

"He said he would, but then started to give employees more freedom. They could take care of customers as they saw fit. He loosened some internal controls that were driving everyone crazy. Everyone thought these changes were going in the right direction, but he missed the profit target a couple of quarters in a row. The board wasn't happy, and decided it was time for a change. I was the change.

"On the way out the door, my old friend told me to keep the box with the goggles under lock and key. If I wanted to keep my job, he said, do what the board wants. He said the goggles gave him too many ideas that he couldn't ignore. These ideas were right, he said, and they made sense. But, the board was just too impatient.

"I assumed the stress was getting to him and he was starting to lose it. Or, he was looking for a way to blame his firing on something other than his own mistakes. I ignored the goggles nonsense and never thought about them again. Until now," he added.

"We're sorry," began Aiden. "I still have my original list of people to cut."

The CEO looked thoughtfully and sat quietly for a minute. "No, I think you two are on the right track. When George Packard founded this company, he wasn't worried about the daily stock price or maximizing short-term shareholder value. He was the only shareholder, and he knew if he kept his customers happy and gave his people room to do their jobs, profit would follow. He became wealthy, and after him, George Junior grew the company and the family fortune even more. Junior's son wasn't interested in the business, though, and the family brought in professional managers. The company went public and appointed an independent board of directors. I'm just a temporary occupant of this chair, sitting here only as long as the board is happy.

"The last guy who had this job tried to stand up to the board and got himself booted. But maybe I'll have better luck. They like me, and I know what they want to hear. I just have to convince them that making things more difficult for our customers and our own people might save a few dollars in this quarter but isn't going to be good for our shareholders in the long run. Missing a quarterly target or two is better than long-term damage to revenue growth.

"I owe you two.... You went out on a limb to suggest a course of action that's right for the company."

The CEO stood up slowly and squared his shoulders. "Now, come with me and show me what you did. I think it's my turn to try on those goggles."

## GOGGLES FOR *YOU*

My intention for this book is to give you and every other reader your very own pair of friction goggles. These goggles will help you discover friction, which I define as "the unnecessary expenditure of time, effort, or money in performing a task," in all kinds of places.

## WHY FRICTION MATTERS

Friction has a far bigger price tag than people recognize. Here are just a few data points to prove why:

- In 2016, an estimated $4.6 trillion dollars of merchandise was left in abandoned e-commerce shopping carts—mostly related to friction in customer experience.[1]
- The US economy loses $3 trillion dollars in productivity annually due to excess bureaucracy.[2]
- China's economy as measured by gross domestic product (GDP) grew a cumulative $82 trillion more than India's from 1987 to 2017, even though the two economies were initially similar in size.[3]

Can friction explain all these distressing statistics? Not entirely, but I'll show you how friction is a key factor in these results and many more. More importantly, I'll show you how eliminating or reducing friction can have long-lasting and even disruptive effects.

## CRAZY COLLEAGUE FRICTION

One quick clarification before we get to Chapter 1. I'm *not* focused on *interpersonal* friction in the pages of this book. While this is an interesting and important topic, it's not one we will touch on.

Instead, we'll see how friction affects the success of businesses and individuals, and even the course of nations. We'll also discuss many ways to reduce friction or, occasionally, use it to our advantage.

If I have one overriding objective in this book, it's to help you identify friction everywhere—in your work, personal life, and community. Once an enemy is visible, he or she is far easier to defeat. And, when we eliminate friction, we make our lives and the lives of those around us better.

## YOUR FRICTION GOGGLES

The good news is that by reading this book, you will come to spot friction more easily than ever before. Once you start seeing friction, you can't unsee it. Every time I talk about friction in a speech or workshop, afterward people notice themselves pointing and exclaiming, "Friction!" when they encounter some unnecessary difficulty. That friction was there before, but suddenly these people are aware of it and ready to call it by its name.

And, I want you to do more than see friction, I want you to *do something about it*. If you are in a leadership position, declare war on friction. Stamp out ridiculous rules, pointless procedures, and meaningless meetings. Become a relentless advocate for the customer and minimizing customer effort. We'll learn how to do all of that together in the pages of this book.

Let's get started.

# PROLOGUE

# Engine of Disruption

*Fortune can bring about great changes in a situation through very slight forces.*
—Julius Caesar, Roman leader and general

The battle that defined Julius Caesar as a great general and future Roman dictator for life was in Gaul, now modern-day France. He faced daunting odds. His army numbered 60,000 legionnaires, but he was deep in enemy territory and a Gallic force of 80,000 was entrenched in the impregnable hilltop fortress of Alesia.

Caesar first had his men build a wall to encircle and isolate the fortress. This wall was 12 feet tall, ran for 11 miles, and had battlements and fortifications at frequent intervals. When he realized that Gallic reinforcements would arrive and attack from behind, Caesar had his men construct a second, even longer, wall to protect their rear flank. The new wall enclosed the first and was 14 miles long.[1]

Eventually, another 250,000 Gallic warriors arrived to join the battle. They attacked the Romans from the rear even as the soldiers in the fortress poured out to attack from the front. A fifth of the Roman army died in the battle, but the combination of well-engineered fortifications and superior military tactics enabled Caesar to rout both attacking armies. The Gauls remaining in the fortress realized their situation was now hopeless and surrendered.[2]

That Caesar and his army defeated vastly superior enemy force wasn't nearly as remarkable as where the battle took place: hundreds of miles from the Mediterranean Sea or any other major body of water. Ships were the fastest mode of transport in that era. Not only did a 60,000-man Roman army have to reach Alesia by a lengthy land route, they had to keep themselves connected to supplies of food, weapons, tools, and construction materials. They built 25 miles of continuous walls deep in enemy territory.[3]

Like today's master of disruption, Amazon, the Romans had a powerful understanding of both technology and logistics. Indeed, as advanced as Amazon's robotic warehouses and far-flung delivery networks are, Rome was even more innovative and dominant in its day. Amazon took advantage of the Internet and leveraged existing delivery technologies. The Romans created their infrastructure from scratch.

## A NEED FOR SPEED

In the pre-Roman era, land travel was slow. Speed of communication over land was equally slow—information could move only as fast as a messenger could walk or ride. Most roads were dirt tracks twisting through rough terrain. In wet weather, they could become impassable. Rivers and other natural barriers further impeded travel.

With land travel so difficult, the most effective way to move armies and goods was by ship. Carthage dominated much of the Mediterranean prior to the ascendance of Rome, but their control rarely extended far from the sea. Moving troops inland and keeping them supplied was difficult.

Rome, too, was a seafaring power, but in the early days of their empire Romans found a way to extend their power far from the water's edge. They built a system of roads unequaled for well over a thousand years.

## ROMAN ROADS: STRAIGHT, FLAT, AND SMOOTH

The roads the Romans built were amazing feats of engineering and construction technology. Roman engineers understood that the shortest distance between two points was a straight line, and they designed their roads that way. If a valley was in the way, they built a bridge. At times, they tunneled through mountains. The Romans built the roads so that water drained away, and used a mix of stone and gravel to make roads durable and smooth even for wheeled carts and chariots.

The network of roads became the glue that held the empire together. They connected Rome to every corner of its territory and major Roman cities to smaller outposts. The roads linked a phenomenal amount of logistical infrastructure. Along major roads, there were stations where messengers could change horses and lodgings where travelers could spend the night in safety. Troops were strategically placed to keep the roads safe and, at times, collect tolls. Warehouses held supplies to allow quick military action. There was even comprehensive signage in the form of stone markers erected at regular intervals.

> *Roman roads were meant to endure and rarely yielded to the vagaries of topography. Unless prevented by impassable mountains or impregnable swamps, the Romans built their roads straight as an arrow across the landscape. They were in fact a sermon in stone to the world—Romans do not yield.*
>
> —from *Julius Caesar* by Philip Freeman

## SUPERHIGHWAYS

The Roman roads took much of the friction out of land travel. Troops could move 25 miles in a day, astoundingly fast in a time when the empire had to be constantly ready for local uprisings or external attacks. Information traveled much faster—couriers covered 50–60 miles per day, stopping only to change horses and sleep at night. Even faster travel was possible when necessary—one contemporary account has Tiberius covering 200 miles in 24 hours to see his dying brother.[4]

The level of logistical superiority demonstrated by the Romans gave them an enormous advantage in conquering and holding territory. As the battle at Alesia showed, they could deploy huge forces far from their sea-based supply lines.

Eventually, the Romans built 250,000 miles of roads, with 50,000 of them paved with stone. Some 29 military highways radiated from Rome, connecting to 372 "great roads."[5] Faster, easier communications, troop movement, and supply logistics allowed Rome to occupy nearly two million square miles of territory with relatively small numbers of troops. This network of smooth, straight roads was both the "information superhighway" and actual highway of that era. The Romans used it to disrupt their enemies and rule for centuries.

## FRICTION TAKEAWAY

Sometimes, making things easy requires hard work. Building stone bridges across valleys and tunneling through rock were extremely difficult in the Roman era, and very costly in materials and labor. But, the Romans knew this extra work would save far more wasted effort in the years to come. The straight, flat roads endured for centuries and enabled information, troops, and supplies to move much more quickly. Sometimes, they were the difference between winning and losing a battle or even a war.

# CHAPTER 1

# The Friction Evangelist

*When you reduce friction, make something easy, people do more of it.*
—Jeff Bezos, Founder and CEO, Amazon

A couple of millennia after Roman engineers were punching impressively smooth and straight roads through the wilds of the ancient world, Kintan Brahmbhatt has a somewhat similar role at e-commerce giant Amazon.

Officially, Brahmbhatt is Product Design Manager with responsibility for a range of Amazon's products like video and music services. He is focused on improving how the products enable users to interact with these products and supervises a group of product managers.

Unofficially, Brahmbhatt is Amazon's friction evangelist. He visits conferences around the country preaching the gospel of fighting friction. Every one of Brahmbhatt's presentations features this Jeff Bezos quote: "When you reduce friction, make something easy, people do more of it."

Amazon prospers when people do more things: watch video, listen to music, and, of course, buy more products. While many companies focus on motivating their customers to take desired actions with ads, bribes, and other nudges, Amazon is uniquely focused on making things easier to do.

This focus on reducing friction is a key reason for Amazon's emergence as the world's biggest, fastest-growing retailer. It's also driving high growth in many other parts of their business.

## BATTERIES NOT INCLUDED

Brahmbhatt says his first experience with friction came as a child. He was thrilled to open a birthday present to find a long-wished-for remote-control toy car. His excitement turned to dismay, though, when he found that the toy manufacturer had not included the necessary batteries. Even worse, none were at hand in his home. So, the now dejected child had to put the car away until a trip to a store could be arranged.[1]

Looking back from his current perspective, Brahmbhatt points out how easily this point of friction—making customers buy batteries before the product could be used—could have been eliminated. Even inexpensive batteries would have enabled every child opening the box to enjoy the product right away.

Today, Brahmbhatt spends much of his time looking for friction where many people don't even see it.

## WHO'S THAT ACTOR?

One of the characteristics of today's connected consumer watching video content is that he or she may have more than one screen open. A movie might be playing on a big-screen television while the person fiddles with a smartphone or tablet.

In some cases, this is simply multitasking. The viewer can check e-mail or Facebook while not completely losing track of what's going on in the movie or television show. But, sometimes the actions on the multiple screens are related to each other. Amazon's research showed that a common task performed by video content viewers was to look up the actors they were seeing. So, while the action continued on the big screen, they might open a resource like IMDb.com (a comprehensive database of entertainment content, actors, and roles, acquired by Amazon in 1998), to find the movie or show and scan the list of cast members to try to identify the actor of interest. Then, by looking at the actor's profile, they could make the connection to some previous role.

Few consider this mild multitasking as particularly problematic or high friction. Of course, when entertainment content is viewed on a mobile device, the process gets a bit messier. In that case, the viewer must pause the content, switch to a browser or app, do the research, and then return to the content. Though not particularly difficult, it's much more awkward.

Could this process be easier?

Well, to answer that question, you need to be familiar with a feature Amazon had previously created called "X-Ray." Introduced in 2011, X-Ray let Kindle readers look up both unfamiliar words and the book's characters as they read. Readers who previously read books with a dictionary close at hand no longer needed the extra book. And, if a minor character introduced at the start of the book pops up many chapters later, confused readers could quickly refresh their memory.

With this in mind, Brahmbhatt wondered how Amazon could improve the video-viewing experience and differentiate itself from other content providers. A new X-Ray feature to pull up actor data was the simple answer. Now, by pausing the video, you can see who the actors are. If you were struggling to recall a name, your problem is solved. If you want more information about the actor, a click or two will show you.

Amazon further reduces friction by showing just the actors in the current scene. Rather than scanning a long list of the show's entire cast, the relevant names and photos are right in front of you.

## COMPETITIVE ADVANTAGE

This kind of small friction reduction seems nearly trivial, but it's not. First, as streaming content becomes a commodity, providers need to differentiate their offerings. One way to do that is by offering unique content. Netflix, for example, spent $9 million per episode on its series *Sense8* in 2015[2] and spent as much as $13 billion in 2018 for original content.[3]

Amazon's estimated $4 billion original content spend is smaller but still enormous.[4] It allows them to create shows like *Bosch* (based on the best-selling crime novels by Michael Connelly) and *Tom Clancy's Jack Ryan* to ensure they have attractive programming that their competitors don't.

Adding the friction-reducing X-Ray also differentiates Amazon Prime Video from Netflix and other services, but at far less cost.

Even more exciting from Amazon's standpoint, perhaps, is the potential linkage to its core commerce business. Have you tried to track down something you've seen on-screen, like a character's sunglasses or a prop chair behind an executive's desk? It's currently possible with a little Google research, but compared to identifying an actor it's much more work.

Imagine you are watching an episode of *Bosch* and click the X-Ray button. Today, you'd see the role of Harry Bosch is played by actor Titus

Welliver. Soon, I'm guessing, you'll also see that he's wearing Randolph Engineering Aviator sunglasses, with a convenient "Buy now with 1-Click" button. By combining friction-free product discovery with friction-free ordering, Amazon will further extend its dominance of e-commerce.

### FRICTION TAKEAWAY

> Sometimes, friction isn't obvious. Amazon observed how people watched video content to understand what they did and how they did it. Once they saw that looking up cast members was common, they were able to find a way to make that easier. That created a small but immediate competitive advantage and, perhaps, a future revenue opportunity. Look for tiny changes in any process that will make it a little easier.

## THE "NOT-SO-EASY" EASY BUTTON

Amazon's 1-Click button was already a standard feature on their site when Staples introduced their "Easy Button" in 2005. Ads showed a big red button with the word *Easy* on it, echoing their tagline, "That was easy!" Pushing the button make solving difficult tasks effortless. One ad showed the Easy Button building the Great Wall of China just in time to stop an invading army.

Staples followed up by selling a physical version of the button that, when pushed, vocalized their slogan, "That was easy!" Within a year, they had sold more than a million of the buttons, most of which ended up on office desks and counters. The popular buttons provided many millions of free ad impressions. An Easy Button appeared on the desk of the Canadian prime minister. The ad campaign won a Gold Effie, an honor awarded for campaigns that are particularly effective in generating real-world results.[5]

Unfortunately, buying from Staples wasn't as easy as pushing a magic red button. One blogger mocked the button in a series of videos chronicling her frustration as she tried to buy a file cabinet.

My own "not-so-easy" Easy Button experience came a few years ago. My printer was low on ink, and I didn't have a spare cartridge. I knew that Staples had what I needed. As an existing customer, I also knew that they offered free next-day delivery.

I quickly found the correct ink product and dropped it into my shopping cart. There was, of course, no 1-Click button, so I navigated to the checkout page—and this is where the Easy Button failed me.

Despite being an existing Staples customer with previous website orders, I found I wasn't logged in. Furthermore, my browser couldn't autofill my username and password. I don't know if the website was coded to prevent that or if I simply hadn't used that browser to log in before. Either way, I was staring at a lengthy order form that took massive scrolling just to view. The form was about five screens long on my Mac. It wanted billing and shipping address and phone information, payment details, and all the other data you might see on a commercial order form.

I was faced with three undesirable choices. Number 1, I could attempt a guest checkout by filling in the lengthy order form. Number 2, I could try to track down my login information. Or, number 3, I could perform a password recovery by e-mail, assuming the site recognized my e-mail address.

After scrolling up and down the discouragingly long order form one last time, I chose a fourth option. I jumped in my car and drove to an OfficeMax store less than 10 minutes away. Within 30 minutes I had the new cartridge installed in my printer.

For all I know, the ink in my Staples.com shopping cart is still there, one small part of the trillions of dollars of abandoned e-commerce shopping carts.[6]

## THE 1-CLICK ENVIRONMENT

While 1-Click gets much of the credit for Amazon's low-friction shopping experience, it's about more than just a button. 1-Click works because Amazon has implemented a host of friction reducing tactics, many of which have to do with security.

### Permanent Login

Amazon keeps you logged in to their site under most circumstances. You don't have to log in each time you visit, and you are never logged out for inactivity. I've joked that the only way you'll get logged out of Amazon.com is if you buy a new computer. That's not actually true, of course. Amazon will ask you to log in occasionally. For instance, if you want to review order history, ship to a new location, or engage in activities other than placing simple orders, you may be asked to verify your password. But for simple order placement, you are always logged in and ready to buy with one little click.

### Credit Cards

Like most e-commerce sites, Amazon will store your credit card information and remember multiple cards. And, your 1-Click order is charged to your default card automatically. But, if you decide to buy Amazon gift cards and e-mail them to other people, they may even ask you to verify your credit card. Setting up a new shipping address may also trigger a security check. Amazon does have powerful security measures, but they are designed to make routine ordering frictionless. Only specific actions with a higher potential for fraud, like sending an Amazon gift card—a near cash-equivalent—will trigger a higher level of security.

### Passwords

Today, bizarre password requirements are one of the most common sources of frustration online. Having to create long passwords with various letters, numbers, cases, and symbols results in passwords that are easily forgotten. Requiring users to change passwords periodically (or after a security incident) compounds the problem. Some sites are coded in a way that won't let your browser automatically fill in your password. Amazon uses none of these techniques. A smooth, easy customer experience is paramount, and these security "best practices" would hamper that. Amazon has never forced me to change the surprisingly weak password I set up more than a dozen years ago.

## SECURITY UNEASE

Apparently, my Staples experience wasn't a complete outlier. A more recent study by Forrester Research compared "security strength" and "security ease" for five online retailers—Amazon, Home Depot, Macy's, Staples, and Walmart. Although they all did well on security strength, Staples was the only one to have a negative value for security ease. Amazon, surprisingly, scored second best in security strength in addition to doing well in the ease rating. A low-friction user experience doesn't necessarily mean loose security.[7] Instead of implementing annoying practices like complicated passwords that expire, implement security measures based on user behavior and the potential for a transaction to be damaging.

## FRUSTRATION-FREE PACKAGING

A key element of Amazon's success is observing customer behavior and making changes to reduce effort and annoyance. They found that customers struggled to open product packaging designed for retail stores. Plastic clamshells and blister packs, which show off the product and discourage shoplifting, were fine for in-person shopping. But customers who shopped at home hated these packages because they often needed sharp instruments to pry or cut them open. Stabbing oneself with a sharp plastic edge was always a possibility. Amazon described the problem as "wrap rage."[8]

In 2008, Amazon introduced "frustration-free packaging" for some products. Typically, these were simple cardboard boxes that were easier and safer to open, cost less, created no plastic waste, and were more efficient to store and ship. Customers loved the change—there was an average 73 percent reduction in negative feedback on products with the low-friction packaging![9] Amazon's relentless focus on the customer allowed them to identify the problem and offer a solution before any of their competitors.

### FRICTION TAKEAWAY

Saying that you are easy to do business with is one thing, delivering on that promise is another. If you really want to make it easy for your customers, don't compare your processes to your direct competitors. They may be even worse. Instead compare yourself to companies like Amazon—your customers shop there, and that's the friction-free experience they expect from you, too.

## THE $4.6 TRILLION PROBLEM

In terms of sheer financial magnitude, e-commerce is one of the best examples of the negative impact of friction.

In 2016, e-commerce sales hit nearly $2 trillion. That's a huge number for a channel that barely existed two decades earlier. But, that number pales in comparison with the estimated $4.6 trillion of merchandise left in e-commerce shopping carts.[10] The monetary value of these abandoned shopping carts is not only more than double the amount of commerce sales, it's bigger than the US budget deficit. This number also dwarfs most of the world's economies.

For the merchants, these abandoned carts are an enormous lost opportunity. On average, more than two out of three e-commerce shopping carts are abandoned without consumers completing the checkout process. I doubt if there is a single struggling online seller that wouldn't be wildly profitable if every cart with merchandise turned into a completed sale.

Think of all the money these merchants poured into driving customers to their site or app—pay-per-click ads, social media marketing, content marketing, search engine optimization, web design, and so much more. These efforts got the customers to the site, got them to examine products, and got them to choose what they wanted to buy. But, all this hard work and money failed to get these customers across the finish line to conclude a purchase.

What went wrong? One study that looked at abandoned shopping carts found that almost all the abandonments were due to some kind of friction.[11] A difficult or confusing checkout process, surprises in checking out, and similar problems account for the vast majority of cart abandonment. Some of the friction is financial—unexpected fees and costs, for example, that are only discovered while checking out. A third of the time, customers cited the need to create an account as the reason for leaving.

## PEOPLE HATE ENTERING DATA

Business Insider reported four of the top five reasons for abandoning a shopping cart involve difficulty in entering checkout data via desktop or mobile device—pure friction. (The fifth, shipping cost, is arguably a form of financial friction.) This is Business Insider's breakdown of cart abandonments:[12]

- 46.1 percent occur at the payment stage.
- 37.4 percent occur at checkout login.

- 35.7 percent occur once the shopper sees shipping costs.
- 20.9 percent occur when the user needs to enter a billing address.
- 20 percent occur when the user needs to enter a shipping or delivery address.[13]

Amazon has none of these issues when customers use the 1-Click button. Indeed, customers who buy that way never abandon their shopping carts because *they have no carts to abandon*! The decision to buy goes from their brain to their finger, and then directly to Amazon's fulfillment system.

## ZERO-CLICK ORDERING

Jeff Bezos and Amazon have been relentless in eliminating any unnecessary effort in placing an order. But, 1-Click ordering has been around since the turn of the millennium. How does one get easier than a single click? Amazon has several answers for that.

### Subscriptions

For years, Amazon has offered subscriptions for products you buy on a regular basis. Want a pack of paper towels every month? Or a water filter cartridge every six months? Amazon will be happy to deliver those things and many others automatically, no click required. They'll even offer you a discount.

### Dash Buttons

A physical version of 1-Click is Amazon's Dash Button. Although the firm discontinued Dash Buttons, they epitomized low-effort ordering. For select staple products, you could get a dedicated button to stick, say, next to the washing machine or inside a kitchen cabinet. When your laundry detergent or paper towels got low, you didn't add them to your shopping list. You didn't jump on your computer or smartphone to place an order. Instead, you pushed the Wi-Fi-enabled button. That's all. The order was placed instantly and delivered quickly.

Some people thought the Dash Button was a joke when it was introduced the day before April Fool's Day 2015. The idea of having branded "buy" buttons stuck around your house seemed somewhat ridiculous. But, it was far from crazy. When do you realize when you are running low on detergent? When you are in the middle of loading your washer. Having a button to push at the moment of need is lower in friction than saying to yourself, "I'm going to have to remember to buy that."

The concept was expected to evolve beyond a few branded buttons. One customizable version was the "Nerf" Dash Button (yes, it existed!) that let you configure it to order 30 darts, 25 round projectiles, or a handful of other Nerf items. (I'm trying to visualize the household that consumes so many Nerf darts that they order a few dozen at a whack and want to simplify the process with a Dash Button.)

Even the setup reduced friction. To access your Wi-Fi network would normally require a configuration process in which you identify the network ID and type in the password. To avoid this process, the Dash Button used your smartphone (which was already connected to your network). The Amazon phone app provided the network connection to the Dash Button without any typing.

While stick-on Dash Buttons proved to be less compelling to customers than subscription purchases, virtual reorder buttons, and voice ordering, they were an interesting experiment in maximizing convenience and capturing intent to buy at exactly the right moment.

## Voice Ordering

While the combination of Amazon Prime and 1-Click may have the largest current revenue impact of any of Amazon's friction-reducing efforts, their Echo/Alexa technology may have even greater long-term impact. Built into products like the Amazon Echo and Fire TV Stick, Alexa eliminates most device friction by responding to and acting on voice commands.

While initially Alexa has been useful mainly for simple things like playing music and giving the weather forecast, she's developing into a powerful interface for doing almost anything. Alexa has more than a thousand "skills" that include sharing bartending expertise, controlling home electronics, tracking fitness data, and much more.

Alexa can also order an Uber, and, naturally, she can place an order with Amazon for anything you wish.

For years, science fiction movies showed humans effortlessly commanding computers to do their bidding with conversational speech. The reality was that we were still struggling with keyboards, mice, and touchscreen. Alexa, along with Google Assistant and Apple's Siri, eliminate most of that friction. While the capabilities of these devices is still far short of the fully conversational computer, they are rapidly improving with new functions being added every day.

## FRICTIONLESS RETAIL

On the retail front, Amazon Go stores, still under development, will allow you to simply walk out with your merchandise. Assuming you don't mind the effort required to get out of your cocoon (where all your entertainment and physical needs are delivered by Amazon), it's hard to imagine an easier way to get what you need.

If science ever finds a way to read minds and anticipate needs before we are consciously aware of them, Amazon will no doubt be at the forefront of implementing the technology. That unexpected package on your doorstep? Open it—it's exactly what you need!

## ALIBABA'S "NEW RETAIL"

*To make it easy to do business anywhere.*

—Alibaba Group Mission Statement[14]

If there's another company on the planet that can rival Amazon's scale and digital savvy, it's Hangzhou-based Alibaba Group. In the United States, most of us think of Alibaba as the Chinese Amazon. The firm is indeed an e-commerce giant, but it has a very diverse set of products and services.

Taobao, for example, is an e-commerce platform and the world's busiest mobile shopping destination. It's also what the company calls a "lifestyle platform" where consumers can discover new products, consume content, and engage with one another as well as with brands and retailers. Taobao and other parts of the Alibaba mobile ecosystem have 700 million monthly users[15] with the average user opening the app nearly eight times a day.[16]

It's evident that Alibaba's founder, Jack Ma, understands friction. The company's official mission is "to make it easy to do business anywhere."[17]

## Seamless Retail

Historically, bringing the physical retail and digital worlds together has been a challenge. For years, some companies kept the two channels entirely separate, or offered a few integrations like in-store pickups and returns for online orders.

Alibaba's Hema stores offer a totally different business model. The stores are fully mobile-enabled for what the company terms a three-in-one retail experience. Hema stores fulfill online orders in addition to offering seamless in-store shopping and dining. The stores also deliver products within a two-mile radius.

Everything from pre-ordering to payment at Hema can take place in their mobile app. Integration with Alibaba's e-commerce platform, Tmall, and their dominant mobile app, Taobao, extends Hema's appeal beyond in-store inventory. About half of its orders are placed online.

While online ordering and home delivery mean that Hema customers never have to step inside a store, Alibaba strives to attract in-person shoppers with a magnetic retail experience. The in-store dining at Hema allows customers to select fresh seafood, including live lobsters, for preparation on-site. Other menu items can be added to the meal via the Hema app. In one Shanghai store, an automated system both carries the customer's food selection to the kitchen and, when the meal is ready, places it on a robotic carrier that delivers the food to the customer's table.

The Hema concept involves a high degree of personalization. Alibaba can leverage its knowledge of the individual consumer's history and store visits to offer relevant content and recommendations. Customers who make in-store purchases can check out with facial recognition.

A key element in making the shopping seamless and fun is that most aspects of the customer experience are within Alibaba. Payment is handled by Alipay. Taobao's mobile app offers multiple shopping options, including Taobao Marketplace and Tmall. It is also a social platform. Users post product reviews at an amazing pace—20 million per day in 2016—and can also share photos and join communities.[18]

The community aspects are a step up even from Amazon's review and question-and-answer process. Alibaba uses an artificial intelligence–based algorithm to identify those users most likely to be able to answer a question about a product. Twenty-five percent of customers who ask a question get an answer within a minute; 60 percent get an answer within 10 minutes.[19]

This makes the Q&A nearly conversational, increasing the social interaction aspect of the app.

## New Retail Results

The emphasis on seamless integration of the physical and digital experiences, in-person shopping and online ordering, and on-site consumption and home delivery—all within the Hema app—seems to be working for both Alibaba and its customers. Hema stores average three to five times the sales per square foot of traditional supermarkets. Customers are loyal, averaging about 50 purchases per year. By mid-2018, Alibaba had opened 57 Hema stores and planned to add as many as 2,000 by 2023.[20]

We think of Amazon as the retail disruptor, but, in China's huge market, Alibaba is pursuing a different path. Amazon's approach to frictionless shopping in their Go store prototype, at least so far, is eliminating the checkout process. Alibaba is reducing friction by combining every way the customer might want to both shop and obtain or consume their product in a single store/app concept.

### FRICTION TAKEAWAY

The high rate of mobile adoption in China enabled Alibaba to create a store environment that depends on the app to make buying and paying a low-effort process. If you think your customers wouldn't be comfortable living inside their smartphones, you might be partially right. But, the world is changing. Younger customers are digital natives and are ripe for innovations that will make life fun and easy. Plan for a world when almost everyone is smartphone savvy.

# CHAPTER 2

# Retail Disruption—Nineteenth and Twentieth Centuries

*Historical growth has always, historically and across industries, come from tackling consumer friction. . . .*

—from *Topple*, by Ralph Welborn and Sunaj Pillai

Amazon's Jeff Bezos and Alibaba's Jack Ma are hardly the first entrepreneurs to disrupt retail. In 1872, Aaron Montgomery Ward and his partner, George Thorne, thought they had a way to make it easier for rural customers to access a wider range of products at better prices—a general merchandise catalog.

In the post–Civil War era in the United States, city dwellers could shop at department stores and other outlets. Rural residents weren't so lucky. Their only option was to buy from small, local merchants. These merchants stocked far fewer items than their urban counterparts and charged higher prices. An individual store was too small to buy direct from manufacturers, so it bought from wholesalers, who were sometimes the department stores themselves.

## THE BIRTH OF MAIL ORDER

A catalog that enabled direct ordering and delivery of a multitude of products would appeal to rural customers with convenience, lower prices, and a bigger selection of merchandise, Ward and Thorne thought. They were right. Within three years, a simple price list had grown to a 72-page catalog. The firm's 1883 catalog was 240 pages listing 10,000 items. Nine years later, their book had more than doubled in size to 568 pages. By the dawn of the twentieth century, the firm known as Montgomery Ward was processing a million and a half orders per year.

Mail order existed before Montgomery Ward, but, not unlike Amazon in e-commerce, Montgomery Ward showed that making shopping easy could create explosive growth.[1]

### Mail Order Optimized

The company that became Ward's biggest nemesis might never have existed had it not been for a shipping dispute. In 1886, a jewelry company sent a Minnesota jeweler a shipment of watches that the jeweler claimed it had never ordered. The shipper didn't want to pay for the return and convinced a local railroad station agent to buy the lot of timepieces for $12 each. The agent's name was Richard Warren Sears.

Sears began selling the watches for $14 each and quit his job to devote himself to the watch business full-time. In 1888, the R. W. Sears watch company was established in Chicago and issued its first catalog. Needing a watch repair specialist, Sears brought in Alvah Roebuck and incorporated as Sears Roebuck. The firm began to add products other than watches to its catalog.

If Montgomery Ward's growth was impressive, Sears Roebuck's was meteoric. It turned out that Sears had a gift for copywriting, and by 1895—just nine years after the disputed watch shipment—their catalog contained 532 pages. By the turn of the century, Sears's revenue edged ahead of Montgomery Wards, and Wards never caught up.

## FIGHTING INTERNAL FRICTION

Both giant mail order firms prospered because they offered easy access to a wide range of products previously unavailable to the rural customer. Filling in an order form took a lot more effort than today's method of clicking "Buy Now," but it took much less effort than traveling to a distant physical store. Sears proved to be Amazon-like in another way: it focused on eliminating friction in its own operations.

In 1895, Sears accepted a substantial investment from Julius Rosenwald, one of their suppliers, and Rosenwald's brother-in-law. Rosenwald became active in the firm and was instrumental in turning Sears into a well-oiled machine. He addressed customer satisfaction issues by improving product quality and toning down some of Sears's copywriting excesses. Most important, he brought a high level of organization to the company's mail order operation.

By 1906, Sears was processing millions of orders per year—as many as 27,000 in one hour. That may not seem like much by today's standards. In comparison, Amazon processes more orders than that in one minute on peak sales days.[2] Retail giant Alibaba processed more than a billion orders on Singles Day (a sort of anti-Valentine's celebration that is now a huge shopping holiday in China) in 2018—that's 700,000 orders per minute, on average![3] But, in the first decade of the twentieth century, each of Sears's orders came by postal mail. Each had an envelope that had to be opened, items to be listed for shipment, and a check to be recorded and deposited . . . all by hand.

The remarkable efficiency achieved by Sears was attained without computers, robots, or, in the earlier years, even telephones.

## FROM MAIL TO RETAIL

Both Montgomery Ward and Sears Roebuck began opening retail stores in the 1920s. The firms diverged in their strategies. Montgomery Ward stuck to its rural roots, while Sears turned in a more urban direction. But Sears didn't emulate department store competitors by locating downtown. Once again, it focused on what was easiest for consumers. To best service a new class of customer, car owners, Sears located stores outside the central city where it could offer plentiful free parking. By 1931, Sears was generating more revenue in stores than via its catalog.[4]

Montgomery Ward never caught up to Sears, which continued to prosper for many years to come. Ward's management made a series of poor choices, including failing to anticipate the post–World War II boom in the United States. Both firms, though, were Amazon-like disruptors in their early decades. They pioneered low-friction ways to let rural Americans shop, and then used their positions of strength to serve a much broader market.[5]

## ABANDONING THEIR ROOTS

Ironically, Sears and Montgomery Wards planted the seeds for their own disruption. In the years after World War II, Sears moved aggressively to open stores in city suburbs. The economic boom that followed the war and a mobile, car-driving customer base propelled this growth. Montgomery Ward was slower to recognize this potential but eventually followed suit. The revenue potential of urban areas was clearly bigger than that offered by dispersed rural customers, so that's where the two chains opened stores.

This left the rural base with the same traditional shopping options. They could shop by mail order from Wards, Sears, and other firms. They could shop at small "Main Street" stores with limited inventory and high prices. Or, they could travel to the city to shop at Sears or a traditional department store.

The status quo in rural areas hadn't changed much since Montgomery Ward and Sears Roebuck first introduced full-line mail order catalogs in the 1880s. But one merchant saw an opportunity to reduce the in-person shopping effort required of non-urban residents.

## RURAL SHOPPING MADE EASIER

In 1962, Sam Walton opened his first store in rural Arkansas. He had owned and operated a "five-and-dime" store in Bentonville, Arkansas, for a dozen years, and decided to try a more ambitious concept with a larger merchandise store in Rogers, Arkansas. He opened a second store shortly after, and the Wal-Mart (later simplified to "Walmart") concept was born. As the chain expanded in the years that followed, it put stores in locations close to rural towns and small cities, but which offered easy access and plenty of parking. The chain also emphasized low prices, which its small-town competitors couldn't easily match.

The impact of a Walmart opening was devastating for "Main Street" stores in nearby communities. Many small stores went out of business. When Walmart announced it would open a store nearby, residents usually split into two factions. Some protested that a nearby superstore would destroy the viability of their downtown shops, while others welcomed the convenience and savings from a large new store.

Taking a page from the mail order giants that preceded it, Walmart built an impregnable base of rural stores first. Then, it used the high-volume cost advantage gained from these stores to begin moving closer to big cities. Today, the firm operates almost 11,200 stores in 27 countries.[6]

Despite its size and seeming invincibility in the face of retail competitors, Walmart itself is subject to disruption by e-commerce giants Amazon and Alibaba. Shopping at a nearby Walmart is easy, but not as easy as having your goods appear on your doorstep with just a few clicks. Walmart eventually saw this as a serious threat and launched its own aggressive programs to drive mobile and e-commerce sales, as well as develop advanced retail technologies.

## FRICTION TAKEAWAY

Sam Walton saw that Sears and Montgomery Ward had become complacent. Their mail order approach to serving rural customers had been the foundation of their business, but they were now focused on bigger markets. Walton found an economical way for these customers to buy what they wanted without the delays and shipping expense of mail order. Once again, "easy" proved to be a winning strategy. Only after Walmart was a major force did the company enter busier cities. If you can find a part of your market that has difficulty doing business with your competitors, attack there first before meeting them head-on.

# CHAPTER 3

# Transportation Disruption

Transportation didn't change much for most of the two millennia after the Romans revolutionized land travel with their network of flat, straight roads. Elaborate carriages and Conestoga wagons might have looked strange to a Roman charioteer, but he would have understood their function instantly. The nineteenth century saw the development and proliferation of railroads, the first major reduction in transport friction. Even today, the comparatively low physical friction of steel wheels on steel track makes traditional rail transport a cost-effective freight alternative.

But, the automobile changed everything. Cars didn't have to be fed and didn't generate manure. Over time, they became more efficient and reliable, supplanting horses and horse-drawn vehicles completely. Of course, the auto brought its own set of problems—pollution, congestion, and traffic fatalities. But, nobody thinks it's time to go back to horses.

## MILLIONAIRE PROBLEMS: CAN'T FIND A LIMO

Garrett Camp returned to San Francisco from Paris in 2008 with an idea that he couldn't quite give up on. He was still CEO of the web-sharing site StumbleUpon after having sold it to eBay for $75 million a year earlier. Camp's idea was for a sort of timeshare limo service. In Paris, he and fellow entrepreneur Travis Kalanick had been unable to hail a cab, and they thought an app that could dial up a "black car" on demand would be useful.

By 2009, Camp was working on a company named UberCab as a side project. Camp persuaded Kalanick to join him in the project with the unlikely title of "Chief Incubator." The service was still focused on an upscale consumer who would pay for a black car if one was readily available.

In 2010, after a short test in New York, UberCab launched its service in San Francisco. Later in the year, they received their first round of funding: $1.25 million. At about the same time, they received a cease-and-desist order from the city of San Francisco, which objected to the firm's use of the term "cab" in its name.

While this demand was a small precursor of far more serious challenges to come from the taxi industry and its political allies, it had one positive effect. The firm dropped the word "cab," changed its name to "Uber," and acquired the uber.com domain.

The following year, two more rounds of financing raised $48 million in venture capital. Then 2013 saw two major developments: Uber launched UberX service that used normal passenger vehicles instead of black cars, and they raised $3.5 billion in additional funding.[1]

Uber expanded globally, burning through cash but establishing footholds. Wherever they went, they were opposed by taxi operators but were almost universally loved by customers. Lyft and other ride-sharing competitors emerged, but Uber remained atop the valuation chart. A 2018 capital raise valued the firm at $62 billion.[2]

## FRICTION TAKEAWAY

Camp and Kalanick started Uber to address a point of friction they personally experienced when they couldn't hire a limo in Paris. That's a good starting point for a business idea—if something is annoying, slow, or effortful for you, it is probably the same for others. But the real success came from looking beyond limos and seeing how much friction could be eliminated for the much larger population of taxi users. Uber became the biggest of unicorns and threatened an industry that dated back to the horse-and-buggy days. As we'll see, friction elimination explains much of their success.

## TAXIS ARE TAXING

In most cities, the taxi experience has changed very little since, say, 1950. But, the act of taking a taxi was so commonplace that nobody recognized the many elements of friction it entails. To put it simply, taxis were taxis. Nobody had found a better way to get a ride, nor even imagined that there could be a better way. The taxi operators themselves, often operating in a regulated or monopolistic environment, had little incentive to innovate.

### Finding a Taxi

The time-honored way of obtaining a taxi is to walk to a busy street, watch for an unoccupied taxi, and wave frantically to get the driver's attention. This is a high-friction process for both the driver and passenger. The driver must roam streets hoping to spot a potential customer. While experienced drivers know where to go to increase the probability of finding customers, there's still plenty of wasted fuel and driving minutes.

Customers also experience plenty of friction. Often, there are no taxis in sight. When it's raining, more people want cabs. This creates an imbalance of supply and demand, and customers may stand in the rain flapping their arms for extended periods.

Taxi stands, airport queues, and other approaches have been created to reduce this matching friction but have their own issues. These methods bring both sides of the taxi transaction together, but the queues may be empty of vehicles when demand is high. When demand is low, drivers may have to sit for extended periods waiting their turn.

Ordering a taxi by phone is another solution to the matching problem. It often works, but it's frequently unreliable. The taxi often arrives early or late. And, sometimes, the taxi doesn't arrive at all. Late arrivals can be particularly worrisome for the rider. If your airport cab was supposed to arrive five minutes ago, what does the delay mean? Was the driver slightly slowed by traffic and a mere block or two away? Or, was there a major blockage that will entail a very late arrival? The worst scenario, of course, is that somehow a breakdown in the dispatch system occurred and no cab at all is coming. You have no way of knowing as you nervously glance at your watch.

## Where Are We Going?

Assuming one finds a taxi, the friction is far from over. While official taxi meters usually eliminate the need for price negotiation, in some areas passengers are still confronted by a driver who demands a fixed price. Of course, the passenger who has just landed in an unfamiliar city (or country) is unlikely to know if a price is a fair one or outright extortion.

Another element of friction is finding a cab that accepts credit cards. This is finally getting easier in many countries, but in some locations riders may still have to query several drivers before finding one equipped for card or mobile pay transactions.

We've all had difficulty explaining to a driver (who may not speak the same language as us) exactly where we are going. "Airport" is usually easy, but an obscure residential address may be more difficult. Even popular destinations can prove challenging, as when one is delivered to the wrong Marriott hotel.

Once one is underway, the friction continues. Does the driver really know where he's going? Is he taking the fastest route, or is he going a longer way to increase his fare? It's not just third-world countries that have greedy drivers—even major US cities like Las Vegas periodically have to crack down on such offenders.

## Time to Pay

Exiting the taxi is the final burst of friction. Paying with cash is usually quickest, unless the driver can't make change. Even with today's technology, paying by credit card often takes a few minutes of fumbling, printing a signature form, awkwardly signing it, and waiting for a receipt.

Tipping can be highly problematic. Tip protocols and driver expectations vary by country and location, and as a passenger I often wonder whether I am over- or under-tipping. In one US airport, I once had an incensed driver curse and demand a much larger tip because my ride was short and he would have to go to the back of the queue for his next ride.

## Why Do We See It Now?

When we go through the taxi experience in detail, the friction is obvious. But, for decades we rarely saw it. When we did have a below-average experience, like a prearranged taxi that never appeared or a driver that got lost, we just assumed that it was an annoying but inevitable part of taxi transportation.

Uber and its ride-sharing peers opened our eyes. Suddenly, when most of the taxi friction was removed, we could see it for what it was. With Uber, we know in advance what a ride will cost. We can see exactly how far away our ride is. We can see how the driver has been rated by others and apply our own rating at the end of our ride. We can follow the route we are taking and predict our time of arrival. And, when we complete our ride, we simply say goodbye—no fumbling for cash or dealing with a balky card reader.

Uber has experienced its share of problems. Kalanick led the firm with a relentless focus on the customer, but he built an internal culture so toxic that he was ousted from his management role. In addition, Uber has been declared illegal in some cities after protests from taxi drivers. And, the company's drivers have complained about low pay and unfriendly business practices. But, Uber's strongest advocates are its customers. There is no doubt that in cities where politicians have allowed Uber to operate it's because so many residents and visitors can't imagine going back to the traditional, high-friction taxi experience.

### FRICTION TAKEAWAY

Everyday experiences we take for granted may contain plenty of friction. Uber, Lyft, and others didn't just try to fix one part of the taxi experience, they optimized every part of it to minimize customer effort. Could smartphones or some other transformative technology provide ways to reduce customer effort in your business?

## DRIVER FRICTION

Most of the press coverage Uber gets focuses on the positive aspects of their customer experience or the negative aspects of how their drivers are treated. Low pay, lack of benefits, and lack of an employer/employee relationship are common complaints. With their nearly total focus on the customer, Uber originally made tipping difficult or impossible. Drivers demanding tips was a well-known problem with traditional taxis, and apparently Uber management decided it was best for customer experience to avoid the issue completely.

Eventually, Uber began to offer tipping options—as usual for the firm, the interface was very simple. A few suggested amounts based on the fare and the market mean the rider can decide with one tap on his or her phone.

Less often discussed is how Uber and similar services reduce friction for the driver.

## Training and Onboarding

*One of the best parts about driving for Uber and Lyft is how frictionless onboarding can be.*

—Harry Campbell, author of *The Rideshare Guide*

What drivers need to do to get started with Uber varies by jurisdiction, but in most cases it's a lot faster and easier than becoming a taxi driver. Uber doesn't require a commercial driver's license and only performs a fairly simple background check that normally takes less than a week. Generally, vehicles must be less than 10 years old (15 in some locations) and have four doors. According to Harry Campbell, author of *The Rideshare Guide*, a driver can normally be approved in a few days and start making money on the first day. And, with Uber's Instant Pay option, drivers can be paid the same day they earn the money.

In contrast, many cities around the world have stringent requirements for taxi drivers. Perhaps the most demanding regime is in London, England. To drive an iconic "black cab," drivers must memorize 320 routes and 25,000 streets. This daunting effort, known as acquiring "The Knowledge," typically takes two to four years of study.[3]

Memorizing tens of thousands of streets in the age of Google Maps and Waze seems as quaint as, say, the guards' uniforms at Buckingham Palace. Or, as out-of-date as requiring cab drivers to know how to care for horses. Nevertheless, London "black cab" drivers compete with "minicab" and Uber drivers for riders, making the disparity in difficulty of training a major bone of contention.

Most cities aren't as demanding as London, but many do have special licensing requirements or demand fingerprinting and criminal background checks for taxi drivers. Unless required by law to follow specific procedures, Uber uses its own faster methods to screen drivers.

## Finding Riders

Connecting drivers with riders is facilitated in the ride-share apps. Unlike taxi drivers, rider-share drivers don't have to wait in a queue at an airport, hotel, or taxi stand. Queues are a relatively efficient matching process, but if many other taxis are available, sometimes the wait can be hours.[4] Also unlike taxi drivers, ride-share drivers never roam city streets, hoping to get hailed by a pedestrian.

Drivers only make money when they are carrying a passenger, so any time between rides is wasted. If they are creeping forward in a slow-moving queue or hunting for passengers on city streets, they are also wasting fuel.

Ride-sharing apps facilitate the matching process. A driver can wait wherever he or she wants, engine off, until the app suggests a nearby rider. The driver can decide whether to accept the ride based on location. I encountered an Uber driver in London who looked for airport rides at the end of his day. He lived not far from the airport, and selectively choosing a trip in that direction ensured that he was making money on his commute home.

The driver and rider meet at a location pinpointed by the app for both of them. In my experience, this has occasionally been a rare source of ride-hailing friction. Airports and commercial facilities may have auto access at multiple levels, for example, and a single GPS point doesn't always fully specify the location. Sometimes, tall buildings interfere with precise location. These inaccuracies can waste time and even result in cancelled rides, so Uber is improving the location of the "blue dot" that represents the rider using advanced GPS technology.[5]

Most of the time, though, the driver and rider come together quickly and efficiently.

## Destination Friction

The next bit of friction that is eliminated is explaining to the driver exactly where you are going. Streets sound similar, for example. In Atlanta, there are 71 streets with "Peachtree" in their name![6] Chain hotels and restaurants may have multiple outlets in one city, all sounding similar.

Stepping into a taxi that just found you on the street requires at least a minute or two of back and forth between rider and driver and any number of things can go wrong. That's more wasted time for both parties. Should the driver misconstrue the details of the destination, the time lost could be much greater.

With Uber or Lyft, that's never a problem—the rider has already specified the exact destination, and it's loaded into the driver's GPS. As soon as the passenger is in the car, the driver can be on her way with near-zero possibility of a destination error.

The use of real-time traffic information in the driver's GPS ensures efficient routing. Even the incomparable knowledge of a London "black cab" driver won't help if there's an accident blocking the best route. The passenger can follow the route using the app if he or she wishes, keeping abreast of the projected arrival time and ensuring that the driver isn't deviating to a longer route as some revenue-hungry taxi drivers do.

## Rider Offloading

Finally, the end of trip routine is as frictionless for the driver as it is for the passenger. They say goodbye, with no worries about payment. The rider can add a tip later using the app, avoiding fumbling for appropriate change. Both parties know the other will rate them after the ride, encouraging courteous and friendly behavior.

We've focused primarily on the near-frictionless customer experience for the rider, but friction for ride-share drivers is far lower than for taxi drivers. When the rider is saving time, the driver is too. Ride-share drivers are more efficient, carrying riders for a greater portion of their time than taxis. Furthermore, new driver onboarding is almost always faster in the ride-share world than for taxi drivers. Ride-share drivers are in complete control of their work hours, and can further increase efficiency by working for multiple services, including food and other delivery firms.

## Taxis Are Officially Disrupted

Overall, the smoother, more flexible experience for both rider and driver explains the explosive popularity of ride-sharing services. Until taxi services can offer a similar experience, they will survive only by bureaucratic intervention.

## FRICTION TAKEAWAY

Uber and its ride-sharing peers wisely focused on customer experience first. But, they knew that making their drivers more productive would be essential to attract and retain drivers as well as maximize value for both rider and driver. Wasted time means either lower earnings for the driver or higher prices for the rider. Reducing wasted time is a win for everyone. As on the rider side, Uber and Lyft have tried to take friction out of every part of the driver experience, including easy onboarding of new drivers and nearly instant payment. Reducing friction for your employees or contractors will help them *and* your customers.

## DISRUPTING USED CARS

I've heard people say they'd rather get a root canal than shop for a used car. I've done both and can confirm that, on average, a root canal is more pleasant than buying a used car.

Used cars have been around since the first automobile drove off with its new owner. And, for most of the twentieth century, there were three primary ways to buy a used car.

**Person to Person.** Buying a car from an individual owner can be cost-effective. There's no middleman who expects to profit. But, it's a potentially risky proposition for both sides of the deal. If something goes wrong with the vehicle after purchase, the buyer may have little recourse. The seller may worry about being blamed for problems later. Transactions usually must be conducted using cash or some other secure payment method. Neither party can fully trust the other.

**New Car Dealers.** New car dealers are often a safer way to buy a used car. They generally have a well-equipped service department, and sometimes offer warranties. The buyer feels more protected but almost always pays a higher price for that security blanket.

**Used Car Lots.** Then, of course, there are the infamous used car lots. The perception of the sales process at these businesses is so bad that the term "used car salesman" has become shorthand for any

> high-pressure, fast-talking, and perhaps dishonest salesperson. No doubt there were, and still are, used car lot operators who are honest and straightforward in their dealings with customers. The consumer, though, may have difficulty distinguishing the good ones from the bad ones.

Historically, many used car dealers seemed willing to do anything to get a car off their lot and into a customer's hands. Mechanical problems might not be disclosed or could be covered up with temporary fixes. Financing would be arranged right on the lot, with terms that greatly favored the seller. Used car lots were frequented most often by shoppers who lacked the financial resources to shop elsewhere.

The often sketchy nature of the used car business meant that most operations were small and local. If a used car dealer ran into too many customer problems, it was easy to move, change the name, or otherwise reconstitute the business.

The customer experience in buying a used car left a lot to be desired. Even at reputable new car dealers, transactions were conducted with unequal bargaining positions. The dealer knew far more about the car, its condition, and its true market value than the buyer. All of this made consumers looking for a used car dread the buying process.

## THE LOW-FRICTION SHOWROOM

The impetus for a better way to sell used cars didn't come from a car dealer or auto manufacturer. As so often happens with disruptive innovation, an outsider saw the problems in an industry and felt there was a better way. Seeking to diversify, electronics retailer Circuit City launched a new concept for used car sales, CarMax.

The customer experience was designed to be a vast improvement over traditional used car lots. The first store opened with 500 vehicles in stock, none more than five years old or with more than 70,000 miles. A computer kiosk in the showroom let customers and salespeople browse through the inventory easily. There was a service facility on-site. Most importantly, the prices of the cars were fixed. The no-haggle policy, which persists today, made the salesperson a helpful ally, not a greedy adversary.[7]

Within two years, CarMax had opened three more stores and notched annual sales of $77 million. One year later, the startup hit $304 million in sales, a remarkable number in an industry where the average dealer generated just $2 million annually.[8] Customers clearly preferred the easy, no-hassle CarMax experience.

By 2002, sales rose to $3.2 billion, generating $91 million in net profit. That year, Circuit City spun off CarMax into a separate, publicly traded company.[9] Since that time, the two firms' fates diverged. By 2009, Circuit City was bankrupt and closed all remaining stores.

## Easy, Easy, Easy

CarMax, meanwhile, continues to emphasize their low-friction experience. The headline describing their shopping experience reads "We Make It Easy," which is followed by "We're committed to making every step in the process easier." They emphasize that there's no haggling, and they offer a five-day full-refund return policy if the customer isn't happy. Financing is "stress-free."

CarMax will buy your car, too. Their motto? "Sell Your Car the Easy Way!"

"Easy" seems to be working for CarMax. In the 12 months ending in February 2016, the company reported selling over a million vehicles, with more than 600,000 of them going to retail customers.[10] In 2017, their sales hit $17 billion with net income of $664 million. Their revenue earned them the #174 spot on the Fortune 500, up 17 from the preceding year.[11]

## Better Experience, Higher Prices

How can CarMax be so profitable selling a commodity like used cars? A bit of research by auto news site Jalopnik showed CarMax generated more profit per car than other publicly traded dealers.[12] And, the article provided a simple explanation: CarMax charges more than other used car dealers. A random sample of cars for sale at CarMax found their prices were somewhat higher than similar vehicles elsewhere. The article was intended to be cautionary, suggesting that car buyers should shop around before committing to a deal at CarMax.

I prefer to look at the same information in a more positive way: customers are willing to pay a little more at CarMax because buying a car there is easier and less stressful than the alternatives.

## FRICTION TAKEAWAY

Circuit City executives translated their experience in one industry to a very different one. They and competitors like Best Buy had taken much of the friction out of buying televisions and electronics gear. The even larger used car industry suffered from many of the same issues. By changing assumptions and improving customer experience, CarMax became huge and profitable even as its parent failed. Importantly, CarMax is more profitable than its competition because customers are willing to pay more for a low-friction experience.

# WHEN JAPAN DISRUPTED THE WORLD

In the early years of Nissan exporting cars to the United States, engineers in Japan were stumped. American owners were reporting that their cars wouldn't start in cold weather. The same models seemed to start just fine in Japan, even when the weather was equally cold.

Finally, they found why the problems were occurring in the United States. In Japan, where car ownership was still a luxury, owners would put blankets over their car's hoods at night. The foolish American owners expected their cars to just start in the winter. They couldn't be bothered with tucking their car in with a cozy blanket each night.[13]

Blankets aside, the earliest Japanese cars imported after World War II were dismissed as unimportant by Detroit executives. They were small, poorly made, and lacking the features that American car buyers wanted. But, by the time the oil crisis made small cars much more appealing, the Japanese automakers, particularly Toyota and Nissan, were ready to shake the foundations of Detroit.

## Starting from Scratch

In the years after their crushing defeat in World War II, Japan's economy grew at a far faster pace than the victors in that conflict. Part of the growth story was that Japan was starting from a postwar low point, but there were other key elements. With much of their manufacturing infrastructure destroyed, Japan had no choice but to rebuild from scratch. This enabled them to leapfrog established rivals by using newer technology as they built more modern facilities. They also enthusiastically adopted the statistical quality control practices championed by American engineer, professor, and management consultant William Edwards Deming.

## Kaizen

Beyond technology, postwar Japan found a new way to operate their businesses. They used what came to be known as lean manufacturing strategies and adopted the principle of "kaizen"—continuous improvement. Conceptually, it's a sort of virtuous cycle of measurement, testing, and small changes with a dose of innovation. Integrated with the quality control practices derived from Deming's work, kaizen became a powerful driver of quality and efficiency.

Practitioners of kaizen tend not to look for sweeping changes or totally new ways of doing things. Rather, they constantly measure the results of the current process and test changes that may further improve those results. Simplification is a key concept. If an assembly like an automobile carburetor was composed of many individual parts and fasteners, instead of merely looking for ways to assemble it more efficiently a kaizen practitioner would try to simplify the assembly. Pieces that were previously separate and which needed to be assembled with screws, for example, might be molded as a single piece.

## You Say "Muda," I Say "Friction"

*Muda [is] the Japanese term for waste that encompasses wasted materials, effort, and time.*

—from *The Machine That Changed The World* by Daniel Roos, Daniel T. Jones, and James P. Womack[14]

Underlying the concept of kaizen and lean manufacturing is the constant reduction of "muda," which translates roughly as "waste." The meaning of muda in this context is very broad. It can mean obvious waste, like scrap raw material or defective products. But, it can also mean things like wasted effort, needless transportation, time spent waiting, and excess inventory.

All these sound like friction, and none more than wasted motion and effort. A key element in the Japanese approach to lean manufacturing is to make the work as easy as possible. This might have seemed to be a strange concept to American managers in an era when they were trying to get uncooperative union workers to work harder. But, eliminating "waste of motion" wasn't about coddling Japanese workers, it was about productivity.

For example, if the parts needed for assembly were at the same level as the place where they would be attached, no lifting would be required. Not only is lifting time consuming, it can lead to injury (and lost production) even if the parts aren't heavy. Placing the parts in a way that the worker did not have to turn to get them would further reduce wasted motion. Similarly, tools should be close at hand.

To eliminate motion-related muda, Japanese engineers observed every movement of the worker, no matter how tiny, to see if it could be reduced or eliminated. And, the workers themselves were expected to identify muda in its many forms. Waste, they were told, would lead to higher car prices and lower sales.[15]

One contemporary account described how shocked American workers were to see how little effort their Japanese counterparts wasted:

> The Japanese workers in the video, following the carefully choreographed steps in their programmed worksheets, were moving at an unbelievable pace, sprinting around cars and switching tools with the sleight-of-hand speed of a magician. When they finished with one car, they raced to the next, not pausing to wipe the sweat from their brows.[16]

Working this way was, quite literally, a foreign concept.

## In the Opposite Corner: Deliberate Friction

The cooperative effort to eliminate friction in the manufacturing process in Japan contrasted with a more antagonistic relationship between management and workers in the United States. Armed with stopwatches and clipboards, US manufacturing engineers timed workers performing tasks and graded their effort. If they thought the workers could go faster, the engineers would increase the target output. Quite naturally, the workers saw this as a ploy to get them to work harder for the same pay. Their union might demand that any new expectations for output be negotiated. Often, workers deliberately slowed their work pace if they knew they were being timed.

Sometimes, American workers found ingenious ways to fool the engineers. One anecdote I recall from my business school days involved an assembly process for a steel frame using nuts and bolts. The workers discovered there was an optimal way to assemble the frame so that the nuts could be spun easily into place by hand and then quickly tightened. But, when the engineers with stopwatches came to observe, the workers altered the order of assembly so that the frame was under stress. In this condition, the nuts didn't spin easily. They had to be turned with a wrench using considerable effort. The workers were literally adding friction to their process!

To complete the charade, the workers put on a show of struggling mightily to tighten each nut quickly. Watching the Herculean effort from the profusely perspiring workers, the engineers didn't dare increase production standards. Of course, as soon as the clipboards and stopwatches were gone, the workers reverted to the easier process that gave them time to relax.

Ironically, these American workers had identified and eliminated muda as efficiently as their Japanese counterparts. But, they failed to share that with management so that the overall process could be improved and production increased.

## Global Dominance

The cooperative focus on eliminating friction in manufacturing served the Japan automakers well. Their costs were lower and quality higher. Driven in part by high gasoline prices, by 1975 they were exporting nearly two million cars per year. In the ensuing decades, they expanded manufacturing to locations outside Japan and largely followed the same approach. By 2000, Japan was the largest car producer in the world.

While automakers in other countries eventually caught up to the Japanese firms in cost and quality,[17] the latter remain among the leaders. Today, Toyota remains the number one global automobile firm by revenue.[18]

## FRICTION TAKEAWAY

Seeing and eliminating "muda" is a great concept, not just for assembly-line workers. As we'll see later in the book, just about every organization has its share of muda that, if eliminated, will make the work easier and let people get more done. Instead of trying to get people to work harder, make their job easier.

# CHAPTER 4

# Digital Disruption

Super Bowl ads usually feature celebrities, animals, and other kinds of appealing imagery. The idea of spending millions of dollars to show a nearly all-text ad in this most elite (and expensive!) of placements seems ludicrous. But, in 2010, that's what Google, which had never run such a high-profile television ad, did.[1] Their "Parisian Love" ad tells an epic love story entirely through the Google search window.

A series of web searches tells the tale. The first entry, typed by unseen hands, is "study abroad paris france." Soon, the searches progress to "cafe near the louvre" and "impress a french girl." Eventually, the phrases turn to jobs, churches, and "how to assemble a crib." The ad was one of the most liked by consumers that year, and generated tremendous buzz online.

While the searches told the story of finding love in Paris, the visuals provided the real message: finding *anything* (even love!) takes just a few keystrokes at Google.

## THE "EASY" PATH TO DOMINATING SEARCH

Google's dominance in search is unchallenged. They attract 90 percent of searches globally, with their closest competitor garnering a mere 3 percent.[2] Considering the effort that companies like Microsoft and Yahoo have put into search over the years, Google's share is nothing short of amazing.

Two factors have led to Google's lead in this space:

- They are very good at producing the result the user is looking for.
- They make it very, very easy to get that result.

In their earliest days, their PageRank and link-based algorithm enabled them to produce results that were much more accurate than the search engines that preceded them. A user searching for "general motors," for example, is probably looking for the official General Motors website. Google, even in its earliest days, would show the General Motors website, gm.com, as its top result. Other search engines, which relied mostly on page content, might show a GM fan page or, more likely, a spam page that had been optimized for the search term. Other search engines improved their algorithms as time passed, but Google improved, too. No other search engine could keep up with Google's quality.

Accurate results save users time and effort. In the earliest days of web search, I recall having to scroll through dozens of results at AltaVista, Lycos, or Excite to find what I was looking for. Plowing past redundant, irrelevant, and sometimes spammy results was a high-friction experience for the user. It was not uncommon to have to load multiple pages of results before something useful appeared.

Providing relevant, accurate results at the top of the first page was one way Google made things easier, but not the only way.

## Simplicity Wins

Even in those early days, Google's home page was nothing more than a search box surrounded by white space. Competitors like Yahoo! and AltaVista thought of themselves as portals, not search engines. The search box on their home page was a tiny part of a page dominated by ads, content links, news feeds, images, and more. Compared to Google's elegant focus on one thing—search—the other portal pages were noisy and distracting. The combination of simplicity and accuracy drove Google's dramatic growth.

Google continued to improve its algorithm, adding more variables and trying to reduce the impact of would-be spammers. Even though search engine optimizers were sometimes able to game the results, Google's quality remained better than anyone else's.

## "Did You Mean . . . ?"

Even as their algorithm became more sophisticated, Google developers also focused on ways to reduce user effort to accomplish their objective.

One way Google found it could reduce friction for users was fixing spelling errors. In the early days of search, spammers gobbled up domains and optimized pages for misspelled words. It might be nearly impossible to rank for the word "poker," since gambling-related terms are extremely competitive, but what about "pokre"? If you typed, say, "play pokre online" into AltaVista or Yahoo! in the early days, you would get results for "pokre," which would usually be websites designed to take advantage of that incorrect spelling. Even if only 0.01 percent of searchers mistype the word in that way, the traffic might be enough to generate a profit from clicks on gambling ads.

The Parisian Love ad highlights Google's ability to spot spelling errors. At one point, the unseen user types in "cafes near the louve," and the first link displayed reads, "Did you mean: cafes near the *louvre*?" Of course, the user clicks on the corrected spelling, and gets a list of cafes near the famed museum.

Without the spelling suggestion, he or she would see a list of irrelevant results. The user would have to fix the spelling and redo the search, if he or she even spotted the error and knew the correct spelling. Google saves the user effort by recognizing his or her intent and suggesting that in a prominent location.

In fact, when user intent seems to be very clear, Google goes a step further. The results for the corrected spelling will be shown, with the heading, "Showing results for: cafes near the louvre." A second link will offer results for the way the user originally spelled the word. The default is to display what the user was looking for, eliminating any user effort to correct the spelling.

## We Know What You Want

But, the big friction-reducer highlighted throughout the Parisian Love ad is Google's predictive autocomplete feature. We take this capability for granted today, but when Google began offering this it seemed almost magical. With each character typed into the search box, Google displays what the user might be looking for.

So, our story begins with someone typing into the Google search box. The first letter, *s*, causes Google to offer choices like "southwest airlines," "sears," and the ominous "swine flu symptoms." With *st* entered, suggestions like "staples," "starbucks," and "star trek" appear. Adding the *u* produces "stub hub" and "student loans" as the top offerings. These options are changing as fast as the user types. Eventually, with more letters entered, "study abroad paris france" is suggested and the unseen user clicks it.

Depending on what you are searching for, the suggestions can save most of your keystrokes. Not only that, it can guess at your intent and suggest different possibilities that might yield better results. For example, when I typed "mac keyboard sticking," my suggested choices included "mac keyboard spacebar sticking" and "wireless mac keyboard keys sticking." Neither of those matched the characters I typed exactly, but both offered a refinement of my search that might yield better results and a quicker answer to my problem.

## Beyond Search

Google's Chrome browser does something similar in the address bar. As you begin to type, it will offer a mix of web addresses and search terms based on your own history as well as popularity. For years, less technical users have apparently been confused by the browser's address bar (where you can type a web address) and the search box (where you can type a word or phrase to search for). Google made things easy for everyone by providing search functionality in the address bar.

## No Click, No Effort

Google never stops trying to make it easier for its users and further minimize effort. Google is doing what its users want: provide the fastest, easiest answer to any question.

One metric that illustrates how successfully Google is minimizing user effort is the number of "no-click" searches. In most cases today, a no-click search means that the user got the information he or she needed without having to click on a result. For desktop searches, more than a third didn't generate a click as of early 2018. On mobile searches, fully 61 percent were no-click, up from 33 percent in late 2015.[3] Google is rapidly closing in on delivering what its users want with no need to look beyond their results.

Google's relentless pursuit of minimum user effort to get the desired information has enabled it to retain its dominant position. Competitors like Microsoft's Bing keep advancing their technology but don't seem to be able to gain on the leader. As search expert Rand Fishkin put it, "There's basically no one else on the web sending out any decent quantity of traffic—it's Google or nothing."[4]

### FRICTION TAKEAWAY

Can you anticipate your user's or customer's needs and offer time-saving choices? If customers are searching your website, are you offering them suggestions as they type? If they type something that either gets no results or seems like an error, do you offer some results that seem to be related to the query? Google saves its users significant time by guessing at their intent early and often. Google suggests searches that may not match what the user typed but seem to match the intent of the search. Be sure you are gathering data on both unsuccessful and successful searches to improve both your search function and your site itself.

## BILLIONS FOR EYEBALLS

Amazing fortunes have been made in the software and application space. Some of the richest people in the world, like Bill Gates and Larry Ellison, built their wealth as shares in their companies, Microsoft and Oracle, appreciated year after year. Those companies had hugely successful software products that earned enormous profits.

In recent years, though, profitability (or even revenue) hasn't been necessary to produce wealth. Many pundits were shocked when Facebook paid a billion dollars for photo app Instagram. The founders were young, and the company had not yet produced significant revenue.[5]

As shocking as a cool billion for a photo app was, the subsequent acquisition of messaging firm WhatsApp by Facebook for $19 billion was jaw-dropping. That company, like Instagram, had little revenue.[6]

Traditionally, businesses are valued based on a multiple of their earnings. Sometimes companies lack earnings but achieve high valuations because they have patents or other hard-to-copy advantages. WhatsApp and Instagram had neither earnings nor proprietary technology.

Furthermore, both applications had lots of competition. Photo sharing and messaging are some of the most common activities on mobile devices, and many app developers have targeted those markets.

So, what set these firms apart and gave them valuations in the billions? The answer is simple—they attracted a huge number of users. None of their countless competitors came close.

Both Instagram and WhatsApp grew to a size where the network effect kicked in. Sharing and communication apps deliver the most value when your friends and many other people are using them. It's no fun sharing photos if almost nobody sees them, and exchanging messages requires everyone to be on a common platform.

Once these apps pulled away from the pack, their growth was almost assured. Any user looking for a fun way to share photos would obviously choose the platform used by the most people, and specifically by the user's friends.

Facebook could have attempted to build its own apps and exploit its own powerful network effect, but doing so would have been time-consuming and costly. Furthermore, Instagram and WhatsApp were already achieving widespread adoption. Both companies would have been able to consolidate their dominant positions while Facebook was trying to convince its users to switch. Facebook, ultimately, valued time and market share more than cash, leading to the record-setting deals.

## HOOKING USERS, DECODED

So, if what made these apps so valuable was their market share, the next question is, how did they achieve leadership status in such a crowded market space? How did they get enough traction that the network effect kept them growing?

My friend Nir Eyal became a bestselling author by answering that question. Already a successful entrepreneur who had built and sold a couple of businesses, Eyal studied hundreds of products, both successes and failures, to determine why some became habits and many others didn't. He wanted to explain why Instagram, WhatsApp, and even Facebook grew their user bases at an exponential pace while apparently similar applications didn't. He found that the network effect is important, but it's far from the whole story. In fact, on their path to dominance in their space, all these apps used a somewhat similar approach to forming user habits.

As he was cracking the code of what made some apps addictive, Eyal blogged about his findings. A friend and fan, Ryan Hoover, thought that knowledge would make a useful book. With Hoover's help and encouragement, Eyal self-published *Hooked: How to Build Habit-Forming Products.*[7] The book launched with minimal promotion. Even worse, most bookstores wouldn't carry it because Eyal published the book through their mortal enemy, Amazon. Despite these handicaps, *Hooked* became a cult bestseller in Silicon Valley—every app and software developer wanted to create the next big thing. Sales of the book and Eyal's notoriety grew. Eventually, a major publisher, Penguin, contacted Eyal and negotiated a deal to publish a new hardcover edition of *Hooked* and distribute it through bookstores nationally.

## The Hooked Model

What made *Hooked* so popular is the relative simplicity of its core concept. Eyal explained how products became habits by using the *Hooked* model, a circular series of four steps:

1. Trigger
2. Action
3. Reward
4. Investment

The concept is simple to explain, though perhaps harder to execute in the real world. A trigger (say, an e-mail promoting the product) gets the user to try it. The action phase involves doing something, like opening the app. The reward phase is where the user gets relief for what he or she came for, like scrolling a feed to feel connected to friends. The investment phase is the effort that makes it better with use, for example, posting a photo or liking someone else's post.

Successful apps use the action to load the next trigger. For example, a post on Facebook can trigger an e-mail or visible notification when your friends like it or comment on it. This brings you back to the app to continue the cycle.

The model works in a circular loop, with the user's brain continuing to seek the rewards offered by the app. The more cycles the user goes through, the more using the app becomes a habit.

The most successful apps, Eyal says, no longer need external triggers like e-mails to initiate a user session. Rather, internal triggers take over. Bored while you are standing in line at Starbucks? Fire up Instagram. Lonely? See what your friends are doing on Facebook. Once an app becomes a habit driven by a user's emotions or feelings, it's very difficult for competing apps (or even other activities) to dislodge or replace it. Indeed, these apps often displace other activities and habits in their users' lives.

## Less Friction, More Adoption

Friction hinders Eyal's "action" phase. If something is difficult or confusing, people won't do it. Have you ever downloaded an app or program that sounded interesting, opened it up, struggled to figure out what to do next, and decided to wait for a better time to try it out? We all have, but that "better time" often never comes.

In cases like that, the trigger worked—the product was opened or downloaded—but the user took no further action. Perhaps the user couldn't figure out what to do first. Or, he or she tried to do something, and it didn't work. Maybe the directions looked too complicated. Unless users are highly motivated, even a little friction in the onboarding process can stop them in their tracks.

### THE POWER OF FREE VS. FRICTION

Research by Duke professor Dan Ariely and others has shown that "free" is very appealing to our brains.[8] We are drawn to free things in a way that is out of proportion to the value. For most of us, the monetary difference between a free item and the same item for one cent is nonexistent—the value of that penny is so low many people won't bother to pick one up from the sidewalk. But, experiments show, free things are far more compelling.

The apps we have been talking about are all free to users—the companies make money by selling ads or user data. Even apps and software products that monetize by subscriptions often start with a "freemium" model.

If an app offers users compelling benefits, it's often better to let users start without demanding a payment method. Businesses like Evernote and Dropbox achieved enormous success by delivering serious value to their unpaid users. After these tools became habits and an essential part of their lives, users were willing to pay to access more features, get more storage, and so on. These free-to-use versions were highly functional so that users were encouraged to go through the *Hooked* cycle and form a habit.

And, over time, the "investment" phase of the model becomes a barrier to change. If you have hundreds of recipes or thousands of articles in Evernote, will you be eager to switch to another storage system? If you have thousands of Twitter connections, would you look forward to starting over on a new network? Once you have reached the point where switching is difficult, it's a lot easier to get you to upgrade to the paid version of a product.

The freemium strategy has paid off for Evernote. They signed up a million users in just 15 months, and hit two million 7 months after that. Their adoption rate accelerated, and less than three years after launch they hit six million.[9] A few years after starting up, Evernote reported that just 0.5 percent of new users converted to paid status, but for two-year users the number was 20 percent.[10] In the 12-month period ending in July 2016, Evernote added 50 million users![11]

Today, Evernote has 225 million users globally. The vast majority remain free users, but the number that convert to paid, including 20,000 business enterprise users, has made Evernote wildly successful.[12]

## PAY ME NOW, OR PAY ME LATER

Not all apps and services are free. The apps we have been talking about monetize by selling advertising or user data, or by charging only users with a high level of activity. Providers of other apps and services may not have those options, or may not want to use those business models. Some expect users to pay a subscription fee if they continue to use the product, while others may charge for enhancements or add-ons.

How and when payment information is collected can make a big difference in app adoption. A common point of friction is asking new users for a payment method, even if no immediate payment is required. For example, a software firm might advertise a free trial and then prompt those who respond to that trigger with a credit card form. They won't charge the user during the trial period, but users won't have to provide payment information later if they continue to use the product.

Getting a payment method up front seems like a great idea from the standpoint of the business. It ensures new users are somewhat serious about the product, reducing support contacts from customers who will never pay. And, the behavioral science is sound—many users won't cancel after the trial period expires due to inertia. It's easier to do nothing than trying to figure out how to cancel before the credit card charges start.

The downside of this approach is that the number of users who sign up will be much lower. Sometimes there are conscious reasons for balking at providing a credit card. Perhaps the user thinks it unlikely that he or she will ever pay for the service so providing a credit card seems pointless or risky. Other users may fear that they will forget to cancel at the end of the free trial and end up being charged. Some may not trust the company if they haven't heard of it before.

For some users, a credit card requirement is simply friction. Having to get a purse or wallet, fish out the credit card, copy the number, look for the hard-to-read security code on the back, and so on, is annoying. If I really want or need a product, of course, I'll do it. (Or, I'll get it from Amazon where they remember me.) But, if I was trying a product out of mere curiosity, I might well decide not to bother. After all, I'm already risking my time by testing a product I'm not certain about. Adding a bit more friction with a credit card requirement can be enough to discourage me.

## FRICTION TAKEAWAY

Making a product free for users eliminates a major friction point and leads to the fastest growth. For a paid business model, make getting started with a digital product as frictionless as possible by using the freemium approach without initially requiring a credit card. Continue to keep friction low by minimizing effort to start using the product. Deliver plenty of value in the free version so that

> some users make it a habit. For Evernote, every note users store adds to their "investment," as Eyal would say. If you offer features in the paid version that habitual users of the free product will eventually want or need, you'll convert enough to be successful.

## A TALE OF TWO APPS

How did a pair of would-be entrepreneurs in the United Kingdom attract funding and millions of users, despite being kicked out of both the United States and Hong Kong in a matter of months, just as their business was getting traction? Among other things, the story involves a focus on friction.

In the early days of social media, users soon found the tools offered by Facebook, Twitter, and other networks were limited. Typically, their websites (and they were mostly websites, since the mobile revolution was in its infancy) offered a single option for posting, viewing activity, consolidating performance metrics, and so on. Power users wanted more flexibility to manage multiple accounts, to schedule posts to appear at specific times, and to view activity in specific formats.

Third-party tools began to fill the gaps. Twitter, for example, began its explosive growth in early 2009. Before midyear, more than half of all tweets posted were from applications other than Twitter itself. The leading third-party app was Tweetdeck, accounting for a 20 percent share.[13] It offered a multicolumn display where the user could watch activity for more than one account, specific keywords or hashtags, or sets of users; view direct messages; and so on.

One could make the case that these third-party apps were friction reducers—they made social media tasks easier than using the native sites, hence their rapid adoption.

Across all social media platforms, Hootsuite emerged as the tool of choice for power users like social media managers. First conceived as a Twitter post scheduler in 2008,[14] it grew into a powerful tool that consolidated monitoring and posting across multiple channels, including Facebook and LinkedIn.

Since its early days, Hootsuite has used a freemium model. They let people use the product for free, but with a limited feature set. As you added capabilities, like multiple users or larger numbers of accounts, you had to pay. As noted previously, the freemium model is a great friction reducer. It avoids initial credit card friction and eliminates any risk for users in evaluating the product. Hootsuite's early goal was to convert 5 percent of their users into paying customers.[15]

Their strategy worked. By mid-2010, Hootsuite had 400,000 users managing more than a million social media accounts.[16] By March 2018, their total user base topped 16 million.[17]

## Buffer Is Born

While Hootsuite was achieving dominance in the space, would-be entrepreneurs Joel Gascoigne and Leo Widrich also saw the need for better social media management tools. Based in the United Kingdom, they followed a classic Silicon Valley game plan. Before writing a line of code, they tested the waters with a one-page website promoting their planned product. Visitors could show interest by getting on a waiting list. The number of signups were encouraging enough for Gascoigne to proceed with programming a simple app the pair decided to call Buffer.

In December 2010—just seven weeks later—they launched the app. It had few features and worked only with Twitter. After a tense four-day wait, the first paying customer signed up. Signups trickled in over the next few weeks, mostly free but a few paid. By May 2011, revenues were $1,000 per month. The founding duo decided they had achieved "ramen profitability"—enough monthly income to survive on a noodle diet. Gascoigne quit his day job and Widrich dropped out of the prestigious Warwick Business School. A few months later, the pair decided to move to the epicenter of the Internet world, San Francisco.

As soon as they arrived in San Francisco, they began looking for funding to allow them to ramp up product development and user acquisition more quickly. They continued to add features to the app to allow managing accounts across different networks and integrating with other popular apps. Their pitch deck to potential investors included the bold claim that they planned to become "the default sharing standard in any app." They closed on an initial seed round of $450,000 in December 2011.[18]

The Buffer success train was almost derailed by bureaucratic friction. Neither Gascoigne nor Widrich had met the requirements for a US visa, and they were forced to leave the country just a month after they closed their first round of funding. The duo decamped for Hong Kong and continued work on Buffer.[19]

Gascoigne and Widrich may have been great entrepreneurs, but they weren't particularly good with immigration law. After a mere six months in Hong Kong, visa troubles forced them to move again, this time to Tel Aviv. There, they grew the team to seven members.[20]

By May 2013, they finally sorted out their US visa problems and returned to San Francisco. They decided to operate as a distributed team, with remote workers around the globe. By September 2013, they hit the million-user milestone.

Today, Buffer is adding users at a rate of 30,000 per week.[21]

## Low-Friction Onboarding

*What if scheduling a Tweet could be as easy as sending it now?*

—Joel Gascoigne, cofounder, Buffer[22]

What enabled Buffer to get traction when Hootsuite had a two-year lead in both development and marketing, not to mention a huge base of users? Quite simply, it was Buffer's nearly frictionless onboarding process for new users. Hootsuite and other established social tools were powerful but also complicated. Want to schedule a group of tweets? Hootsuite offered the choice of uploading a "CSV" or "RTF" file. Even creating a post now to appear a few hours later wasn't particularly intuitive to a novice.

A key element in Buffer's strategy was to offer fewer functions than the all-inclusive Hootsuite, which was a sort of Swiss Army knife for social media. As one reviewer put it, "In terms of complexity, Buffer is almost the polar opposite of Hootsuite. You don't get such a wide range of features, but what you do get is a cleaner and easier to use tool."[23]

With its different look and shunning of complexity, Buffer changed the game for social media posting tools. Its user interface was incredibly simple and intuitive. The user simply connected a social media account and was ready to schedule posts.

One simplifying strategy Buffer used was to begin with a default schedule. The user didn't need to enter a scheduling menu and decide which times of day were best. Buffer had these preset. The times were editable, of course, but a new user didn't need to learn how to do that to get started.

Behavioral science shows us that doing nothing is always easier than doing something, so Buffer built in default times.

The next way Buffer made it easy to start using its app was to suggest quality content to share. It recognized that users who wanted to build their following needed to post content that others would find valuable. An account that posts only self-promotional content is boring and won't attract new followers. Buffer solved this problem by offering its users pre-vetted content. Buffer users could supplement their own content and spend less time hunting for content their followers would appreciate. (Eventually, Buffer found their content suggestions didn't scale well and eliminated this feature. A few users posting similar links is fine, but hundreds of thousands of nearly identical posts would be annoying and spammy.)

## Effortless Action, Visible Rewards

In short, Buffer made getting started easy by having ready answers to the questions: *When should I post?* and *What should I post?* They made scheduling posts effortless—the action phase of Eyal's Hook model. This not only increased the probability that users would use the tool but also built their investment. Mindful of the need to trigger users to keep going, Buffer would dispatch an e-mail as soon as a user had no remaining posts queued for a particular social profile.

The reward phase came when other users liked or shared the posted content. Buffer provided analytics tools that let a user quickly see which posts generated more activity. Seeing that posts were liked, shared, or replied to made the user want to post more.

## Frictionless and Friendly, Too

Buffer also rewarded users with encouraging and often amusing messages. Scheduling a tweet might get a "Great job!" message. And, their approach to messaging reduced friction from the kind of negative feedback that is all too common in digital products. Typical software error messages are factual—they tell you that you did something wrong. Sometimes, they are scary and cryptic, like "Error 7698, try again." Buffer's messages are cheery and make the user feel good about moving forward.

When a user deletes a scheduled post, instead of a simple confirmation the user might see one of these:

- "Dun, dun, dun . . . another tweet bites the dust!"
- "Your tweet has been sent to a better place . . ."
- "That one just wasn't meant to be!"

When the user looks at post statistics, he or she sees, "Your latest posts are looking good, keep it up!" Just scheduling a post gets, "Great! The post has been added to your queue."

The friendly, likable approach carries over to Buffer's human representatives. One of my own early support requests got a prompt reply from Adam, whose title was "Happiness Hero." It began, "Thanks for reaching out to us on this one! You definitely ask a great question and something that should probably be added to our FAQ since it comes up quite a bit." It finished with, "We are here for you, Roger! Cheers!" and included a PS, "We're always around and love hearing from you. Please get in touch if you want to ask something or even just to say hello :-)."

This breezy style was replicated by other reps I interacted with on other issues. Their approach made you feel like they were really excited to hear from you and help with your problem. That's very different than the more typical, "Sorry, but our product doesn't do that."

## Actually, You Shouldn't Say That

The choice of language Buffer uses to communicate with customers is no accident. Buffer support staffer Carolyn Kopprasch wrote that one "happiness hack" she employed was to eliminate the word "actually" from customer communications.[24] She contrasts these two sentences:

- *Actually, you can do this under "Settings."*
- *Sure thing, you can do this under "Settings!" :)*

The second one seems much friendlier. Why? The exclamation point and smiley help, but replacing "actually" is the key element. The word seems to imply, "This feature is there, you just missed it." Kopprasch says they never want customers to feel stupid, wrong, or corrected. That's a small detail, but lots of little details like that create the brand's persona and keep users engaged with the product.

In 2014, Nicole Miller was the firm's "Community Champion." Describing her job, she said "I send out love to our customers all day."[25] The firm sends out many handwritten notes to customers, often eliciting a surprised and pleased reaction from customers used to impersonal e-mails.

## Likability

Research shows that a likable persona is more likely to elicit cooperation. Dr. Robert Cialdini, author of *Influence* and *Pre-Suasion*, found that complimenting someone was one way to invoke liking, one of his seven (originally six) principles of influence. So, when you take an action and immediately see a message like "Great job! You scheduled your first post!," it triggers a little burst of positive emotion around the brand.

In a software space where technology can often be intimidating, this kind of reassurance can keep users engaged even if they are still stumbling through their first use of a product. Every software product has a learning curve, and the number of users who drop out prematurely can be high. Buffer's combination of eliminating friction combined with positive reinforcement has helped grow its user base and minimize churn.

## Simpler Than Ever

When Buffer recently redesigned their free offering, they strove to make it even simpler than ever. The redesign took out prompts, less-used features, and popups—all with the objective of making its use intuitive for new users and the software as "smooth and hassle-free" as possible. Buffer cofounder and CEO Joel Gascoigne notes that "If we were able to streamline how the Buffer product works, then people would be able to understand Buffer faster and see the impact sooner."[26]

### FRICTION TAKEAWAY

> Buffer grew quickly despite heavy competition and other obstacles by focusing on making it unusually easy for people to sign up for and start using its product. It used creative tactics like establishing

preset schedules and suggesting shareable content to get neophytes posting. An ultra-friendly persona was part of both automated and human interactions. Getting started on Buffer was about as frictionless an experience as one could imagine, and it paid off in explosive growth.

## DISRUPTION DECODED

*Amazon appeals to our hunter-gatherer instinct to collect more stuff with minimum effort. . . . Easy stuff is the best stuff, because it consumes less energy and gives you time to do other important things.*

—from *The Four: The Hidden DNA of Amazon, Apple, Facebook, and Google* by Scott Galloway

Scott Galloway is a rare individual. He's a serial entrepreneur, for one. Many self-described serial entrepreneurs chase new opportunities because their previous one didn't work out. Galloway, on the other hand, has had a series of successful start-ups—he founded business like L2 (sold to Gartner Group for $134 million),[27] RedEnvelope (went public for $31 million before running into trouble under other management),[28] and Prophet. And, not only is he a college professor at New York University's Stern School of Business, he's a faculty star. In 2012, he made the Poets & Quants list of the "World's 50 Best Business Professors."[29] His video series, *Winners and Losers*, has generated tens of millions of views.[30]

Lately, he has focused on four digital giants—Amazon, Apple, Facebook, and Google. He admires their prowess and success, while also urging caution about their growing power. Google, he thinks, is almost a god to many of its users. They trust Google to provide wise, unbiased answers to the most intimate and unusual questions.

One of the behaviors that Galloway has identified relates to product design at these firms. While many companies are constantly seeking to add value to their products by building in ever more features and functions, Galloway suggests that "removal" is an important strategy. While competitors focus on delivering "more for less," he says, much of the success of Apple, Amazon, and the others is based on "removing obstacles and time killers from our daily lives."[31]

He describes the traditional shopping trip—drive to the mall, park, walk a considerable distance, be overwhelmed by a plethora of irrelevant merchandise, carry your purchase back to your car, and drive home. Amazon, he notes, has removed all that friction—a few clicks, and the product you want will be delivered to your door in 48 hours. For free.

"Friction is everywhere," Galloway says.[32] Well, except at Amazon.

CHAPTER

5

# The Science of Friction

At this point, we've seen some very different examples of how reducing friction can disrupt entire industries. We've got many more practical examples to come, but I'd like to spend a short time on the science that underlies the effects of friction on human behavior.

I think you'll find this chapter interesting and helpful, but if you want to skip over it, don't worry—there won't be a test, and the rest of the book will still make perfect sense. (Well, at least as much sense as if you *don't* skip it!)

## THE LAW OF FRICTION

Given what we know from the work of Daniel Kahneman, BJ Fogg, Richard Thaler, and other scientists, not to mention philosophers through the centuries, I propose this fundamental law of friction:

**Decreasing friction increases action.**

A slightly more formal way of stating this would be:

**The level of action is inversely proportional to the level of friction.**

From this basic law, we can derive more specific correlates:

- When you make something easier, people do more of it.
- When you make something more difficult, people do less of it.

- When you make something easier, it is more likely that people will do it.
- When you make something more difficult, it is less likely that people will do it.
- When you tax something, people do or consume less of it.
- Given two options, people will choose the one with less friction.

You can probably come up with other variations suited to your own application, but the underlying principle is the same.

The rest of this chapter will look at the science behind this simple law.

## FRICTION ON ICE

Have you ever watched the unusual sport of curling? Except for serious fans, most of us experience curling once every four years when the Winter Olympics turns it into prime-time television fare. At first glance, curling looks a lot like shuffleboard on a skating rink. A player glides down the ice and releases a heavy granite stone toward a distant target. As with shuffleboard, scoring is based on proximity to the target.

What happens next makes curling different from every other sport. As the stone lumbers toward the target on the icy surface, two other team members called "sweepers" accompany it. They wield little brooms and brush the ice furiously in front of the stone. This frenetic sweeping alters both the distance and the direction of the stone, and the sweepers adjust their effort to direct the stone as close to the target as possible. They only sweep the ice in front of the moving stone, since they aren't allowed to touch the stone itself.

While the frenzied sweeping action may appear strange or even comical to some, it's an art that can lead to Olympic gold. And, sweepers have been part of curling since the game was first played on frozen lakes in Scotland.

What all that brushing does is *reduce friction*. Ice is already a low-friction surface, as anyone attempting to navigate a frozen sidewalk can attest. But the rapid brushing warms the surface of the ice, making the ice in front of the stone even more slick. Despite the considerable weight and momentum of the stone, the sweeping has a big impact on its final resting place. The stone can travel as much as 10 feet farther and its direction can be altered significantly.

**FRICTION TAKEAWAY**

> Humans can be a lot like curling stones. They are heading in a direction and changing their course without physical contact looks impossible. But, instead of trying to push them in a new direction, *we can steer them by selectively reducing friction in their path.*

## THE INVISIBLE FORCE

*Transaction costs, one often hears, are "the economic equivalent of friction in physical systems." Like physicists, economists can sometimes neglect friction in formulating theories; but like engineers, they can never neglect friction in studying how the system actually does—let alone should—work. Interestingly, however, the present-day economics of organization also ignores friction.*

—from *The Secret Life of Mundane Transaction Costs* by Richard N. Langlois

Friction is a force we experience countless times per day in our physical world, but which eluded discovery for millennia.

The first person to investigate physical friction in a scientific way was none other than Leonardo da Vinci, one of the greatest minds of any age. He recognized that the motion of two objects in contact with each other was resisted by some kind of force. He set out to investigate it with a clever experiment involving a round rod in a semicircular groove. When he attached a weight to one side of the rod, it resisted spinning in the groove until the weight was heavy enough.

But da Vinci's early friction research remained hidden in his notes and wasn't discovered until long after his death. Eventually, other scientists followed a similar path and friction became a well-documented force. Today, every student of physics learns about friction.

### Always Present, Often Ignored

Here's the odd part about friction in the physical world—even though every physicist knows about it and acknowledges its existence, it is often ignored in basic calculations. Beginning students learn the laws of physics as if friction simply didn't exist. An object dropped from a high point (think Galileo and the Tower of Pisa) is influenced by gravity but not by air drag in their simple calculations.

Why do physicists often ignore friction? The main reason is that calculations go from simple to complex very quickly. The motion of a block sliding down an inclined, frictionless surface affected only by gravity is easy to predict. When you include friction in the calculation, you need to think about the area of contact, the characteristics of the two surfaces, and so on. The math gets messy, and perhaps too complicated for beginners.

This book isn't about physical friction, but we'll see that businesses, governments, and even individual people take the same shortcut as physics teachers. They find the effects of friction hard to quantify, so it's usually much more convenient to ignore it.

If NASA decided to simplify its calculations by ignoring friction, no space mission would ever succeed. With this book, my objective is to show how it can be just as dangerous to ignore friction in other areas of endeavor.

## FRICTION ECONOMICS

As a young boy in London, Ronald Coase's parents sent him to a school for "physical defectives" due to his weak legs—hardly a promising start for a future Nobel Prize winner. He was sent to a phrenologist, who, after carefully feeling Coase's skull, proclaimed him to be "in possession of much intelligence" and praised his mental vigor. The phrenologist recommended a career as a banker or an accountant, and suggested raising poultry would be an ideal hobby.

Coase wisely ignored the phrenologist, skipped the chickens, and instead studied economics. While an undergraduate at the London School of Economics, he delved into what made businesses work efficiently. This work led to Coase authoring his seminal paper, "The Nature of the Firm." He was just 27 years old, but challenged the established economic doctrine related to firms and markets.

In that paper, Coase proposed the idea that "transaction costs" determined the viability of enterprises. These were costs that companies incur in buying and selling things, and that could be eliminated when firms grew and brought these operations in-house. These transaction costs were a friction element, a sort of financial tax that could be eliminated by greater integration.

According to Coase's ideas, Henry Ford's early cost advantage in the auto industry could be explained not just by its innovative assembly methods but also because the company made its own parts and even steel. Faced with high rubber prices driven by a British cartel, at one point Ford even established rubber plantations in Brazil to supply raw material for tires.

Much later, New York University (NYU) law professor Richard Epstein summed up Coase's paper by repeating a single word: "Friction, friction, friction, friction."[1]

Since the dawn of economics, as in the simplest version of Newtonian physics, economists ignored friction. In *The Org*, Ray Fisman and Tim Sullivan discuss Adam Smith, the eighteenth-century Scottish philosopher and father of modern economics. They write:

> But what Smith's account is missing, among other things, is the real cost of doing business in an open market. These factors—what Coase labeled "transaction costs"—find no place in the mathematical models that the followers of Adam Smith developed to explain the superiority of the market's invisible hand to the controlling hand of bosses. . . . Coase's conception of the market involved a lot more friction and discord than Adam Smith's original vision.[2]

For another 20 years, mainstream economists continued to pay little attention to transaction costs. They assumed such costs could be safely ignored, much as a physics student might ignore the friction of air drag on a heavy object falling a short distance.

By the 1960s, continued work by Coase and others brought transaction costs back into the discussion. In 1960, Coase wrote another paper, "The Problem of Social Cost." The paper describes what other economists labeled the Coase theorem. While that theorem relates to the use of property and harm to others, it had its roots in Coase's thinking about transaction costs. The paper became the most cited law review article of all time. At last count, Google Scholar showed a remarkable 33,404 citations.[3]

## Coase vs. Blackboard Economics

In 1991, more than half a century later, Coase was awarded the Nobel Prize for Economics for his work in transaction costs.[4] The Royal Swedish Academy of Sciences called his work a "radical extension of economic micro theory."[5]

When Coase died in 2013 at the age of 102, his friend and colleague, NYU law professor Richard Epstein, wrote that even in his final year, Coase bemoaned his colleagues practicing "blackboard economics." He was starting a publication, *The Journal of Man*, to focus on how people behaved in real contexts. Coase didn't live long enough to see the publication, ultimately titled *Man and the Economy*, launch in 2015. He survives on the masthead as "founder."[6]

*To put it otherwise, what [Coase] did was make friction the main event in all cases, not just a sideshow.*

—Richard Epstein, NYU law professor[7]

In some ways, Coase's work prefigured that of later behavioral economists. His early transaction cost insights were based on visits with executives from Ford, General Motors, and Union Carbide. Coase made the point in his writings that his peers should spend less time with their models and more time in the real world.[8]

Perhaps Coase didn't quite go far enough. Two later Nobel Prize winners, Daniel Kahneman and Richard Thaler, authored (along with Jack Knetsch) a paper that showed people were more irrational than even Coase predicted. The paper discussed the endowment effect, which predicts that you will value an item that you own more than the same item owned by someone else.[9]

Another Nobel Prize winner, Oliver E. Williamson, also found that transactions within a firm could be more efficient. He shared the Economics prize in 2009 with Elinor Ostrom.[10]

## Beyond Transaction Costs

*Opening the black box of the firm revealed that it was Pandora's Box: positive transaction costs were everywhere.*

—Oliver E. Williamson, Nobel Prize Lecture, 2009[11]

Ironically, even as Coase was finally being acclaimed for his insights into the firm, the problems with giant companies were becoming increasingly apparent.

Early in the twentieth century, Coase's insights about firms minimizing transaction costs when the activity took place inside the firm made sense.

Size usually did increase efficiency and lower costs. Ford made automobiles affordable by building the biggest, most integrated factory and supply chain the world had ever seen. Sears Roebuck disrupted retail by publishing an all-encompassing catalog more than 500 pages long, and building the world's biggest commercial building—a 3-million-square-foot mail-order plant.[12]

While scale and integration can indeed increase efficiency and reduce costs, it can also add complexity to an enterprise. There are more layers of management, and, with so many diverse activities, focus on core competencies can suffer. Ford's bold move to vertically integrate was initially successful, but ultimately the company decided to leave tasks like making steel to firms where that was the primary focus.

It seemed that although transaction friction was important, at some level friction from bureaucracy and complexity was even more so.

## EMPLOYMENT FRICTION

Handmade handkerchiefs fascinated young Christopher Pissarides while he was growing up on the island of Cyprus. Cypriot women would buy silk thread from his father's shop and eventually return with elegantly embroidered handkerchiefs. The labor performed by these women transformed low-value materials into a beautiful and far more valuable finished product.[13]

In a way, seeing the transformation of these handkerchiefs presaged Pissarides's love for mathematics, a discipline in which basic building blocks can be transformed into elegant models. He went on to study economics first at the University of Essex and then at the London School of Economics, where he earned his PhD.

Early in his study of economics, Pissarides made an observation: there were people who wanted jobs but couldn't get hired, even though firms were actively trying to fill vacant positions. The economic models of the time couldn't explain this conundrum, as they predicted perfect matching—job openings would be filled if there were willing workers.

Just as simple physics equations ignore the messy mathematics of friction, the supply and demand equations used by economists were ignoring "frictions" in the job market. (Economists favor the plural form of friction.)

Pissarides had compassion for the plight of people who wanted to find work and couldn't. This situation could be devastating at the personal level, but it also represented the waste of a valuable resource. His focus on solving the problem of why economists couldn't get unemployment predictions right resulted in Pissarides developing an entirely new equation, being knighted by the Queen of England, and sharing the Nobel Prize for Economics with Americans Peter Diamond and Dale Mortensen.[14]

## Supply Meets Demand, Sort Of

Everyone who has taken a basic economics class learned about supply and demand curves. For most commodities in competitive markets, supply and demand vary with price. When prices go down, buyers demand more but sellers are willing to supply less. Higher prices have the opposite effect. Each of those tendencies forms a curve, and where the curves intersect equilibrium is reached and transactions take place. The concept of supply and demand curves goes back to the seventeenth century.

*Financial Times* columnist Tim Harford notes that supply and demand curves don't work very well in the labor market. When unemployment is high, that is, the supply of labor is higher than demand, the traditional model suggests that wages will fall, demand for labor will increase, and in short order everyone who wants a job will have one. That simply doesn't happen in the real world.

In an interview for a UBS "Nobel Perspective" piece focused on Pissarides's contributions to economic theory, Harford notes, "The truth is getting a job or hiring a worker isn't a transaction like buying or selling apples, it's more like finding a boyfriend or girlfriend, neither the employer nor the job seeker are willing to settle for just anyone, they both want someone who fits their needs."[15]

Harford extends the dating analogy by proposing that unemployment is a natural state, just as people start out as single until they find a suitable partner.

There are many frictions in the labor market. Jobs may be in the wrong place geographically. Worker skills may not match up to employer needs. Fixed pay structures, union contracts, and other factors can prevent employers from raising (or lowering) wages to achieve supply/demand equilibrium. Availability of alternate support systems like government unemployment benefits can affect a worker's willingness to take a particular job. Countless human factors mean that not every person will take an available job or get hired for it.

## The Internet Changes Everything

As in other areas, the Internet has helped reduce friction in the employment market. Today, the ease of matching employers and employees has been dramatically increased by firms like Indeed, Monster, ZipRecruiter, and many others.

Compared with the era when most matching was done through local newspaper classified ads and a few national publications, today neither hiring firms nor job seekers are limited geographically. Either can cast as wide or as narrow a net as desired. The search algorithms employed for matching likewise aid both parties. Employers can identify individuals with the exact characteristics they want, even if those individuals aren't publicly engaged in a job search. Similarly, individuals can find job openings that fit their skills in a quick and efficient way.

Even the low-tech, free listing site Craigslist greatly reduced matching friction. Craigslist eliminated the often prohibitive cost of classified advertising for both employers and job seekers. Its rudimentary search function made scanning ads faster than reading newspaper listings. And, creating a listing could be accomplished in seconds. Listings would appear immediately and could be removed at any time.

That isn't to say that all the employment friction discussed by Pissarides is gone. While it's much easier to find a match, that doesn't mean that every match will be consummated. Individuals and firms still have preferences and priorities.

Nevertheless, eliminating much of the matching friction created billions of dollars of revenue for Internet-enabled search firms. Indeed alone is approaching annual revenue of a billion dollars, and hundreds of millions of visitors visit their website each month.[16]

While online firms prospered, their effect on traditional newspapers was devastating. For America's newspapers, overall advertising revenue fell from $63.5 billion in 2000 to $23 billion in 2013.[17] That includes all forms of advertising, but employment classified and display ads were a highly profitable category. Beyond employment ads, Craigslist killed most newspaper revenue from other categories of classified ads as well. After decades of near-monopoly status for employment and local classified advertising, newspapers have been forced to search for new business models.

## WHAT, HUMANS AREN'T ROBOTS?

The Nobel Committee has awarded 49 prizes for Economics, and almost all have been for work in traditional, equation-based economics. Two, however, have been awarded in the relatively young area of behavioral economics—Daniel Kahneman in 2002 and Richard Thaler in 2017.

Behavioral economists have shown that people don't always behave in the rational, logical way that traditional economists and their models predict. Real people make irrational decisions. Presenting a choice framed as a loss will get different results than the identical choice framed as a gain. My coffee mug is worth more to me than your identical coffee mug.

Behavioral economists eschew the mathematical formulas of their colleagues and instead conduct research to determine what people really do. Often, these behaviors aren't what traditional economists predict.

Behavioral economics and thinking about friction go hand in hand. One of the insights that has done the most to change the world has been that simple "nudges" can change behavior. For example, Thaler showed that one way to increase retirement plan enrollment was to opt new employees into the plan automatically—this costs nothing, but it achieves substantially higher enrollment rates.

Thaler and his colleague, Shlomo Benartzi, proposed a second technique to get people to save more. Automatically scheduling small annual increases in savings, called "automatic escalation," increased savings in US retirement plans by $7 billion in one year.[18]

### The Path of Least Friction

By making desirable outcomes the default choice, behavioral scientists exploit what some call "passive decision making" or, more colloquially, "the path of least resistance." In most cases, research shows, people will do whatever requires the least amount of current effort. Since it takes less effort to do nothing than to fill out a form, the desirable option, like saving for retirement, should be the one that requires no form.

In other words, the basic tenet of these strategies is that people will choose the path with the least friction.

## FRICTION VS. MOTIVATION

In my Persuasion Slide framework (see the Appendix), friction is the mortal enemy of motivation. Motivation, represented by gravity, propels the child down the slide. Friction resists that motion, slowing the descent. Occasionally, too much friction can stop the child midslide. (The Persuasion Slide is derived from the Fogg Behavior Model [FBM], whose creator, Stanford professor BJ Fogg, we will meet later in the book.)

Most of the insights in this book are based on the interplay of motivation and friction and how they affect human behavior.

If an action is to be completed or behavior to be changed, there must be motivation present. For example, if I know that a favorite author of mine has released a new book, I'm motivated to buy it. Or, if I visit the website of an author I don't know, I might be motivated by her compelling description of the value I'll gain from reading her new book.

Whether I began with an internal desire to read the book or that desire was created by effective marketing, I'm motivated to buy it. If I'm looking at the book's Amazon page, I'll likely take the frictionless route of 1-Click ordering, and the transaction will be complete. For me (and millions of other readers), that's the normal course of events.

But what if the book isn't available at Amazon? Improbable, I know, but this actually happened to me not long ago when the sole electronic format for a book I wanted was the Nook version. (The publisher was an arm of Barnes & Noble, creator of the Nook. To promote their own technology and perhaps to spite archrival Amazon, they didn't release the book in the vastly more popular Kindle format.) Getting the book in electronic format not only required me to make a purchase on a website that didn't have all my information stored, I also had to install a different app to read it.

In this case, I was motivated enough to put up with the annoying friction. I was going to discuss the book with its author, and I didn't have time to wait for a paper copy to be delivered. So, motivation trumped friction and I made the awkward purchase.

Under any other circumstance, though, the outcome would have been different. If I didn't need that exact book in that exact moment, the additional friction might make me pause to think about whether I really wanted the book. Did I really want to set up an account at a new e-commerce site? Would I actually read it, or would I just let it languish on my "to read" list?

Since it wouldn't appear in my Kindle library, would I forget I owned it? Is there a similar book I could get with fewer hassles? These aren't the thoughts you want in a potential buyer's head.

That's not to say motivation couldn't overcome even the slick 1-Click friction advantage. If I was shopping for an expensive camera and found I could save a couple of hundred dollars somewhere else, I'd probably at least check out the alternative.

It's clear that Amazon understands this—they aren't always the lowest-priced vendor, but they are almost always competitive. They know if their price is reasonably close to the best, their customers won't expend the additional effort to shop elsewhere.

## When Motivation Wins

High motivation can overcome friction. Just about all of us in the United States file our taxes every year despite the bewildering array of forms we are required to complete. We do it because we are motivated by some combination of a sense of civic duty and the knowledge that the IRS will severely penalize us if we don't. Most of us reduce that friction by employing professional preparers or using software that offers a much lower friction user experience.

Similarly, filling out loan application papers is almost always a high-friction process. But, if we have found our dream house and need the bank's help to buy it, we submit to the bank's onerous, invasive, and time-consuming procedures. If we want the house and aren't wealthy enough to write a check for the full amount, we have no choice.

If you are trying to get humans to take some action, you can always try to increase their motivation. You can make the alternative to compliance very unpleasant if you are a government agency. Or, if you are selling a product, you can make your price lower than competitors'. But these alternatives are rarely better than making the action easier to accomplish.

**FRICTION TAKEAWAY**

> Instead of costly attempts to boost motivation, friction reduction is almost always less expensive and sometimes faster to accomplish. Making things easier often costs little or nothing. If you offer less friction than your competition, you may even be able to charge slightly higher prices.

## THE LAW OF LEAST EFFORT

The concepts that underpin this book aren't new. The phrase "path of least resistance" has been used since 1825,[19] originally as a science and engineering term but later adapted to human behavior.

In 1894, French philosopher Guillaume Ferrero wrote a treatise, *L'inertie mentale et la loi du moindre effort*. That translates to, *Mental Inertia and the Law of Least Effort*.[20] Earlier thinkers had made similar observations, but Ferrero seems to be the first to formalize the idea as an explanation of human behavior. Six years later, "The Principle of Least Action as a Psychological Principle" was published in the October 1900 issue of *Mind* by W. R. Boyce Gibson.[21]

The Law of Least Effort, sometimes called the Principle of Least Effort, says that given a choice, people will choose the option that requires the smallest amount of work.

The concept didn't seem to get much attention for most of the twentieth century. Perhaps it seemed too obvious. One exception was a 1949 book by George Kingsley Zipf, *Human Behavior and the Principle of Least Effort*.[22] Zipf traced the idea back to fourteenth-century friar and philosopher William of Ockham, who proposed a Law of Parsimony. One definition of parsimony is "economy in the use of means to an end."[23] Today, that law has evolved into what we know as Occam's razor, which states that the simplest solution to any problem is most likely the correct one.

### Cognitive Effort

Nobel Prize winner Daniel Kahneman found the concept worth discussing. In his seminal book on human behavior, *Thinking Fast and Slow*, Kahneman wrote:

> A general "law of least effort" applies to cognitive as well as physical exertion. The law asserts that if there are several ways of achieving the same goal, people will eventually gravitate to the least demanding course of action. . . . Laziness is built deep into our nature.[24]

Even New Age guru and alternate medicine advocate Deepak Chopra believes in the Law of Least Effort. It's the fourth law listed in his book *The Seven Spiritual Laws of Success*.[25] He calls it "the principle of least action, of no resistance." While most of his discussion veers into a rather strange discussion of "Nature's intelligence" and how love holds Nature together, Chopra does mention that his use of the law involves eliminating friction. In fact, his chapter on the law is the first use I recall of the awkward adverb "frictionlessly."[26]

**FRICTION TAKEAWAY**

> The Law of Least Effort underlies the premise of this book. People avoid unnecessary effort, i.e., friction, as a matter of course. I don't have to do a behavioral study to predict that given the choice between an elevator and adjacent stairway, almost everyone going up more than one or two floors will take the elevator. When you want to steer the behavior of others, the Law of Least Effort should be the first tool you reach for.

## THE FRICTION CURVE

This section is as theoretical as we're going to get. Don't worry, it's not too long. And it's not even too complicated.

The simplest friction curve is one where the more friction there is, the less of the desired behavior you get. So, Amazon maximizes the number of orders it gets by minimizing friction. There will be an upper limit to the number of orders—there's a finite number of shoppers who want items and can afford them. That upper limit of orders will be hit when there is no friction.

As ordering becomes more difficult, the number of orders will go down. Eventually, there will be so much friction that there are no orders at all. That kind of curve might look like Figure 5.1.

Figure 5.1 **Simple Friction Curve**

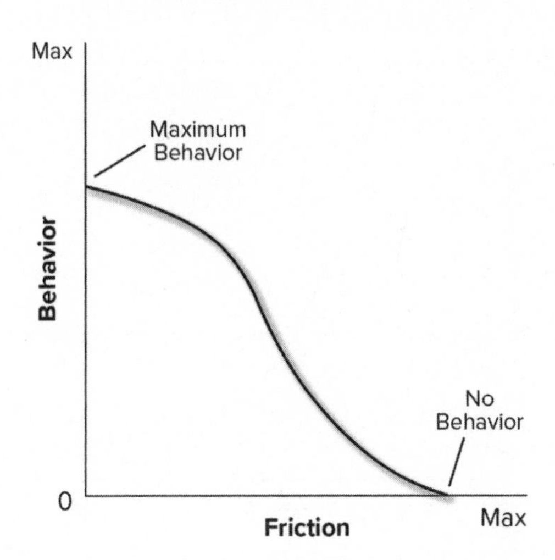


The shape of the curve may vary. Low-motivation behaviors may fall off quickly as friction increases. You may want to eat more broccoli, but if the store you normally shop at doesn't have any, you are unlikely to keep looking for it.

High-motivation behaviors can continue despite high friction. Despite the complexity of the US tax code, most people still file tax returns to avoid unpleasant consequences.

Think of this curve as a very general representation of how friction affects behavior, and don't worry too much about the exact shape.

## Taxes and Fees

Since taxes and fees are a form of friction, it's no surprise that their effect follows a typical friction curve, as shown in Figure 5.2.

Once again, the shape of the curve will vary. Typically, the curve will start out flat—adding a tax that is inconsequential in amount won't change behavior much. As the level becomes significant and noticeable, behavior will start to change.

When changing behavior is difficult, the short-term effect of a tax may be minimal. For example, if the gasoline tax is tripled, people will still keep driving. Over time, though, that behavior will change. In response to the

Figure 5.2 **Effect of Taxing an Activity**

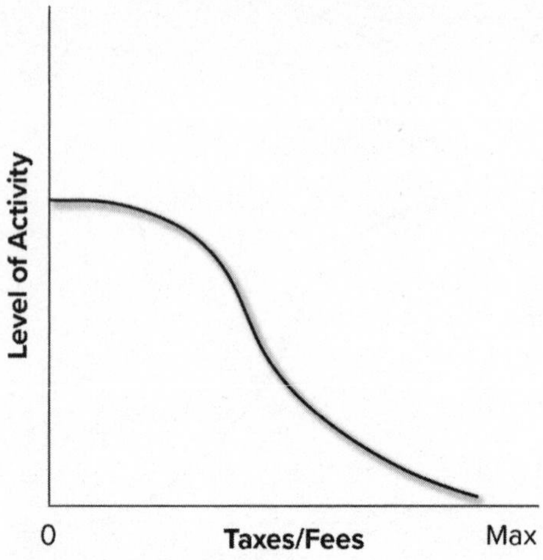

Level of Activity

0 Taxes/Fees Max

higher prices, people may buy more fuel-efficient vehicles, use mass transit, carpool, or choose to drive less.

If behavior change is easy, then the curve may be steeper. Adding a steep tax to broccoli will cause shoppers to choose cauliflower and other vegetables.

## Laws and Regulations

We think of rules, laws, and regulations as always adding friction. Up to a point, that's true. The more red tape you add to an activity, the less you'll get of it. If starting a business requires a months-long approval process through multiple agencies, you will get fewer start-ups than if it only requires filing a one-page form with no approvals needed.

But, the minimum point of friction isn't no laws or regulations at all. As much as businesspeople complain about red tape, they would find it difficult to operate without any effective legal structures at all. They would have no way of enforcing contracts, collecting overdue bills, defending their trademarks, or any of the other protections businesses count on. When they complain about laws and regulations, it's usually about burdensome rules that raise their cost of doing business without (from their point of view) providing an equivalent benefit to them, their customers, or society as a whole.

Figure 5.3 is a graphical representation of that idea.

Figure 5.3 **Laws and Regulations**

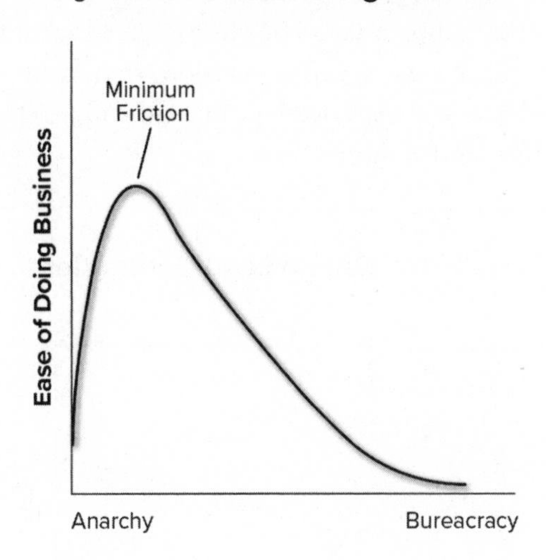


The optimal point is when the rule of law allows businesses to operate efficiently and protects society from bad actors but doesn't impose undue red tape or enforce rules without a clear benefit.

## Example: Lead Generation

A slightly more complex example of a friction curve is a business trying to collect sales leads on their website. This is usually done by a web form. Lead generation experts have learned that the shorter and simpler the form, the more leads you will get. A form that is too long or complex will get no leads at all. If you reduce your 10-question form to just four blanks, you'll get more leads.

The minimum friction option is usually to ask for one piece of information only—an e-mail address. That's what many newsletters ask for—there's almost no incremental cost to send an e-mail, so it makes sense to maximize the leads. Another low-friction way to get a sales lead is to have the customer send a brief text message to a specified number. That gives the recipient just the phone number, but it's enough to begin communication.

Maximizing the absolute number of leads isn't always the best business outcome. If human salespeople must contact the leads, or if something is to be sent by postal mail, the cost of servicing these leads could be high. Adding friction in the form of a couple of qualifying questions will reduce the number of leads. But, the leads collected would be of higher quality and the action taken by the company could be more targeted and effective.

Figure 5.4 shows what a lead generation friction curves might look like. The dashed line represents lead quality—the more effort visitors put in, the higher their level of motivation.

Figure 5.4 **Online Lead Generation**

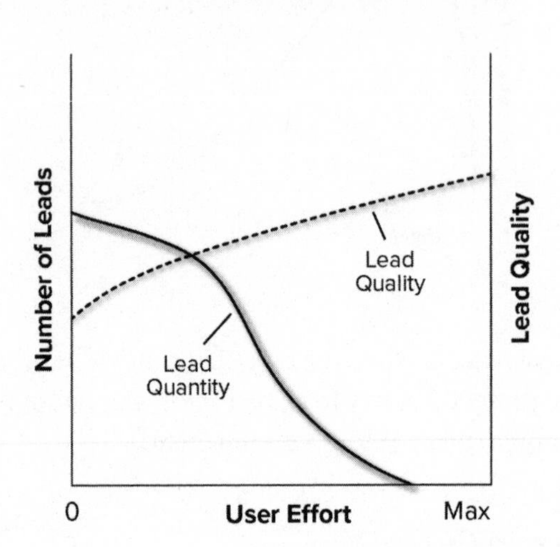


So, minimum user effort will maximize the number of leads. But, what is the *optimum* level of user effort? It depends on the cost of servicing those leads. If there is no cost, as in the case where the response is an automatic e-mail, then it makes sense to minimize friction and gather the maximum number of leads.

Often, of course, there is a cost associated with each lead. For example, a business might send a color brochure in response to inquiries and then have a salesperson telephone them to follow up. In any condition where there is a cost associated with each lead there will be an optimal level of friction—just high enough to screen out the lowest-quality leads, but not so high as to deter any legitimate responders. (See Figure 5.5.)

Figure 5.5 **Lead Generation**

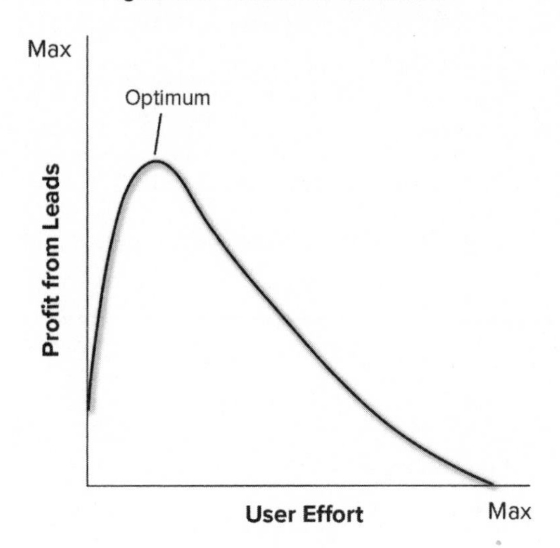


## Your Unique Friction Curve

The sample curves here aren't precise mathematical models. They are meant to illustrate how human behavior can change when friction is added or subtracted. These curves also show that while less friction is usually better, there may be a level of friction that produces the best results in a given situation. Use these curves as starting points to think about your specific goals and how manipulating friction can help achieve them.

# CHAPTER 6

# Decision Friction

*Thinking is to humans as swimming is to cats;*
*they can do it but they'd prefer not to.*
—Daniel Kahneman, Behavioral Economist
and Nobel Laureate

Most of us don't spend a lot of time thinking about thinking. Except for solving difficult math problems and similar tasks, thinking seems effortless. In fact, our brains experience a range of difficulty in thinking and making decisions. Understanding what constitutes "effort" for our brains is the first step in knowing how to change behavior.

## CHOICE PARALYSIS

If you ask people whether they would prefer more choices or fewer, virtually everyone will reply "more." Why limit yourself?

And, for a business, offering several variations of a product is often a practical and effective strategy. Different market segments may have varied needs and preferences. Today's stores offer a plethora of choice and seem to be well optimized to maximize sales. It certainly seems likely that supermarkets sell more jams and jellies by offering a huge variety of brands and flavors as compared with just one brand of grape jelly.

But too much choice can be a bad thing. A classic experiment at Columbia University evaluated the effect of choice on that exact product:

fruit jams. They offered shoppers samples of jam and logged sales of the preserves under two conditions.

In one condition, there were just six flavors. In the other, there were two dozen.

Intuitively, one expects that the larger assortment would sell more total product. A gooseberry fancier might not find his or her preferred preserve in the selection of six. An exotic combination, like Peach Pecan, might appeal to a buyer who didn't find pedestrian flavors like cherry or strawberry all that interesting.

The bigger jam display did succeed in attracting attention—50 percent more shoppers stopped to check out the product and taste a sample. But, the effect on sales was surprising.

Thirty percent of the shoppers presented with six choices bought some, compared to only 3 percent of those who saw 24 possible flavors. That's *10 times higher* sales for the limited selection.[1] It seems that the much larger number of choices produced a sort of "paralysis of analysis" and inhibited sales.

*The fact that some choice is good doesn't necessarily mean that more choice is better.*

—from *The Paradox of Choice: Why More Is Less* by Barry Schwartz

Too many choices can create friction. A customer who was moving briskly to complete an order now slows down to ponder options. Many customers may make a choice and regain their momentum. Some won't. They'll decide to choose later or do something else while they think about it. This loss of momentum may be irreversible.

The paradox of choice has been demonstrated in many domains. There's not necessarily an optimal number of choices that is best in every situation, and in your specific area you may have to test different approaches to find out when the benefit of more choice turns into a liability.

Humans also have tools to avoid being overwhelmed by choice. The typical shampoo section in an American supermarket can have five or more tiers and run for dozens of feet. A shopper could spend an entire day in the shampoo aisle and not get to every product. But, most consumers manage to escape the shampoo aisle without being trapped for hours. That's because they use heuristics, or rules, to minimize cognitive effort. For example, different shoppers might buy

- The brand they always buy.
- A product that is on sale today.
- A brand they trust.
- A product with attractive or unusual packaging.
- A product in a large size that is also inexpensive.
- A special-purpose product, e.g., for colored hair.

Combining multiple heuristics, say, spotting a familiar brand that's also on sale, can lead to a quick decision despite the impossibly large number of choices.

## AMAZON, THE EVERYTHING STORE

Amazon seems like the perfect counterexample to the idea that offering too many choices is a bad thing. They offer near-infinite choice. In any given category they carry not just an ample selection but almost every product available to the market. And, even for an individual product, there may be multiple sellers, sometimes dozens. Despite the bewildering array of choices, Amazon has overcome choice friction to become by far the largest e-commerce company.

From a practical standpoint, their exhaustive selection is one excellent reason to shop there. If I read about a product that sounds interesting, I'll head for Amazon first because I know it will be there.

Amazon uses a variety of techniques to combat paralysis of choice. First and foremost, its review system provides a powerful way for consumers to distinguish between apparently similar items. Amazon's five-star rating system allows quick visual discrimination, and the text reviews help customers compare in more detail.

Amazon guides customers by flagging products as "Amazon's Choice" or "Bestseller." The order in which products are displayed helps as well. Although customers can choose different sort criteria manually, Amazon displays what its algorithm thinks are the most relevant matches by default.

It also offers sorting and filtering options to bring those products most appropriate for the shopper to the top of the page. If you are looking for a particular price range, a specific brand, or only highly rated products, a single click will show only those items.

For some products, Amazon presents a side-by-side comparison of similar products. While that might appear to be offering a customer more choices, the tabular data also points out differences between the items. Research shows that even inconsequential differences between similar products help us make a choice.[2]

## Still More Choice?

Another feature at Amazon that one might expect to trigger paralysis of choice is its additional promotions. Just as the shopper has reviewed the product details, he or she is presented with additional products in the form of "Customers Also Bought," "Sponsored Products," "Customers Also Viewed," and so on. Conventional wisdom suggests this is a disaster—Amazon seems to be going out of their way to overwhelm the customer with possible alternatives. Digital conversion experts know that adding *any* distractions to a sales page can cause a customer to navigate away or start considering other options.

In fact, these displays of related and similar products help guide the customer to the best choice. Does it introduce a little friction? Probably. But does it save some customers from making a less-than-optimal decision because they chose bad search terms? Almost certainly. While sometimes these "also bought" items are similar to the original item, they can also be complementary items that increase the total sale.

A customer visiting Amazon for the first time might be a bit overwhelmed by both the number of choices and the amount of information on each page. But, regular Amazon shoppers have figured out how do deal with the mind-boggling amount of choice. They use the visual cues and the filtering tools Amazon provides and, in most cases, make a decision. With Amazon Prime members now totaling more than 100 million, almost everyone shopping at Amazon is a repeat visitor.

It's analogous to the supermarket situation. Most of us can race through a shopping trip without being paralyzed by choice. But, if we are going to buy a product in an unfamiliar category, we may slow down, read labels, compare prices, and look for clues to make an informed decision.

If we know what we want to buy at Amazon, we can do it in seconds. But, if we aren't sure of our choice, Amazon provides all the tools we need to make a decision.

It's important to remember that Amazon is constantly testing changes on their website—hundreds of tests on an ongoing basis. If you see a feature on their site that doesn't disappear in a week or two, you can be sure that it helps, rather than hinders, sales.

### FRICTION TAKEAWAY

If you are going to offer customers many choices or options, reduce decision friction by guiding them to the best choices. Use flags like "Recommended," "Highest Rated," "Bestseller," etc., to help customers decide. Reviews and ratings provide social proof. Show comparative information for popular products in the same category.

## DECISIONS, DECISIONS

While many possible options can create friction, even the simplest choice can as well. Paper or plastic? French fries or mashed potatoes? Often, we build in choices where no choice is really necessary.

Psychologists have demonstrated using a variety of experiments that making a decision depletes a finite (in the short run) resource in our brain. To put it simply, when we make decisions, resist temptation, solve problems, and perform other executive tasks, we are drawing on a resource in our brain that eventually needs to be recharged.

One classic study demonstrated how making decisions depletes a person's mental resources. (It also showed how far desperate undergraduate students will go for course credit and small amounts of money.) One of the experiments in the study measured the "self-regulation" of subjects by seeing how long they can immerse their hands in near-freezing water. Some of the subjects did this after making a series of complex decisions involving t-shirt colors, scented candles, and other products. Other subjects made no decisions but rated several products instead. The experimenters found that the subjects suffering from decision fatigue removed their hands from the icy water more quickly.[3]

Another test in the same study showed that decision making reduced self-control in a way likely to increase procrastination. In this case, the experimenters had some subjects spend eight minutes either carefully choosing courses in their major from written descriptions or simply reading about the courses. Next, they were told they would take a math problem-solving test (perhaps no less stressful than freezing water for some) and that studying had been shown to improve performance. All subjects were then given 15 minutes to study, read a magazine, or play a video game.

The subjects who made choices spent less time studying and more time on the "fun" activities, again demonstrating the depleting effects of decisions.[4]

Still another variation of the experiment tested how long subjects would work on unsolvable puzzles before giving up. Those subjects who didn't have to make choices persisted longer. From these and several other experiments, the researchers concluded that making decisions does deplete one's resources. This can reduce their self-control and impair their ability to continue with a task that requires effort.[5]

**FRICTION TAKEAWAY**

> Every decision in a process can reduce the probability that the person will make the final, big decision to complete the process—submit the form, place the order, buy the car, and so on. Eliminate decisions and anything else that requires conscious deliberation if you want someone else to take action.

## DANES AREN'T HORRIBLE PEOPLE

Organ donation is a socially desirable activity. Donated organs save lives, but patients are often forced to endure long waits because a matching organ isn't available. When Columbia University researchers Eric Johnson and Daniel Goldstein analyzed donation data in 2003, it was clear that many European countries have responded generously to this need. Almost 100 percent of the citizens in France, Belgium, Hungary, Poland, and elsewhere volunteered to donate their organs after death.[6]

There were a few outliers, though. Just 27 percent of Germans signed up to donate their organs. And the citizens of Denmark participated at a rate of just 4 percent![7]

The obvious conclusion is that Danes are selfish jerks and don't care about their less fortunate neighbors desperately waiting for organs.

Just kidding! In fact, Danes likely aren't any worse people than their peers in high-donation-rate countries.

Friction is the culprit.

In the countries with extremely high donation rates, enrolling as an organ donor is friction-free. Citizens are simply opted in automatically when they renew a driver's license or register to vote. Any friction is associated with *not* donating—one must opt out.

In the low-donation-rate countries, citizens must *opt in* to be donors. Even though the process might be as simple as checking a box, many don't. The comparatively low rate in Denmark is blamed on several factors, including an opt-in system that involves specifying which organs will be harvested. Another factor is that few Danes are placed on life support and surviving relatives are asked about organ donation at a difficult and emotional time.[8]

In countries where organ donation is not automatically opted in, friction is costing lives.

## THE POWER OF DEFAULTS

The organ donation example may be extreme. It's a big decision. As you struggle to stay alive after a traumatic accident, do you want an organ-harvesting team checking with your doctor to see if you are dead yet? On the other hand, wouldn't you like to think you could save a child's life if you had the bad luck to ram a tree with your motorcycle?

Most of the decisions we place in front of customers are far less consequential. Would you like to get our newsletter? Daily, weekly, or monthly? Is your order a gift? Will you like us on Facebook?

Even though these decisions seem trivial, each one imposes a bit of a cognitive load and consumes some resources. If you can, avoid forcing your customer to make any unnecessary decisions, at least until they have completed your desired action—placed an order, requested information, and so on.

The easiest way to avoid decision fatigue is to eliminate the decision completely. Sometimes processes are based on legacy practices rather than current requirements. Whenever possible, eliminate these.

People tend to accept the default for multiple reasons, according to Goldstein and Johnson. First, making an active decision can be unpleasant and stressful. Second, making a choice other than the default can require effort, like filling out a form. Finally, the default condition generally represents the "status quo." Changing from the status quo might trigger a "loss aversion" response, making the default the easier choice.[9]

### FRICTION TAKEAWAY

> Assuming a decision is necessary, whenever possible make your desired choice the default. The choice, of course, should be both legal and desirable for the other party. Don't opt people into your mailing list if that doesn't comply with the relevant law. Don't opt people into your highly profitable expedited shipping if 98 percent usually choose a slower but free method. Default choices are a powerful nudge because they eliminate friction, but they should be used wisely and ethically.

## THE TIRED BRAIN

One of the most striking illustrations in how decisions create fatigue emerged in a study of Israeli parole judges. At the beginning of the day, they granted parole requests about two-thirds of the time. By just before their meal break, they were granting almost none, despite a similar mix of cases.

After the break, the parolee success rate was back to the early morning level. But, once again, the rate dropped as the afternoon progressed until, at the end of the day, it was near zero.

The scientists who analyzed the data were baffled at first but eventually determined that the judges were suffering from a sort of mental energy depletion. As their cognitive resources declined, it became increasingly easy to take the easy way out and deny parole.[10]

The consequences of denying parole are minimal, except for the prisoner. The consequences of making a bad decision and releasing a dangerous person are much greater for the judge. So, a simple "no" needed far fewer cognitive resources than granting parole.

Clearly, this kind of decision is a difficult one. In consumer terms, it's probably closer to buying an expensive appliance than ticking off a box to get a newsletter. Nevertheless, the principle is the same. Making decisions requires mental effort and consumes scarce resources. This affects our behavior, but we aren't self-aware enough to realize it.

## FRICTION TAKEAWAY

You can't know the level of cognitive resources other people are coming to you with. Any decision point, large or small, is friction. If you are hoping for the other person to take some action, eliminate any decisions that aren't absolutely necessary. Where choices must be made, present a default if one option is the most commonly chosen.

# CHAPTER 7

# Customer Experience and Friction

In recent years, companies have increasingly focused on improving their customer experience. The ubiquity of social media means that bad interactions are no longer a private matter. The worse the failure, the more likely it is to be shared. Ask United Airlines. They experienced one of the worst branding disasters ever when a horrendous video of a passenger being dragged off a flight, bloodied and screaming, went viral and gained global media attention.[1] Disaster struck again a year later. A puppy died in an overhead bin after a United flight attendant told a passenger to put the pet carrier there.[2]

No amount of advertising and positive brand-building can offset stories like these. I've flown a half-million miles on United in the past five years and know that these incidents were not representative of the airline or its team members. But, ask casual travelers what they know about United and they will likely mention one or both of these events.

Beyond the threat of debacles like these, companies recognize that customer experience is a key competitive battleground. But, what kind of experience do customers really want?

## DELIGHT IS FOR DUMMIES

Many marketing experts emphasize the importance of customer delight. Customers won't be impressed if you meet their expectations, the reasoning goes, but will remember if you exceed those expectations.

Perhaps the most delightful delight story comes from the Ritz Carlton Hotels. The chain is very focused on customer satisfaction and exceeding customer expectations. Each employee can spend up to $2,000 to resolve a customer problem—no managerial approval needed. Ponder that for a moment—how many businesses would empower each of their employees to spend that much money simply because they thought it would make a customer happy?

Ritz Carlton staffers can be creative, too. When a young guest left his stuffed giraffe, Joshie, behind, the staff at the Amelia Island Ritz Carlton didn't just ship the plush toy home. They created a photo album of Joshie's continued vacation adventure. Photos showed him reclining poolside, hanging out with other stuffed animals, and having a great time. One photo showed the little giraffe driving a beach buggy. Along with the Joshie himself, the hotel staff shipped the album, some Ritz Carlton swag, and even a hotel ID with Joshie's name and photo on it to the youngster's home.[3]

Naturally, everyone in the family was delighted. The parents shared the hotel's over-the-top effort on social media, and the story went viral. Although this took place a few years ago, I still hear customer service advocates trot out the Joshie story as an example of how to delight your customers.

But, there are three problems with that advice:

- ***Your* story isn't going to break the Internet.** There's no doubt that the effort the Ritz Carlton staff put into orchestrating the Joshie resort experience paid for itself a thousand times over in free publicity. But, can you name a similar delight story from another company that went viral in the same way? No? Neither can I. Viral social media explosions like this are exceedingly rare.
- **Joshie doesn't scale.** Every customer can't be the recipient of a Joshie-like production that takes hours of time to execute, even at a five-star luxury brand like Ritz Carlton. At more economical brands like Hilton Garden Inn or Best Western, Joshie moments will be few and far between.
- **Delight doesn't drive loyalty.** This is the surprising clincher. Even when so many businesses are trying to delight their customers, the data shows that delight isn't a big factor in keeping customers loyal.

That's not to say that delighting your customers is a bad thing, it's just that the type of delight that you can deliver at scale isn't the most powerful way to earn loyalty.

## Reducing Friction Tops Delight

Unless you are part of a large company, you probably haven't heard of CEB Global. Today, they are part of the somewhat better-known Gartner Group. Despite their relatively low profile, CEB's members include 83 percent of Fortune 1000 companies and the same share of FTSE 100 firms. Their customer base exceeds 10,000 in 110 countries. One of CEB's singular efforts has been to both measure customer effort and gauge its impact on customer behavior.

CEB's research delivers some real surprises. They think most customers want a satisfactory experience, not surprise and delight. While "satisfactory" may seem like a low bar, CEB's data shows:

- Ninety-six percent of customers who put forth high effort to resolve their issues are more disloyal.
- Fifty-nine percent of customers report moderate-to-high additional effort in a service interaction.
- Customer service interactions are nearly four times more likely to lead to disloyalty than loyalty.[4]

## Quantifying Customer Effort

CEB developed a metric that they call the Customer Effort Score. It's meant to be an alternative to (or perhaps augment) more established metrics like Customer Satisfaction (CSAT) and Net Promoter Score (NPS). The score is determined by asking customers a simple question—they ask to what extent the customer agrees or disagrees with the statement, "The company made it easy for me to handle my issue." Customers can choose one of seven values ranging from "Strongly Agree" to "Strongly Disagree."[5]

Does that sound subjective? Could it reflect personal biases and vary between customers? Could it change over time for the same experience? The answer to all three is yes, but that's not a problem. CEB would argue that it's the customer's *perception* of effort that counts. Your process for placing an online order may be better than most, but if I do most of my shopping at Amazon using their 1-Click button, I'm likely to find filling out your forms to be high effort.

One study of 75,000 executives showed that "exceeding customer expectations" added 10–20 percent to the cost of servicing those customers. The metric may be more qualitative than quantitative, but one can't disagree with the concept that it costs more to exceed expectations than to meet them.

Meanwhile, a survey of 97,000 customers shows the remarkable effect of customer effort on loyalty:

- Nine percent of customers who had low-effort experiences reported being disloyal.
- Ninety-six percent of customers who had high-effort experiences reported being disloyal.[6]

In addition, CEB found that customers whose expectations were exceeded were no more likely to be loyal than those whose expectations were merely met.[7]

Older CEB data shows that

- Ninety-four percent of low-effort customers repurchase.
- Four percent of high-effort customers repurchase.
- Eighty-eight percent of low-effort customers increase their spend.
- Four percent of high-effort customers increase their spend.[8]

In this era of pervasive social media, word of mouth is ever more important. It turns out that customer effort has a huge effect on what people say:

- One percent of low-effort customers say negative things about the company.
- Eighty-eight percent of high-effort customers say negative things about the company.[9]

## What Is High Effort?

Effort is subjective and personal to each customer, but CEB identified some of the common items associated with high effort:

- Multiple contacts to solve a problem
- Having to change channels, e.g., web to phone
- Impersonal treatment and generic advice
- Transfers, and having to repeat information
- Perception of additional effort[10]

Is there anything more infuriating than being transferred from person to person in an organization and having to repeat your personal information or describe the problem each time? Or dealing with a representative who is following a script and won't deviate no matter how hard you try to cut to the chase? Unfortunately, these and other annoying things are built into all too many customer interactions.

**FRICTION TAKEAWAY**

> Delighting your customers occasionally is fine, but it shouldn't be your primary strategy if you want to build loyalty. Instead, increase sales and loyalty by reducing customer effort. Resolve issues in a single contact, preferably with one person. If changing people or departments is necessary, be sure your systems transfer the customer information, too, so that the customer doesn't have to re-authenticate himself or herself, or repeat a long explanation.

## Responsive vs. Prescriptive Sales

Much of CEB's work has focused on customer service in general and problem resolution in particular. But, they have looked at the effort customers exert while purchasing in the business-to-business market as well. In these cases, there is an interaction between two people, a salesperson and a buyer. The results of their research may surprise you.

Most salespeople try to provide customers with the information they need to make a wise purchase, but CEB has found that there's a right way and wrong way to do that.

The wrong way is what CEB calls "responsive." When a customer has a question, the salesperson provides information in response. A responsive salesperson is careful to outline the possible options to the customer and stays flexible in response to customer needs and opinions.

Responding to customer questions with ample information and describing the full range of options sound a lot like "best practices." But, this information-oriented approach has some major downsides. CEB data shows it can make the purchasing process *more* difficult and increase the likelihood of buyer regret by 50 percent.[11]

This relates in part to the well-established "paradox of choice" described by Barry Schwartz in his book of the same name.[12] People often say they want more choice, but more choices make deciding difficult and increase post-purchase anxiety.

The better approach is "prescriptive" selling. The salesperson reduces customer effort, a.k.a. friction, by guiding the customer through a specific solution that has been shown to work in similar situations. The buyer isn't forced to work through alternatives and decide (perhaps with limited expertise) which product or approach will be best.

CEB's data shows that a prescriptive selling approach increases the "likeliness of purchasing ease" by 82 percent and drops the probability of buyer remorse by 37 percent.[13] Not only is the low-friction process easier for the customer, it's more satisfying.

## FRICTION TAKEAWAY

Avoid the temptation to explain every option and possibility in a sales process. Don't overwhelm the customer with information. Instead, understand what the customer's problem is and propose the best way to solve it. You'll close more sales and, at the same time, have fewer instances of buyer's remorse.

# ENGINEERING A FRICTION-FREE EXPERIENCE

*It's kind of fun to do the impossible.*

—Walt Disney, Entrepreneur

When Walt Disney launched Disneyland in 1955, he wanted it to be a happy place, "a source of joy and inspiration to all the world."[14] Although unbridled commercial development around the small theme park in Anaheim limited Disney's control over customer experience, by and large he achieved his objective.

Disney and his successors saw an opportunity to create a far more seamless experience with their next project, Walt Disney World in Florida. With more than 27,000 acres (43 square miles, twice the area of Manhattan!), guests never have to leave the Disney environment. Not only were there multiple attractions, there were hotels, restaurants, shops . . . everything a guest might want. A huge network of underground tunnels allowed workers to move about and perform necessary tasks invisibly.

Although Disney didn't live long enough to see the giant Florida park open, it was a resounding success. Millions of people from around the globe flocked to the property. Still, the experience wasn't perfect. The very popularity of the attractions caused long lines for rides. Just getting into the park could be slow at peak times. Still, most visitors felt these aggravations were a necessary part of the process and didn't let them diminish their enjoyment of the experience.

## Dealing with Lines

The first time I visited Walt Disney World was decades ago. At the time, the smart advice was to enter the park earlier than the posted gate opening time. To avoid an initial crush of visitors, Disney opened the parks a little before the advertised times. Once in the park, clever guests would head immediately to the most distant attractions. Most visitors would follow a sequential path after entering the park, creating long lines at the first attractions they encountered. Our clever visitor would return to these later in the day when the surge had moved farther into the park.

Disney management realized that waiting in lines wasn't a great customer experience, so they tried to mitigate the damage. They posted wait times, often a bit longer than the actual wait, so that guests could decide whether to get in line or move on. They disguised the length of lines with circuitous paths and visual barriers. And, when wait times were longer, they dispatched entertainment like jugglers or costumed characters to amuse the weary guests.

In 1999, Disney rolled out its FastPass, a sort of ride reservation system. The guest could get a ticket to board a ride in a specific time window, greatly reducing the time spent standing in line. One limitation was that a guest could only reserve a time slot for one attraction at a time. While far from perfect, this paper ticket-based scheme was a novel way to reduce wasted time at amusement parks.[15]

## Dangerously Complex

By the mid-2000s, it seemed Mickey Mouse was losing his touch. Reportedly, guest satisfaction was declining not just because of high ticket prices but also because of long lines and other pain points. Ominously, half of guests surveyed said they wouldn't return.[16]

When Disney executives dug into the reasons for guest satisfaction, they found that lines were far from the only problems. Crowds were everywhere. To pack in as much fun as possible, families would move frequently between different attractions, sometimes crossing through the center of the park *as many as 20 times*. Even ticketing was complicated enough to frustrate visitors.[17]

Parks vice president at the time was Jim MacPhee, who noted that the park experience was in danger of becoming "dangerously complex and transactional."[18]

Jay Rasulo was chairman of Walt Disney Parks and Resorts at the time. He asked John Padgett, VP of Business Development, for his perspectives on how to grow the business. Padgett was part of a small team formed by Rasulo to take eight weeks to drill down on what should be done.

## What vs. How

Early in the process, Padgett decided that historically, Disney's focus had been on the "what" of the park—the rides, attractions, restaurants, and so on. To attract more visitors, Disney would add another ride or attraction. Padgett realized that there was already more than enough "what" in the park. In what might be a mild exaggeration, he told me that Disney World had more "what" than guests could experience if they came every day for a year.

The key to a better Disney World experience wasn't more "what." Rather, Disney World needed to work on the "how" of the park experience. "If we changed *how* guests experienced the 'what,' they could consume many more experiences, leave with higher guest satisfaction, higher intent to return, and ultimately have a higher perceived value for their overall vacation," Padgett said.[19]

## A Frictionless Experience

*The strategy was to create a frictionless experience, not create a wearable. The wearable was the facilitator.*

—John Padgett, former VP of Business Development, Walt Disney World

The objective, Padgett says, was to eliminate friction at every touch point. That included transportation, entry to the park, the attractions, the resort room, food and beverage . . . everything from start to finish. The initial focus wasn't on technology, but rather what that frictionless experience would look like.

Only when they had sketched out the "how" did they start to think about the technology that would be able to provide this seamless guest experience.

In a classic example of creative inspiration from an unlikely source, Padgett was flipping through a *SkyMall* catalog on one of his many flights to Orlando. He paused at an ad for something called the Trion:Z, a magnetic wristband that purported to reduce muscle soreness and, at the same time, improve one's golf swing.[20]

Somehow, an idea blossomed inside Padgett's head that had nothing to do with magnetic golf enhancement. What if Disney's visitors could wear a wristband that was a digital identifier that served many purposes? It could be a room key and credit card, much like one's credit card–style key at a hotel. But, it could do so much more—it could give them speedy entry to the parks, connect them with their photos, and let park staff greet them by name. Padgett calculated that the wristband could replace as many as

20 pieces of paper guests had to keep track of and carry, including tickets, discount coupons, vouchers . . . the list went on and on.[21]

The technology would have to be robust enough that no swiping would be needed—merely being close would be sufficient. The group began secretly experimenting with the technology, which became known as the MagicBand. Ultimately, full-size mock-ups were housed in a huge, unused soundstage so that every element could be both tested and demonstrated in as realistic a setting as possible.

The park would need both short- and long-range sensors to interact with the bands. Short-range sensors would enable room entry and purchase transactions, while longer-range sensors could track the flow of visitors around the park.

The MagicBand vision expanded to include things like recognizing children who were celebrating a birthday and delivering pre-ordered food to the right table automatically. It even extended beyond the park itself. What if visitors could arrive at the Orlando airport, scan the MagicBand they received before they left home, and board a waiting Disney bus? Hotel check-in could be streamlined, too—no waiting in line to fill out forms.

## The Billion-Dollar Gamble

*I'd say it's been my biggest problem all my life . . . it's money.*
*It takes a lot of money to make these dreams come true.*

—Walt Disney

One challenge with a transformative system like this is that partial implementation won't work. It's not unlike the startup of FedEx—an overnight delivery system wouldn't be useful if it only served a few destinations. One jet wouldn't work—a fleet was required, along with the associated delivery infrastructure to serve a national market.

To achieve its goal of simplifying and enhancing guest experience, the MagicBand had to work everywhere in the park and interact with many separate processes that had never been connected.

## IBFW

Not only would the new technology be everywhere, it would have to work flawlessly. A tech meltdown with tens of thousands of visitors in the park would be a disaster of unthinkable proportions. The often-repeated phrase on the development team was, "It better work!" Less formally, it was shortened to IBFW—"It better frickin' work!"[22]

Padgett highlights the difficulty of selling an enormously expensive project that was mostly invisible to guests. And, they were proposing to fix something that didn't seem to be broken. Disney World already offered what was arguably the most seamless vacation experience on the planet. They pressed forward, though, because they were confident that even a small difference in the "friction coefficient," in Padgett's words, would cause a big jump in guest satisfaction and intent to return.

In 2011, Disney CEO Bob Iger went before the board to describe the MyMagic+ technology. At the end of his presentation, the board applauded. Later, they approved an investment of nearly $1 billion in the ambitious but risky project. To put this in perspective, MyMagic+ was the largest single capital investment ever made in a theme park.[23] Considering that technology infrastructure isn't going to be a big consumer selling point like a new "land" or major ride, that was an impressive display of faith in the MyMagic+ team.

## The Magic Era Begins

MyMagic+ began rolling out in 2013 and concluded, at least in its first iteration, in 2014. Despite a mix of technical difficulties, delays, and internal bickering, the rollout was accomplished without a major disruption of park operations and guest experience.

In 2016, a new version of the MagicBand came out. This band looked a bit more like a slim, faceless watch. The band fits adults, but a kid-size band can be popped out for smaller wrists. And, for those who don't want to wear a band, an oval disc that contains the technology can be removed and placed in a pocket or purse.

The bands come in many Disney-themed styles, from princesses to Star Wars. And, third parties offer "skins" that let visitors dress up their band in too many ways to count. The band itself is becoming a visible, personalized part of the Walt Disney World experience.

And, by shipping the bands to guests well in advance of their vacation, Disney adds still more value to the vacation. First, there's the "unboxing" process that builds excitement. Once opened and visible, the bands serve as a reminder of the impending vacation. That's important—researchers have found that the happiest time for vacationers is the period of anticipation leading up to it.[24] Having that reminder kicks expectations into a higher gear. And, of course, guests can start sharing the experience with their friends via social media that much earlier.

The other key finding from that study was that post-trip happiness levels were boosted only by the most relaxing vacations. While a visit to Disney World is a lot more active than sipping piña coladas on a private beach, taking the friction out of things like luggage transfers, hotel check-in, park entry, standing in long lines, and so on, can't help but have a positive effect on post-trip happiness.

## The Bottom Line

Has MyMagic+ delivered on its promise of a smoother, more seamless guest experience? The answer seems to be yes. Lines are shorter, or, in some cases, gone. Getting into the park is 30 percent faster. For some attractions, lines still form but the waiting time seems shorter because of band-driven guest interactions. Intent to return metrics are up, as are "likely to recommend" numbers—overall satisfaction rates are about 70 percent.[25]

And, perhaps most significantly, in-park spending is up. The MagicBand reduces time spent standing in lines, giving guests more time not only to enjoy themselves but to spend money. "Time in park" is a traditional theme park performance metric. The more time you can get people to stay in the park, the more they will spend. For most of theme park history, that meant getting visitors to commit more days (hence, attractive multiday discounts) or to keep them in the park longer with events like evening parades and fireworks.

The MagicBand increases a different metric—"*available* time in park." Time spent waiting in lines for rides, waiting for food service, and walking from one distant attraction to another are all frictional losses, both from the guest's standpoint and that of the park operator.

As pointed out by John Maeda in *The Laws of Simplicity*, there are two conditions: quantitatively fast (wait time is shorter) and qualitatively fast (wait time is more tolerable).[26] Both speed-up methods are used at Walt Disney World. When lines can't be eliminated, Disney tells you how long the wait will be (usually a high estimate) and often provides in-line distractions and entertainment. The MagicBand technology keeps staff informed as to where lines are building so that interventions can happen quickly.

Finally, like Amazon's 1-Click buy button, the MagicBand technology makes spending faster and easier. If you don't have to fumble in your pocket or purse for a credit card or cash, you are more likely to make a purchase. If you know you can preorder a meal and be served promptly when you arrive at the restaurant, you are more likely to stop for a bite to eat. It's our recurring theme—when you make something easier, people will do more of it.

**FRICTION TAKEAWAY**

By rethinking every element of every guest interaction, Disney reduced points of friction that were thought to be unimportant, inevitable, or someone else's problem. The changes Disney made let guests ride more rides, visit more attractions, and have a more enjoyable experience overall. And, Disney's revenue and traffic metrics improved as well. Just because you offer an experience that is already better than your competition doesn't mean that you should stop improving. Removing friction will keep your customers loyal and your competitors off balance.

## NO-EFFORT VACATIONS

The cruise industry has been one of the fastest growing segments of the leisure travel industry. Fewer than 4 million passengers were carried in 1990, but by 2017, the total topped 25 million. That represents $46 billion in revenue.[27]

There are many reasons why people choose cruising over other vacation options. Some feel cruising saves money compared to comparable travel experiences. Others enjoy the social aspects of spending time with fellow vacationers who are, quite literally, in the same boat.

Many of the top reasons people cite for cruising involve friction reduction. To see multiple cities (or islands) in a single, self-organized vacation requires effort both in planning and execution. Travelers must figure out transport between locations, both local (say, a taxi to the train station) and longer haul. They must choose each hotel from many possibilities, and then book it. Every time there's a change in location, the traveler must pack and unpack. Every meal represents a decision. Some may be planned in advance, others must be discovered on the fly. Some choices will work out, others won't.

For some travelers, the extensive planning process for a multi-destination trip is part of the fun. Indeed, one study showed that making travel arrangements was stressful but also generated happiness.[28] Other travelers may not have the time to do destination research or may worry they are making less-than-optimal choices.

For those travelers who prefer to simplify both the planning and logistics of a vacation, cruises are an ideal choice. One picks the cruise line and the itinerary, and the work is mostly done. Many cruises offer inclusive air travel along with port transportation. The traveler needs only to pack and show up at the airport at the designated time.

Only all-inclusive resorts offer a similar low-friction vacation, and they don't offer the opportunity to visit multiple destinations in a single trip.

## UP-SELLING FRICTION

Even though cruising greatly simplifies the vacation experience, not all cruises are the same. Most cruise lines include a multiple dining choices and ample entertainment, but the tendency these days is to do extensive upselling on the ship. Specialty restaurants, fancy coffeeshops, spa services, alcoholic beverages, shore excursions, soft drinks, and even bottled water represent revenue-boosting opportunities.

From the passenger's point of view, every additional charge is a friction point. Not only is there the annoyance of digging out one's card and waiting for the staff member to return it with a receipt, there's the subtler "pain of paying." Researchers at Carnegie Mellon and Stanford showed that making a purchase lit up areas of the brain associated with pain, particularly if the price seemed too high. According to Carnegie Mellon's George Loewenstein, "sushi-style" pricing is the worst—when each small element of consumption is priced separately, it's a more painful experience.[29]

Cruise lines combat this by offering packages that let passengers pay for unlimited consumption for things like alcoholic beverages, soft drinks, specialty coffees, and so on. Even this practice can add friction, though, as staff members aggressively promote these offerings. On one recent cruise I took, the upselling began in the cruise terminal and continued in all areas of the ship. In the first 24 hours, at least 10 ship's staff tried to sell me a beverage package. (One lesson from this: incentivizing service employees can increase sales, but perhaps at the expense of customer experience.)

## Eliminating Customer Effort

Some cruise lines consciously work to deliver on the promise of near frictionless travel.

Jason Montague has a boyish face and a palpable sense of enthusiasm when he talks about cruising. While one might mistake him for a genial cruise director, Montague is president and CEO of Regent Seven Seas Cruises and was part of the founding team at Regent's sister line, Oceania Cruises.

Montague has deep roots in hospitality and customer experience. His first job was a restaurant dishwasher at the age of 13. He progressed through almost every job in the restaurant—prep chef, waiter, and more. He confesses that the best job was parking valet. "It was an upscale restaurant, and I got to drive some great cars!"[30]

When he left his hometown to attend the University of Miami as a finance major, his restaurant experience stuck with him. He began working in the school's food service, eventually progressing to a leadership role.

The years of front-line exposure to customers served him well even as he progressed in the world of finance. After several years of consulting experience, Montague was tapped by Cuban émigré and cruise line entrepreneur Frank Del Rio to help start Oceania Cruises. The line became part of a holding group that later added Regent and ultimately became part of Norwegian Cruise Lines. Montague's initial role was as vice president–treasurer, but he later led both Oceania and Regent as president/COO. Today, he's CEO at the latter.

In an industry that minimizes friction, Regent offers perhaps the lowest friction of any line. Regent offers all-inclusive cruising. All dining options, including specialty restaurants, are included. Almost all shore excursions are part of the cruise price. All beverages, from specialty coffees to premium liquors, are included. (Well, almost all . . . that rare 25-year Macallan scotch and a few other unusually costly items aren't free.) On Regent, it's entirely possible to spend a couple of weeks on board and use your cruise card only to enter your stateroom.

While most cruise lines have tried to reduce friction by making additional charges faster and easier to process, it's hard to beat the smooth experience of no transaction at all.

Montague notes that Regent is at the luxury end of the cruise line spectrum, and delivering impeccable customer experience is critical. Avoiding frequent charges and upselling is part of that, along with high-touch service provided by a large, well-trained staff.

Where can friction be reduced even more? Technology may help with the occasional slowdown in the initial passenger check-in and boarding process. Regent's ships are far smaller than most, which also reduces bottlenecks when many passengers return from shore excursions at the same time.

Does the Regent experience work from a business standpoint? Montague points out that of the three lines that make up Norwegian Cruise Line—Norwegian and Oceania are the other two—Regent has the highest rebooking rate. The line is continuing to add capacity at a measured pace, with another ship launching in 2020. Despite having some of the highest prices in the cruise industry, Regent is thriving.[31]

### FRICTION TAKEAWAY

What's better than making transactions faster and easier? Eliminating the transaction entirely. Do you have extra charges that could be built into the purchase price without a negative effect on total revenue? Do you offer a single-price, all-inclusive option? Customers will frequently pay more for an all-inclusive option than what they would spend in an a la carte price scheme—it's convenient, and avoids what's called the "pain of paying."

## MAGIC MEDALLION

Another approach to getting the friction out of cruising comes from the largest cruise ship operator, Carnival Corporation. Their nine-brand portfolio ranges from Carnival, a value line that caters to families and younger passengers, to Cunard, a luxury line known for transatlantic crossings and iconic ships like the *Queen Mary 2*. Unlike the Regent all-inclusive experience, to varying degrees the Carnival brands expect shipboard charges to be an important part of the revenue for each cruise.

Unbundling services isn't necessarily bad. A passenger who, say, doesn't drink alcohol or go on port excursions might find the value proposition in an all-inclusive cruise lacking compared with a cruiser who fully utilizes the included services. Even an affordable cruise includes a lot—lodging, a variety of dining, entertainment, and activities. An inexpensive cruise is nothing at all like flying a discount airline, and passengers can choose those additional services they find attractive.

Of course, on lower-cost cruises there are more frequent transactions onboard. An increase in friction is inevitable. Soft drinks, specialty coffees, alcoholic beverages, and some food options will all require a purchase transaction using the cruise card. Even passengers who, say, purchase an all-you-can-drink beverage package still need to have a no-charge transaction processed each time they order.

## A Magical Approach to the Cruise Experience

To greatly reduce not only transaction effort but to serve passengers better and anticipate their needs, Carnival is going all-in on technology. Who is leading their charge? None other than John Padgett of Disney MagicBand fame. In his position as Chief Experience and Innovation Officer, he's spearheading the development of a technology infrastructure uniquely designed to improve the cruise passenger experience.

Padgett is seeking to go beyond the MagicBand experience in the cruise environment. "Simplicity is the baseline," he notes, and identifies an important goal: a high level of real-time personalization. Cruise lines are in the business of creating unique experiences and memories, he says, and personalization enhances those memories.[32]

A cruise ship is a self-contained city but can interact with different ports and different countries every day. Padgett views the cruise experience "horizontally." By that he means that it's not just the individual experiences one has on or off the ship, it's the transitions between those experiences that can make the difference in overall guest experience.

Padgett and his team are introducing the OceanMedallion, a wearable (or pocketable) device that has two main objectives:

1. Reduce friction in both transactions and transitions.
2. Take personalization to a level higher than has been seen before.[33]

## Great Experiences, Not Great Technology

Padgett wants the technology to fade into the background. Cruise ship guests do not crave great technology, he says; they desire great experiences. The Medallion requires no interaction from the guest. There are no buttons, no screens, no lights. Guests need only wear it or carry it. Padgett says the Medallion "takes out all the friction and complexity of engaging [guests] with experiences while simultaneously personalizing them to each and every individual. We're democratizing elite service to everybody."[34]

Waiting in lines is part of many business experiences, and it's usually assumed to be an unavoidable, if undesirable, necessity. Lines are often a part of the cruise experience, particularly on ships with thousands of passengers. Given that the size of the largest ships has more than doubled in the past decade, the risk to the cruise industry of commoditizing further with "en masse" experiences is very real.

Padgett wants to get rid of lines. He notes:

> Every second, every minute that a guest is in any form of line, they're not consuming an experience. And if they're not consuming an experience, you're not maximizing their experience. If you're not maximizing their experience, you're not maximizing their value perception.[35]

The Medallion, among other things, is intended to eliminate lines by letting guests know when they can participate in activities without waiting. Everything from boarding the ship to dining in the ship's restaurants can be streamlined.

Padgett sums up: "Our goal with the OceanMedallion is to take what would previously be seen as an elite level vacation, like at The Ritz, or the Four Seasons, or on our Seabourn Cruise Line, and democratize that to our larger brands . . . giving a better price-value relationship to the consumer, and better scale for us."[36]

From a business standpoint, there are multiple benefits to the Medallion. If guests truly experience a better cruise and pack in more enjoyment, the value of those cruises will be higher, and they could command a higher price. And, if transactions like buying a cocktail can be completed simply by having the Medallion in one's pocket, an increase in the number of transactions can be expected. Ship casinos have long been a source of profit for cruise lines, and Medallion technology promises to extend the opportunity to gamble to screens and personal devices anywhere on the ship.

And, the Medallion will help the crew, too. Padgett says it will reduce friction and cut the learning curve in delivering a highly personalized experience. Even on a luxury line with a one-to-one crew-to-passenger ratio, it still takes time for staff to learn customer names, preferences, and other details. A "MedallionClass" experience is intended to deliver personalization at the first guest interaction point without any learning curve.

Simplicity is the overarching design criterion. In fact, the ultimate goal of the Medallion goes beyond simplicity—it's invisibility. Padgett notes, "Guests don't care about technology. Guests care about experiences. So, we've gone to extraordinary lengths to make sure that the technology becomes embedded in the experiential environment. We minimize the perception of connectivity by hoping that the medallion itself is not perceived as a piece of technology because it has no on/off button.

"You don't charge it. You don't associate it. You don't do anything with it. You just have to have it."[37]

The OceanMedallion technology has been fully implemented on two ships, the *Caribbean Princess* and the *Regal Princess*. Ultimately, Padgett expects that it will enhance guest experience (and increase profits) on the 100+ ships Carnival operates under 10 brands.

## FRICTION TAKEAWAY

Carnival expects that its OceanMedallion will not only take the friction out of transactions and let guests do more but also allow its service to be highly personalized. Today, we are all usually identifiable when we visit a website or open an app, at least if we have an existing relationship. If you know who a visitor is, can you make things easier for him or her? Can you use past behavior or what the visitor told you about themselves to deliver a lower friction and/or more personalized experience?

## SIMPLICITY AND THE CUSTOMER

*I've discovered how complex a topic simplicity really is . . .*

—John Maeda, Author of *The Laws of Simplicity*[38]

John Maeda says his daughters think he looks a bit like the bespectacled, slightly bug-eyed cartoon character that graces the cover of every book in the *Dummies* series.[39] But, Maeda is no dummy himself. He was the president of The Rhode Island School of Design and a tenured professor at MIT's Media Lab. Later, he left academia behind to work in business and advised eBay CEO John Donohoe as the firm adopted a companywide design culture. That effort ended up becoming a case study at the Stanford Graduate School of Business. He was a partner at the iconic venture capital firm Kleiner Perkins. He's been an advisor to Google and a board member at firms as diverse as ad giant Wieden + Kennedy and audio innovator Sonos. He's won such divergent honors as the White House National Design Award, the Raymond Loewy Foundation Prize, and even a Tribeca Film Festival Award for disruptive innovation.

Despite Maeda's complex set of interests, he is also an advocate of simplicity. His TED Talk[40] on the topic has garnered more than a million views, and his book, *The Laws of Simplicity*, has become a classic. He points out that simplicity is about living life with more enjoyment and less pain. Kids will always choose the bigger cookie (enjoyment) but the smaller pile of laundry to fold (pain, in the form of required effort).

### Apple's iPod—Minimum Friction, Maximum Simplicity

In his book, Maeda explains why Apple's iPod is a simplicity play combined with elegant design. Today, we think of Apple has having invented the digital music player. In fact, there were reasonably successful products in that space well before Apple introduced the iPod. Creative Labs and Rio, to name a couple, had players available years before the launch of the iPod.

The early players, though, got limited traction. They were difficult to use and were adopted more by tech-savvy fans than by mainstream music lovers.

In 2001, Apple cobbled together a new, small-format hard drive and a clean, wheel-based control layout to produce the first iPod. It was initially compatible only with Apple's Mac computers, a factor that limited adoption. But, in the next few years, compatibility for other operating systems like Windows combined with more song storage greatly increased the iPod's reach.

Eventually, the iPod became the dominant music player. A key driver throughout was its simple, intuitive interface. Maeda's Third Law is, "Savings in time feel like simplicity."[41] He cites the iPod Shuffle as a prime example. The Shuffle eliminated the need (and the ability) for the user to choose songs to play. It simply played its contents randomly. This avoided the need for a display, a scroll wheel, a playlist management system, and so on. It also saved time as it removed the onus of music choice once the device was loaded.

The Shuffle eliminated other features found on both its larger iPod siblings and competitive models. It had no calendar, no alarm, and no notes. It played fewer file types.

The Shuffle's simple interface, small form factor, and time-saving effect turned it into yet another hit for Apple. The key lesson is that people liked the Shuffle even though it was designed with far fewer capabilities than its competition. Simplicity and lack of user effort trumped features and power, and Apple sold more than 300 million iPods in the first 10 years of its life.[42] The iPod ruled the category until smartphones eliminated the need for separate music devices.

## Music Made Even Easier

Devices made to play the music one had purchased reached a point of maximum simplicity. But, there were simpler solutions still in store for music lovers. Today, music streaming services like Spotify and Pandora let you access a vast selection of music without having to buy it or manage your collection. The services will create playlists automatically and adjust them to your preferences.

Can things get even simpler? Actually, they can. Now, without lifting a finger, you can tell Alexa (or Siri or Google Assistant) what to play and it will happen.

## FRICTION TAKEAWAY

The music industry has moved relentlessly toward simpler and easier ways to consume music. At first, some of these innovations were actively opposed by the music companies. Don't be like them. Instead, as Maeda suggests, focus on delivering more enjoyment with less pain.

# CHAPTER 8

# Technology Friction

*Complexity is your enemy. Any fool can make something complicated. It is hard to keep things simple.*

—Richard Branson, Founder, Virgin Group

Modern technology is a friction conundrum. Any number of tasks are infinitely easier, from booking an airline reservation to sending a message to someone on the other side of the planet. But, that same technology has given us incomprehensible interfaces, baffling error messages, and overloaded inboxes.

Technology doesn't always increase friction, though. When the user experience is designed to be intuitive and effortless, it does the opposite. Unfortunately, user interfaces are often a product of utilitarian coding rather than the result of observing real user behavior.

Not long ago, a nontechnical friend of mine said he *had* to tell me about his new home router. "It's amazing—I set it up in a few minutes, and it worked right away!" Before he named the brand, I told him I could guess. When I correctly identified the product, he was somewhat surprised. I guessed correctly because not only did I own one myself, I knew the backstory behind the product.

## A PROMISING ENGINEER

Rammohan Malasani grew up in a middle-class Indian family in the early days of personal computers. His family couldn't afford a computer of their own, but young Malasani got lucky. When he began eighth grade, he found his school had several early generation IBM personal computers. Malasani quickly learned BASIC programming, which complemented his existing interest in math.

Malasani's proficiency in math and technology gained him entrance to the prestigious Indian Institute of Technology (IIT) Madras. IIT has one of the most selective admissions processes in the world, accepting a mere 2 percent of those who take the entrance exam.[1]

After earning his degree in electrical engineering at IIT, Malasani was admitted to a master's program at the University of California, San Diego (UCSD). He completed his degree in a couple of years and decided to stay in California. He took a job in Santa Barbara. The company was Centellax, where Malasani learned to design complex integrated circuits.

While still working his at his day job, Malasani and a UCSD classmate, Robert Pera, were spending their nights creating a new, less expensive design for outdoor wireless networking gear. In 2005, the pair cofounded Ubiquiti Networks to exploit their invention. Ubiquiti began manufacturing in Taiwan, and Malasani secured networking giant Netgear as their first major customer.

The company was more successful than the partnership. Malasani left the firm in early 2006, just as it became profitable. He later sued Pera to recover money he said was owed him, while Pera countered by claiming that the key invention was his alone.[2]

Ubiquiti went on to ever-greater success, going public in 2011 and making Pera a billionaire. Malasani, meanwhile, returned to Taiwan and went back to the entrepreneurial drawing board. For a few years, he worked on his Chinese while looking for new opportunities. In 2007, he started Dbii Networks, a small designer and manufacturer of wireless networking equipment. He sold that business within a few years to focus on a totally new concept.

## Taking the Friction Out of Home Networks

Malasani was an expert in designing wireless networking gear but had always focused on the behind-the-scenes commercial side of the business. None of his past work had been in the consumer networking market, which was dominated by giant companies like Cisco and Netgear.

The market for consumer networking gear isn't easy to crack. Products like Wi-Fi routers often sell for less than $100, putting heavy pressure on pricing and manufacturing costs. Traditional retail channels like electronics leader Best Buy and office chains like Staples aren't eager to add new vendors to an already crowded and confusing spot in their stores.

And, there's support . . . consumer network gear can be fiendishly difficult to install properly and requires a costly investment in support infrastructure. Nontechnical customers having to cope with MAC addresses, IP configuration, WPA2 security, and more are a support nightmare.

From the consumer standpoint, getting a home network up and running is often a high-friction process. The typical router is a black box with a row of cryptically labeled blinking lights. Externally, it gives no clues as to how to use it. One generally must connect a computer to it, type in a string of numbers that form the router's IP address, and then go through a series of configuration steps. One wrong setting, and the network won't work. Ironically, the router is usually the gateway to the Internet, so devices that require access via the home network can't be used for troubleshooting.

## A Crazier Idea

If Malasani's first idea, taking on Cisco and the other big firms making home routers, seemed crazy, his method for doing that seemed doubly so. He decided to design a router with a color touchscreen built in, naming the business Securifi.[3]

Everyone he discussed the idea with dismissed it. Why would people want a color screen on a device that spends its entire life under a desk or gathering dust on an inaccessible shelf? And, wouldn't the added cost make it impossible to compete in the brutal home market?

Malasani saw things differently. First, the explosion in the smartphone market was making touchscreens cheaper by the day. So, the cost penalty wouldn't be nearly as high as in the past. More important, though, was that the routers on the market were, in his judgment, awful. Even his tech-savvy friends were afraid to touch their routers or try to change a setting, lest they ruin their weekend trying to get them working again.

The process for installing his screen-enabled router could be fundamentally easier and less intimidating than for a faceless black box that needed a connected computer. The user could plug it in, follow the directions on the built-in screen, and be up and running in minutes. And, if a setting needed to be changed later, the same built-in screen could be used.

## Build a Better Mousetrap . . .

The other huge problem facing Malasani was distribution. This was where he encountered friction—simply having a better product didn't mean he could get it in front of customers. Not only would he be fighting for shelf space with entrenched, well-known competitors, he would have to get past powerful gatekeepers. At a chain like Best Buy, one person makes the decision on what gets on the shelf and what doesn't.

To solve the distribution problem, Malasani turned to our favorite friction-fighter, Amazon. While we think of Amazon's friction-fighting efforts as being focused on making things easy for consumers, they also make things easy for product sellers. Malasani found that all you had to do was put a UPC label on your product and upload the information to Amazon, and you can start taking orders.

So, that's what Malasani did. There was just one problem—there were already hundreds of routers listed at Amazon. Some were from the big networking brands, others from lesser-known vendors offering cheap prices. Getting visibility for a new product amid this plethora of similar products is a challenge.

Malasani's own friction-reduction strategy eventually began to pay off. He marketed the Securifi Almond router with the claim that it could be installed in three minutes. That's something no other vendor could promise at the time. Most importantly, consumers did, in fact, find his router easier to install. Many were able to accomplish the task in something close to the time promised by Malasani.

Another task Securifi dramatically simplified was updating a router's firmware—an essential, if dreaded, part of keeping one's network secure. Most of Securifi's competitors required using a computer to download a file and then connecting to the router and installing it. Installing the wrong file could render the router inoperable. In contrast, updating was effortless on the Almond. A couple of taps of the touchscreen, and the router itself checks for updates. If it finds newer firmware, the display lets the user decide whether to install it. A single tap downloads the update, installs it, and reboots the router. There's no chance of installing the wrong update, and the unit is back in service in minutes.

The friction-free setup and ease of operation resulted in five-star ratings at Amazon, and the virtuous cycle began.

### The Wisdom of Amazon Shoppers

Amazon doesn't employ buyer-gatekeepers like Best Buy or Staples—their customers are the ultimate gatekeepers. Instead of relying on a few experts to choose the best products, Amazon offers everything and lets the wisdom of the crowd pick the winners. A product may offer excellent quality and outstanding performance, but if customers have difficulty setting it up or making it do what they expect, they'll give it a low rating.

Technical product categories with "difficult" products like network gear and backup systems are often populated by top-selling products that have very mixed ratings, often below four out of five. In other product categories, the top products fare much better, with ratings in the 4.5 range and higher. These networking products aren't necessarily bad, but a technical setup process means that some less-adept customers will be frustrated and give the product a bad rating.

The uncharacteristically high ratings for the Almond, driven by the easy touchscreen setup, allowed Securifi to quickly emerge from the rest of the router pack. And, as more customers bought them and posted good reviews, the visibility of the product and the credibility of its reputation continued to increase. Having 20 excellent reviews helps, but having 2,000 is highly persuasive.

This positive cycle enabled Securifi to ship 100,000 routers before they took a penny of outside funding. Within four years, the total was 250,000. The Almond not only had a five-figure review count, it remained the top-ranked unit in its space.

Malasani steered the company to this position by exploiting friction twice. First, he created a product that eliminated much of the friction involved in setting up a highly technical product. Then, he chose Amazon's low-friction entry path to introduce the product to the market.

## SMART ROUTER, SMARTER HOME

Malasani's next move also involves friction reduction. Home automation products to control lights, thermostats, and other items are notoriously difficult to set up. Indeed, after being marketed without much success for more than 30 years, home automation products and systems are only now getting some traction.

Malasani's path to that market is, once again, to avoid the need for complex computer interfaces or specialized additional hardware. The Almond line works with Amazon's Echo, a.k.a. Alexa, to let users control their home by voice. The newest Almonds will offer home control options on the built-in screen as well as by smartphone app. It will even arm and disarm the security system automatically—no fumbling to enter a code when you return with an armload of groceries.

Building home automation into his routers is what Malasani calls a Trojan Horse approach—customers will buy the router for network connectivity but get the home control capability that comes with it. Even if they don't immediately start using it, eventually there will be a huge installed base of Securifi home controllers ready to be activated. And, it will be easy!

### FRICTION TAKEAWAY

Before Securifi, all home and small office routers looked the same: boxes with blinking lights on the front and a place to plug cables in on the back. They were configured using a computer and software. This was a high-friction process, but both the big network gear companies and their customers accepted it as the only way. Just as Uber threw out the playbook and used the smartphone to create a better customer experience than traditional taxis, Securifi got rid of the blinking lights and built in a user-friendly touchscreen. Any one of the big makers of network gear could have built a device like the Almond, but it took an outsider to actually do it. If you deal with an experience that is annoying or difficult but seems unavoidable, do what Malasani did—think outside the box!

## SECURITY FRICTION

The biggest source of digital friction these days is security. With hackers making the news every day, organizations of every size are striving to make their technology secure. This is undoubtedly a good thing, until the burden of dealing with security becomes too onerous for the user. Every time a user has to enter a password, go through a double authentication process, or answer a security challenge question, there's friction. The challenge every security manager faces is to keep the bad actors out while making things as free of friction as possible for legitimate users.

## Just Don't Do It

A few months ago, I visited the website of Nike, the giant shoe company. The shopping experience was fine. I was able to view and search their products, and at one point I had a short interaction with a chat support representative. At least I think it was a representative. If it was actually a chatbot, it passed my personal Turing test with no problems.

I found a pair of shoes that I liked, dropped them in my shopping cart, and went to check out. The first step was to set up an account, as I was a first-time buyer. I entered my information, put in a password I thought I'd be able to remember, and was immediately stymied. My password wasn't up to Nike's standards. An error screen listed the elements that my password had to contain. The first was "At least one mixed case letter."

Huh?

I know what upper- and lowercase letters are, but I had never heard of a mixed case letter. I've used this example in speeches, and, whenever I've asked the audience if anyone knew what a mixed case letter was, nobody has ever raised a hand.

I resolved my immediate issue by trying a bunch of different passwords until I hit on one that wasn't rejected. If I had to guess, I'd say what the instruction meant was, "At least one uppercase letter and one lowercase letter," but I can't be sure.

At least I solved the puzzle and completed my order. How many would-be customers tried once and gave up? How many orders were never finished because of this confusing security requirement? Not long after my experience, Nike announced that they would partner with Amazon to create an official, branded presence on the e-commerce site and boost their online sales. Smart move.

# CAN'T LIVE WITH IT, OR WITHOUT IT

Long before digital technology, we accepted that keeping valuable things safe was important enough to make it more difficult to access them. We put money in banks instead of keeping it in the house. We put expensive jewelry in a home safe, if we were lucky enough to have one. If we didn't have a safe, we hid valuables in places where we hoped a thief might not easily find them. We stored valuables in bank safety deposit boxes that required an in-person visit and an identity check by a bank employee. All these steps made it more difficult for us to get to our own stuff, but the additional safety was a reasonable trade-off.

In the digital world, security has emerged as an enormous point of friction. The ongoing war between those charged with keeping your information secure and the hackers and criminals who want to break in has left users in an uncomfortable no-man's-land of cumbersome procedures and passwords that are impossible to remember.

## Security vs. User Experience

Most organizations strive for a smooth user experience (UX) in their digital products. Not all succeed—some rely on the instincts of their developers or security managers to make design choices. Often, these choices aren't right for the user encountering the website or app for the first time. Smarter organizations employ user experience specialists who rely not just on their own knowledge but on user testing and user behavior measurement.

A frictionless experience may be optimal from the user's viewpoint but might not provide the best level of safety as dictated by the organization's security czar. To put it in physical terms, it might be really convenient for you to leave your Rolex Cosmograph Daytona on top of the dresser in your hotel room, but a security expert would recommend leaving it at home in a bank vault or at least locking it in the hotel room safe.

The tension between UX design and security has been increasing as hackers penetrate more businesses to steal customer information. Security czars demand strong passwords with numbers, letters, and symbols. They force users to create new passwords periodically and prevent them from reusing old ones. They may require users to set up answers to challenge questions like, "Who is your favorite author?" Some implement two-factor authentication, so that even if you know your password you must enter a code sent to your registered mobile phone number.

UX experts push back, noting that the more onerous security requirements are, the more inclined customers will be to go to a competitor's site or app. They also complain that passwords that are difficult to remember encourage behaviors likely to compromise security, like writing the password on a sticky note in plain view.

**FRICTION TAKEAWAY**

Whenever you change your website or launch a redesign, do a quick user test to see how people really behave. These don't require fancy lab setups—there are firms that can record panels of subjects using your site or app quickly and cheaply. And, even if the tests don't expose problems, instrument the site to track granular user behavior. If a few users get an error when they first submit a form, they are probably careless. If half your visitors get an error, they aren't the problem. Instead, the form or its instructions are confusing them.

## FROM REJECTS TO BILLIONAIRES

In 2007, Brian Acton and Jan Koum both applied for jobs at Facebook. They were rejected. In 2014, they connected with Facebook again. This time, it was to close the sale of their startup, WhatsApp, to Facebook for $19 billion.[4] Founded in 2009, WhatsApp had grown to 465 million users when they became part of Facebook only five years later.[5]

What enabled WhatsApp to add hundreds of millions of users in their first five years? As with most success stories, there's never just one reason. But, one key factor was how free of friction their process for onboarding new users was.

To begin with, unlike virtually every other mobile app, WhatsApp didn't require you to create a username and password. Your phone was all you needed. You didn't need an e-mail address, either.

Sam Hulick, author of *The Elements of User Onboarding,* did a "teardown" of WhatsApp's streamlined process.[6] His analysis showed how little wasted user effort there was. For instance, the country code was prefilled in the one piece of data that users had to enter—their phone number. Not only did this save a couple of screen taps, the vast majority of users in the United States would be hard-pressed to identify their country code as "+1." This reduced errors and avoided the need for millions of users to scroll through a list of countries to find the right code.

Even cursor placement reduced effort. By placing the cursor in the spot where the user needed to enter the phone number, the user could start typing immediately. There were two permissions needed, including permission to see the user's phone contacts. In both cases a short, clear explanation was offered to show why these permissions would enable the app to work properly.

The verification process was ultra-simple as well. As soon as the user completed the signup process, WhatsApp sent a text to the phone with a six-digit code. The user could enter that code, or, even more simply, click on a link in the text. As soon as you did one or the other, the app offered to let you enter a name and add an optional photo, and, also optionally, invite your contacts to WhatsApp.

## Two Minutes to Going Live

Hulick timed the process the first time he did it. Even as a newbie, the process took him just two minutes and five seconds—including the verification step. I've visited sites where it took me more than two minutes to fill out their signup form and find a password that met their specifications. In some cases, I've seen the confirmation process alone take minutes or fail on the first try.

WhatsApp's remarkably quick process enabled new users to get up and running instantly. If they invited friends to the app, those friends could get going with equal speed and few barriers to conversion. And, those new users might invite *their* friends. It's easy to imagine how a quick cycle of signups and invites could ricochet around a community and spread beyond, all in a matter of an hour or two.

### FRICTION TAKEAWAY

Can you onboard a user or subscriber in two minutes? Have you designed every element of the process for minimum user effort by prefilling fields where possible and placing the cursor where the user is supposed to start typing? (And, not only for mobile. Remember, on most desktop forms, you will have to take your hand off the keyboard and use the mouse to place the cursor in the first form field.) The odds that you'll add users as quickly as WhatsApp are pretty slim, but a small reduction in user effort can lead to higher conversion rates.

CHAPTER

# 9

# Friction Within Your Business

*Bureaucracy is the epoxy that greases the wheels of progress.*

—James Boren, American Humorist and Writer

Friction doesn't only happen when businesses interface with customers. Internal friction—red tape, wasted effort, pointless meetings, and so much else—all combine to raise costs, reduce productivity, and slow progress to a crawl. In this chapter, we'll look at some of the sources of friction inside organizations and how to reduce, if not eliminate, it.

## THE SLOWING PACE OF BUSINESS

In this high-tech era where business conversation is dominated by talk of failing fast and the rise of billion-dollar unicorns, it would be easy to assume that businesses are moving faster. There's evidence to the contrary: the pace of business is *slowing down*.

One survey of 400 recruiters showed that in 2015 it took an average of 63 days to hire a new employee, up from 45 days just five years earlier. Other surveys showed that the time to complete an office information technology project rose by more than 10 percent and the time to close a business-to-business sale was up 22 percent in that same period.[1]

Tom Monahan, CEO of CEB, the consulting firm that conducted those surveys, attributes much of the slowdown to an increase in corporate control and concern for risk management. Issues like regulatory compliance, privacy protection, and data security have resulted in a proliferation of processes. Most startling was the firm's discovery that in 10 years there was a nine-fold increase in enterprise risk management functions.[2]

The firm's research also found that collaboration needs were on the rise. As firms move to flatter, less hierarchical structures, the need for peer interaction increases. They found that 60 percent of those surveyed interacted with 10 or more coworkers daily, and half of those needed to engage with 20 or more daily.[3]

Monahan doesn't use the word "friction," but it's clear that bureaucratic processes and out-of-control collaboration are behind the slow pace at many companies.

## THE DEVIL HAS MANY NAMES

Friction inside organizations has been called many things. But, when you did a bit deeper, the names are all aliases for the something. Friction by any other name is . . .

### Red Tape

Transaction costs as described by Nobel Prize–winning economist Ronald Coase are an economic concept and don't reflect the full range of friction inside firms and organizations. Other terms are more familiar. One is "red tape." Often associated with bureaucratic procedures in government and business, the term has uncertain origins. The earliest uses in a paperwork context trace back to sixteenth-century and later Europe, where red tape was used to bind religious and administrative documents.

Charles Dickens wrote in his 1850 novel *David Copperfield*, "Britannia, that unfortunate female, is always before me, like a trussed fowl: skewered through and through with office-pens, and bound hand and foot with red tape."[4]

Although red tape has long been associated with legal or important documents, the derogatory context of bureaucratic procedures and delays may have its roots in the United States. After the Civil War, getting access to veterans' service and pension records was a tedious process. These records were, as you might guess, secured with red tape.

### Organizational Drag

One of my favorite terms for internal friction is the much more recent "organizational drag." Like friction, the term "drag" has scientific origins. Drag is a form of friction found when an object moves through a gas or liquid, and is a force that acts in the opposite direction of that movement. A bullet shot into water, for example, will slow down and eventually stop because of drag. In contrast, a space probe could travel indefinitely in the vacuum of space because of the absence of drag.

The concept of organizational drag was popularized by Michael Mankins and Eric Garton, Bain & Company partners and key players in the consulting firm's organization practice.[5] Their thesis is that companies have established procedures to allocate financial capital, but nothing similar for human capital. They believe that an organization's most valuable resource is its people, specifically their time, talent, and energy. This resource is often squandered in attending pointless meetings, handling irrelevant e-mail, and following bureaucratic procedures. They lump the latter time sinks into the term "organizational drag."

### Bureausclerosis

It's not common parlance, but you've got to love the term "bureausclerosis." The first use of the term I found was in a 1996 paper by author and management thought leader Gerald Kraines, who uses it to refer to a condition in which organizations are excessively layered and autocratically managed.[6] The term is also featured in a new book by Gary Hamel and Michele Zanini, *Humanocracy*. Hamel and Zanini have focused on the high cost of bureaucracy, putting the annual number in the trillions of dollars.

Despite the apparent awareness of the negative effects of bureaucracy, we'll see that it is still with us.

## PARKINSON'S LAW

*Bureaucracy expands to meet the needs of the expanding bureaucracy.*

—Oscar Wilde, Irish Essayist, Novelist, and Playwright

One of the earliest critics of bureaucracies was C. Northcote Parkinson, author and the creator of Parkinson's law. His eponymous law states simply that "work expands so as to fill the time available for its completion." In an amusing paragraph that opens his book, he speculated that an "elderly lady of leisure" might spend an entire day in writing and sending a postcard. He describes her hunting for spectacles, deciding whether to take an umbrella for the walk to the post office, and so on, until she has spent hours in the process. A busy man, on the other hand, would occupy himself for just three minutes with the same task.[7]

Ageism and sexism aside (standards were a bit different in 1957), Parkinson did hit on a key insight: work is elastic in its demands on time. This, in turn, drives ever-larger and more complex organizations. In theory, an organization should get larger only as the amount of work forces the hiring of more people. Parkinson argued the opposite: as more people are added, the work expands to fill their time.

Parkinson felt that bureaucratic organizations grew in the number of people employed, regardless of the actual work that needed to be done. He saw two primary driving forces:

1. An official wants to multiply subordinates, not rivals.
2. Officials make work for each other.[8]

## Beware of "Injelitis"

Parkinson coined the name "injelititis" for what he termed "palsied paralysis" in organizations. He traces the signs of the disease from the first signs to the final coma. He also created a set of equations that showed why, left unchecked, bureaucracies grew at an average rate of 5.75 percent per year. To prove his point about administrative growth, he cites the British Admiralty between 1914 and 1928. Despite the number of Navy ships falling by two-thirds and the officers and sailors total declining by 32 percent, the number of dockyard officials and clerks rose by 40 percent. Admiralty officials surged by 78 percent.[9]

## Meeting Triviality

Parkinson was an early critic of meetings, too. He introduced the Law of Triviality, which states that the time spent on any item of the agenda will be in inverse proportion to the sum (of money) involved. While committee members would feel unqualified to criticize an expenditure of tens of millions of dollars, an amount they can't personally comprehend, everyone will debate at length the construction of a small shed or how much should be spent on refreshments.

While satiric in nature and a bit over-the-top by today's standards, Parkinson's work accurately skewered the self-perpetuating nature of bureaucracies. And, long before the science of behavioral economics had been accepted, Parkinson was describing how real people behaved in the real world. Herb Simon, the Nobel Prize winner who created the concept of managerial "satisficing" (not optimizing, but rather doing enough to satisfy), was working on similar issues but in an academically robust way.

### FRICTION TAKEAWAY

> The idea that bureaucracies become increasingly bloated with time isn't new. It wasn't discovered by former General Electric CEO Jack Welch. Parkinson's astute observations of how humans behave in organizations are still relevant today, and the same mistakes he described are still being perpetrated. More people, rules, and procedures add needless friction without increasing the amount of real work being accomplished.

## THE MOTHER OF ALL BUSINESS BOOKS

*The only thing that saves us from the bureaucracy is its inefficiency.*

—Eugene McCarthy, US Senator

Tom Peters won't hesitate to say what's on his mind. He, along with coauthor Bob Waterman, Jr., kicked off explosive growth in the management book genre in 1982. Their *In Search of Excellence* went from an initial printing of 5,000 copies to selling a million in a year. Even then, Peters was outspoken. He emphasized that company culture was far more important than strategy and wouldn't back away from that position. He was a partner at McKinsey, the consulting giant that, among other things, assisted large corporations with strategic planning. Even before *Excellence* was printed, Peters's conflict with his partners resulted in him leaving McKinsey.[10]

Peters left McKinsey with the right to keep his half of the royalties from book sales. I asked him if that seemed like the worst exit package ever. After all, only 5,000 copies of the book would be printed, and few business books went into a second printing. He agreed, and added that he actually had to pay McKinsey $50,000 for his share of the royalties! Of course, what initially appeared to be an awful deal turned into a brilliant move; within a few years, *Excellence* had sold millions of copies.

Peters kept writing books and speaking his mind. In 1997, when the web was in its infancy and years before social media took off, he created the concept of personal branding. An audience member at one of his speeches challenged him as a "corporate stooge." Peters was surprised and annoyed, and retorted, "Hey, don't whine to me. Are you s-o-o-o-o cool, s-o-o-o-o obviously distinct, that you can survive? Do you have a 'signature' that's as unmistakable in its own right as BMW's? Or Tiffany's? Or Nordstrom's?"[11]

Peters developed his off-the-cuff remark into a seminal *Fast Company* article and later into one of his 17 books. Many other authors and consultants piled into the personal branding space in the ensuing decades.

## The Batshit Chapter

Today, Peters's frustration with most corporations is palpable. His latest book, *The Excellence Dividend,* is an unfiltered fire hose of advice and makes liberal use of big, bold type to hammer home key points. The importance of culture as a driver of growth and success is painfully obvious to Peters, but he sees too many businesses that continue to focus on financial metrics. One measure of his frustration is his informal title for one chapter: "The Batshit Chapter" actual titled (just slightly more acceptably) "One More (Damn) Time: Putting People First."

Peters's impatience isn't a new thing. A 2003 *Fast Company* interview with Peters was titled "Still Angry After All These Years." It quoted him, "I'm pissed off at life. Plus, I happen to believe that only pissed-off people change the world, either in small ways or large ways."[12]

## Go Big and Go Home

Peters has strong opinions about bureaucracy, too. He doesn't mince words when he says, "Giant companies are stinkers when it comes to long-term performance."[13] He cites work by McKinsey's Richard Foster that studied the performance of 1,000 large companies over a 40-year period. None of the survivors outperformed the market as a whole. Even more perplexing, the companies that were around the longest performed the worst.[14]

It seems counterintuitive that these long-lived companies underperform their peers. To survive for decades when other firms perished suggests that they are doing something right. The problem, Foster posited, lies in their success: the very structures needed to control existing operations weren't conducive to new ideas flourishing.

At a speech in Kenya, a large company CEO asked Peters if he truly thought there was no hope for big companies. Peters replied, "Yup. No hope."[15]

To temper the doom and gloom, Peters offers big companies a ray of hope: "The odds are stacked against you, hence you in effect have damn near nothing to lose—so swing for the fences and you at least up the odds a bit of performing well."[16]

## The Anti-Mickey Mouse Brigade

Bureaucracy comes with growth, and as early as 1987, Peters urged managers to fight it. "Poke fun at bureaucratic behavior, starting with your own," he advised.[17] Turning bureaucracy-busting into something that's fun will draw attention to the problem and keep people engaged. He suggested having an impromptu office party at the incinerator highlighted by the burning of boxes of unread reports.

Another suggestion is a recurring theme among bureaucracy foes. Peters said everyone should "continuously nominate forms and irritating regulations that they want eliminated." These nominations would be reviewed by a "high court" of mostly line and junior people who would be required to accept at least 50 percent of the recommendations. Periodically, there would be an award ceremony with "prizes for all whose Mickey Mouse regulation-removal ideas have been accepted."[18]

Indeed, Peters once proposed forming an "anti-Mickey Mouse Brigade" within an organization to identify and eliminate dumb rules, forms, and reports.

## JACK WELCH, BUREAUCRACY BUSTER

*Have a passion for excellence, hate bureaucracy and all the nonsense that comes with it.*

—Jack Welch, Former CEO, General Electric

*Business Week* declared legendary General Electric leader Jack Welch to be "the gold standard against which other CEOs are measured."[19] *Fortune* declared him to be "Manager of the Century" in 1999.[20] But, it wasn't always evident that Welch was on track to become one of the most famous and respected executives in business history. In fact, his GE career hit an early low point when he blew up a plant.

As a 27-year-old engineer, Welch oversaw a pilot plant in GE's Plastics division. One morning, he was startled by a huge explosion. Looking out, he was horrified to see the roof of his plant blown off. Windows were shattered, and a pall of smoke hovered over the factory. He was relieved when he learned that nobody had been injured in the explosion, but he faced a grim meeting with his boss's boss.

Welch's career might well have ended in the smoking ruin of that plant, but, to the benefit of generations of GE shareholders, his "big boss" wasn't looking for a scapegoat. Instead, the two discussed what Welch had learned from the disaster and whether the malfunction could be corrected. Welch returned to his factory, chastened but still employed, and no doubt wiser for the experience.[21]

### Nuking the Hierarchy

Blowing up a pilot plant was a minor controversy compared to Welch's early initiatives as CEO.

When Welch took over the reins at GE in 1981, the company was profitable and growing. Other large firms admired GE for its management innovations and emulated them. GE had pioneered the practice of strategic planning and had decentralized into many autonomous business units while other firms retained more centralized management.

Despite the company's business innovations, GE's management structure was still typical for a large industrial firm of that era—a pyramidal hierarchy. This structure had evolved over the decades to allow control over diverse businesses with global operations and was by far the most common practice in large companies.

Of necessity, the number of layers in the hierarchy increased as the organization grew in size and diversity. A single manager could supervise a limited number of direct reports, it was thought, so as the base of the pyramid grew so did the height. Small, autonomous divisions had some freedom to operate but had multiple layers of corporate management above them.

Welch rejected the conventional wisdom of layered, hierarchical management. Where others saw effective control, he saw complexity and waste. When he took over, 25,000 GE employees had a title that included "manager." There were 500 senior managers and 130 vice presidents. He thought there was too much bureaucracy, too many managers, and too many titles. Communication was slow and filtered by senior managers who were out of touch with what was happening on the ground. In Welch's view, GE had become a lumbering giant that was unable to respond quickly to its customers and markets.[22]

Welch's initial strategy to reduce bureaucratic friction was "delayering." When he took over, nine levels of management separated the CEO from front-line managers. He eliminated positions (and often the people who occupied them) to reduce the layer count to as few as four and never more than six.

To reduce the need for bureaucracy and to simplify GE's business, Welch also sold off or closed businesses with low profitability and limited growth potential. He didn't want to be in any business where GE wasn't the leader or a strong number two. Businesses with weaker positions were never going to be winners.

At the conclusion of this radical simplification process, a typical GE business unit had just 10 senior managers compared to 50 at other industrial businesses of similar scale.

Corporate staff wasn't spared, either. Welch cut GE's highly regarded strategic planning department from 30 to 8, calling the practice "archaic." He took 150 separate businesses and reorganized them into 15 lines of business and grouped those into three "circles."[23]

Overall, GE went from 411,000 employees when Welch took command to just 299,000 in 1985. Some of the reduction came from selling low-potential businesses, but more than two-thirds of the headcount reduction was in GE's ongoing businesses.[24] This unprecedented carnage earned Welch the nickname "Neutron Jack," a reference to the neutron bomb that kills people but leaves buildings untouched.

## Less Bureaucracy, More Profit

While there were clearly major cost savings from the delayering, they weren't the primary objective. Welch wanted a more nimble, agile organization where accountability was clear. He wanted information to flow freely and not be impeded by either the need to go through formal channels or be distorted by layers of management.

Results became evident within a few years. By 1986, five years after Welch took over the top job at GE, the firm's stock price had gone from $30 per share to more than $80. Revenues were flat, but Welch's streamlining had profits increasing faster than at most companies and the firm was positioned in faster-growing markets.[25]

Welch summed up his approach: "At GE, we're driving to be lean and agile, to move faster, to pare away bureaucracy. We're subjecting every activity, every function, to the most rigorous review, distinguishing between those things which we absolutely need to do and know versus those which would be merely nice to know."[26]

Bureaucracy busting was a lifelong goal for Welch. He thought that it was one consequence of success. A business unit grows its sales, profits, and staff. Eventually, management becomes complacent and loses its focus on speed and efficiency. In contrast, Welch saw smallness as a virtue. In one speech, Welch expounded on this theory:

> Without all the din and prattle of bureaucracy, people listen as well as talk; and since there are fewer of them, they generally know and understand each other.
>
> Small companies move faster. They know the penalties. . . . Small companies waste less. They spend less time in endless reviews and approvals and politics and paper drills. . . . Their people are free to direct their energy and attention toward the marketplace rather than fighting bureaucracy.[27]

**FRICTION TAKEAWAY**

As organizations grow, the number of managers increases. Inevitably, the number of layers of management grow, too. If Parkinson's theories have any merit, this growth will lead to inefficiencies when managers add subordinates. Organizational drag will increase, too, as more time will be spent communicating both horizontally and vertically. If your organization is having difficulty getting things done, the problem may not be too few managers, but too many.

## Next Target: Horizontal Friction

Welch's delayering efforts had the desired effect of bringing senior managers closer to GE's front lines and reducing waste from managerial roles with no operating responsibility. But, by 1988, Welch realized there was more work to be done. Bureaucracy had been reduced, but not eliminated. Even in the flatter hierarchy, communications still went through defined channels. If sales had a problem with manufacturing, the issue would have to be sent up to a higher-level manager who would then discuss it with his counterpart in the other organization. Eventually, a directive might flow down to the operational level where the problem could be solved.

The solution, Welch felt, was to "blow up the factory." Not literally, as he had done early in his GE career, but to demolish the figurative walls separating the people. Welch wanted anyone to be able to talk to anyone else, regardless of department or position in the hierarchy. Even more radically, he wanted to tear down the last big vertical barrier: the divide that separated workers (often union members) from management. Welch wanted to use their brains. They were, after all, the people most familiar with the work and how it got done.

## Working Out the Friction

In 1989, Welch launched perhaps his biggest bureaucracy-busting initiative: Work-Out. He said it would stop "wrestling with the boundaries, the absurdities that grow in large organizations. We're all familiar with those absurdities: too many approvals, duplication, pomposity, waste."[28]

A key element of Work-Out was getting groups of workers and managers together for a few days to discuss problems and solutions. On the closing day, the group offered proposals. To avoid the usual "we'll look into that" response, top managers had to either accept or reject proposals on the spot or ask for more information. Remarkably, four out of five proposals received an immediate answer.

The Work-Out program quickly began uncovering rules and procedures that were wasteful and pointless. In one case, the editor of a plant newspaper disclosed that even though there had never been a problem with the publication (it had even won awards), seven signatures were needed to approve each issue. The immediate decision was to eliminate all the approvals.[29]

In another session, an experienced machine operator explained that his job required wearing work gloves that wore out a few times per month. When the gloves were unusable, he had to leave his machine and walk to another building. There, he went to the supply room and filled out a form. Next, he had to walk around to find a supervisor with sufficient authority to approve the request, and then return to the supply room to get the gloves. The entire process could take an hour. The immediate and very simple answer? Put a box of gloves near the workstation.

Like so many ridiculous rules and procedures, this glove requisition process turned out to have a history. Years earlier, a box of gloves had gone missing. To prevent future glove shrinkage, some well-meaning manager instituted a procedure that perhaps saved a few dollars' worth of gloves but cost countless hours of worker and machine productivity.[30]

Not all problems were this straightforward. The more complicated problems identified in Work-Out sessions had to be attacked over time. But the program was so effective at increasing worker engagement and productivity that it became widely emulated. Entire books were written to show other companies how to conduct their own, similar Work-Out programs.

## The Welch Legacy

Welch's stewardship at GE wasn't without controversy. His divestment of business units and letting go more than a 100,000 employees caused great pain to individuals and communities. His constant emphasis on identifying and eliminating those managers and employees he called "C" players was criticized as heartless and demotivating. After he left GE, its performance declined rapidly. Both the 9/11 attack in 2001 and the 2008 financial crisis hit GE hard, and critics found fault with the mix of businesses that Welch had built. GE Capital was particularly problematic—it had become an important profit contributor in Welch's later years at GE, but eventually proved to be a big source of losses for his successor, Jeff Immelt.

Nevertheless, it's hard to argue with the results Welch achieved by his emphasis on cutting bureaucracy and simplifying the business. GE stock went up 4,000 percent and the firm became the most valuable corporation in the world.[31] Welch himself was broadly considered to be the prototype for a CEO and agent of change. He exhibited a disdain for red tape and bureaucratic waste throughout his career. He always carried GE's value statement on a laminated card in his pocket, with one of its principles being:

**Have a passion for excellence, hate bureaucracy and all the nonsense that comes with it.**[32]

In 1900, the *Wall Street Journal* proclaimed, "General Electric is entitled now to take rank as one of the . . . best managed industrial companies known to investors."[33] Welch's radical simplification of GE's bureaucracy ensured that the firm began the next century equally well-regarded.

## FRICTION TAKEAWAY

Much of what Welch accomplished in his Work-Out effort came from fostering communication across boundaries. Many of the wins were small, like putting a box of gloves next to the machine where they were needed, but conveyed a message of trust and cooperation. If your organization has bureaucratic barriers to free and frank communication, blow them up!

## THE NAVY WAY

*Red tape will often get in your way.*
*It's one of the reasons I often carry scissors!*
—Richard Branson, Founder, Virgin Group

Michael Abrashoff was a career Navy man who reached a level attained by only a tiny fraction of all naval officers. He was awarded command of his own ship, the USS *Benfold*. That's the good news.

The bad news? Of all the ships in the Navy, when Abrashoff took over, the *Benfold* had the worst readiness rating. Even worse, 72 percent of the crew planned on leaving not just the ship, but the Navy. While perhaps not quite as bad as being assigned to take charge of the *Titanic*'s maiden voyage, this appointment didn't seem to have a lot of upside for Abrashoff.[34]

Conventional wisdom suggested that Abrashoff should simply ride out this unappealing post without making waves. In an entrenched bureaucracy like the Navy, bold initiatives were a path to career disaster if they didn't work. On the other hand, an uneventful stint at the *Benfold* could lead to a promotion and a more desirable assignment the next time.

Abrashoff rejected the easy path and decided to do his best to fix the dysfunctional culture of his assigned ship.

### Blowing Up the Bulkheads

Just a few years after CEO Jack Welch "blew up the walls and ceilings" at GE with his Work-Out initiative, Abrashoff did something similar on the *Benfold*. The US Navy is a classic military hierarchy, with well-defined ranks and command structures. Orders are given and carried out. Or, at least that's how things worked on most ships.

Abrashoff began interacting directly with every sailor on the ship. He met with them individually. He learned their names. When there was a common meal, he went to the back of the line instead of cutting to the front as officers were allowed to do. He listened to everyone's ideas about how things could be done better.

He taught his people to ignore conventional wisdom and dream up better ways to do their jobs. Long-established procedures could be discarded if there was a more efficient or effective way of accomplishing a task. He empowered his crew to make any changes they thought necessary on their own. The only time he wanted to be consulted was if something had the potential to kill or injure someone, damage the ship, or waste taxpayer money.

### Non-Value-Added Chores

A big element of friction on the *Benfold* (and every other Navy ship) was the existence of what Abrashoff called "non-value-added chores." These included repetitive tasks like chipping and painting. While some captains have viewed this kind of work as a useful way to keep idle hands busy, Abrashoff thought they were a huge waste of time and effort. In addition, they had a negative impact on morale.

One sailor suggested that using stainless steel bolts and nuts in place of traditional fasteners would prevent rust streaks on the ship's exposed surfaces. These visible streaks necessitated frequent maintenance. The Navy didn't have stainless fasteners available, so Abrashoff bypassed procurement procedures and used the ship's credit card to order them. The non-rusting bolts and nuts meant that painting could be delayed for an entire year, saving massive time and effort. (Eventually, the Navy began using similar nonrusting fasteners on all its ships.)

Similarly, Abrashoff ignored established practice and procedures by having other steel parts specially treated at a commercial facility. Spending $25,000 on a flame-spraying process ensured these parts wouldn't corrode for years. This completely eliminated the need for regular painting.

Abrashoff even bent rigid Navy rules from time to time. To improve the experience of sailors on leave in Dubai, he hired unauthorized vans to chauffeur them around the city. Another time, he skirted the prohibition on consuming alcohol aboard ship by throwing a giant party on an adjacent barge.

Abrashoff's changes not only made the crew happier, they freed up a vast amount of time that could be used to improve the ship's poor state of readiness.

## FROM WORST TO BEST

Freed from the shackles of bureaucracy and inflexible procedures, the *Benfold* went from the worst of laggards to a star performer. The retention rate for sailors soared—in key areas, it hit 100 percent. With the cost of recruiting and training of $100,000 for just one job, retaining more people represented enormous savings. The *Benfold* ultimately achieved the top readiness score of any ship in the Navy.[35]

The *Benfold* also became the top choice for difficult missions during its time in the Persian Gulf—a mixed blessing, perhaps, but clear recognition of what Abrashoff and his crew accomplished. His egalitarian approach with his people and his creative interpretation of rules built trust and motivation. Even in a regulation-bound, bureaucratic organization like the US Navy, Abrashoff was able to effect change quickly and dramatically.

### FRICTION TAKEAWAY

Abrashoff effected dramatic changes in the way things were done on his ship despite the Navy's bureaucracy and rulebook. His actions motivated and engaged his entire crew and led to exceptional performance compared to the rest of the fleet. In your organization, there are probably rules, defined procedures, and customary ways of doing things. If these are hindering the performance of your people, or making them feel untrusted, don't be afraid to deviate from them if it will make things better. Sometimes it's better to ask for forgiveness later than permission in advance.

## TRUST AS A FRICTION-FIGHTER

In his book *It's Your Ship*,[36] Abrashoff describes a repair shop near San Diego's port facilities. Owned by an older gentleman named Irv Refken, the shop did repairs for the Navy and commercial customers. The shop had a reputation for delivering on time and at fair prices.

At one point, Refken's general manager said they needed a tool room to prevent employees from stealing expensive tools. So, they created a locked tool area and hired a custodian for $35,000 per year.

One morning, Refken was walking through the shop and saw a line of workers waiting to check out the tools they needed for work that day. The same line formed at the end of the day when workers queued up to return the tools. Refken realized that this time-consuming process was costing a lot of money. Even worse, it was signaling that he didn't trust his people.

He immediately abolished the entire process and assigned the custodian to another job. The result: much less wasted time, happier workers, and an annual cost of just $2,000 to replace lost or stolen tools. (This story is remarkably similar to Jack Welch's "work glove" anecdote. There, eliminating the requisition process and just making the gloves available in a box eliminated hours of wasted time.) To further show he trusted his people, Refken got rid of employee time clocks.

Trusting his customers also helped Refken grow his business. Typically, service providers would negotiate a contract for any services the Navy needed and wait until the necessary paperwork was approved before doing any work. Refken understood that sometimes time was of the essence. If an admiral needed work done immediately, Refken had his people start on it with no contract in place. He trusted that the Navy would pay him, and in turn the procurement officers trusted that Refken's price would be fair and the work would be done right. His shop ended up becoming the go-to source for time-sensitive projects.

**FRICTION TAKEAWAY**

> Rules and procedures are often put in place because of lack of trust. Sometimes, these are necessary—you probably don't want your bank to open its vault and operate on the honor system. But often, the savings from these onerous processes are far smaller than the cost of wasted time and effort they engender. Look for places where a small increase in trust will result in a big decrease in friction.

## MEETING FRICTION

*You'll meet the world's brightest, you'll hang with the best!*
*And now that you've met them, you'll work with the rest!*
—from *Oh, The Meetings You'll Go To!: A Parody* by Dr. Suits [37]

A few years ago, during a rare corporate stint, I met with a product manager whose performance was suffering. She seemed unable to create a coherent product improvement roadmap, much less generate truly innovative ideas.

Since she knew the product space well and was certainly bright enough, her lack of progress was perplexing. Even more surprising was her request for training in a mostly unrelated skill. That, I felt, was her way of finding a way out of an uncomfortable position.

As we discussed her situation and how to improve it, a startling fact emerged: in some weeks, she was spending *more than 30 hours* in meetings. Once you factored in other necessary evils like e-mail, the amount of time she had available to reflect, plan, and innovate was near zero. It explained her interest in learning other skills—she wasn't enjoying her time in the office and could see that she would never meet management's expectations for new product innovation.

It's possible that her meeting schedule was a monster of her own creation. She could point to her busy days as proof that she was serving the company's needs while avoiding the more difficult and less well-defined activity of creating new and better products. But her situation isn't all that unusual. It's not uncommon for executives to spend half their time in meetings.[38]

Each of the meetings on that product manager's schedule was individually justifiable. Her products would be discussed, or she might have information that others would need . . . but, the aggregate effect of all these meetings was to ensure there was no way she could do any real work. If nothing changed, failure was inevitable.

As with so many things in life, something that can be valuable and essential can turn into something that is inefficient, wasteful, and destructive. High-performing organizations use meetings sparingly and only when bringing people together in person is the most efficient way to communicate and make decisions. Meetings can grow like cancer in less effective organizations, with a mix of regularly scheduled get-togethers that have outlived their original purpose and ad hoc meetings that include far more attendees than necessary.

## Unfocused and Inefficient

While there are certainly some great workplaces with enlightened management and engaged, energized workers, there are many others where frustration and exhaustion are rampant. Almost always, the latter are plagued by bureaucratic procedures, wasted effort, and a lack of individual empowerment.

According to Gallup, an astonishing 85 percent of workers are not engaged with their employers. Fully 18 percent are "actively disengaged," while the other 67 percent are merely indifferent, or, using their term, "not engaged."[39] Some estimates say half of all meetings may be a waste of time.[40] Another poll found that 69 percent of workers said they were distracted, citing meetings, e-mail, messaging, and other factors.[41]

Another analysis found that one weekly meeting consumed an astonishing *300,000 hours* per year. The 11 business unit heads who participated in this executive committee meeting spent 7,000 hours directly. The numbers rippled out from there—meeting with their own senior people to prepare for the meeting consumed a total of 20,000 hours. These spawned 21 team meetings that consumed 63,000 hours per year. Supporting these team meetings required a staggering 210,000 hours of effort by individuals.[42]

That might be an extreme example, but almost all organizations experience a ripple effect of meeting-driven effort. Meetings that involve higher-level executives will almost certainly spawn either additional preparatory meetings or expenditures of individual effort.

Productivity expert Elizabeth Grace Saunders says, "'Let's schedule a meeting' has become the universal default response to most business issues."[43] This creates a huge amount of waste when poorly planned meetings accomplish nothing or when people are invited who don't really need to attend.

## How Schedule Software Disrupts Productivity

One small study found that just *scheduling* meetings—not actually attending them, just the process of coordinating people, times, and places—took more than five hours per week.[44] Of course, there are now more tools than ever to reduce friction in the scheduling process. Microsoft Outlook, Google Calendar, and similar applications can easily find times where all attendees are available, not to mention a conference room. This ease of scheduling is a mixed blessing, though—one person organizing a meeting can, with a few clicks, commit a larger much larger number of people to wasting an hour of their time.

The fundamental flaw in scheduling software is that by default it considers time where no meeting is scheduled to be free and available. This is fine when meetings are few in number and planned thoughtfully. But, in organizations with a less productive meeting culture, individual schedules can be disrupted and dominated by a constant barrage of meeting invitations.

Productivity experts recommend that individuals schedule blocks of "focus" time to prevent others from committing that time to meetings. This is a good solution, but the person must have the ability and confidence to do that. My overcommitted project manager didn't. Apparently, she felt she couldn't say no to reasonable meeting requests, even though her participation wasn't critical. Lower-level employees are particularly vulnerable to this problem—the meeting requests often come from higher-ranked managers and executives.

Powerful collaborative scheduling tools should, in theory, be big timesavers. Before they existed, executives or their assistants had to call potential attendees (or their own assistants) to try to find a meeting time that worked for everyone. This high-friction process did indeed waste time, but it had the beneficial effect of keeping a lid on the number of meetings and attendees. When scheduling meetings is easy, people schedule more meetings.

## The Cost of Meetings

The consequences of too many bad meetings are enormous. A study by Bain & Company concluded that despite working an average of 47 hours per week, a typical front-line supervisor or midlevel manager had a mere 6½ hours per week of uninterrupted time.[45] And that stretch wasn't continuous—it was merely the sum of schedule gaps of longer than 20 minutes. Is it any wonder so many people feel like they are working harder and accomplishing less?

Similarly, Yves Morieux of the Boston Consulting Group discussed his firm's research. They found that "people spend their time in meetings, writing reports they have to do, undo and redo. Based on our analysis, teams in these organizations spend between 40 and 80 percent of their time wasting their time, but working harder and harder, longer and longer, on less and less value-adding activities. This is what is killing productivity, what makes people suffer at work."[46]

## Setting Limits

Some businesses are ensuring at least one day of uninterrupted deep work (or at least the possibility of deep work) for their people by declaring one day a week off-limits for scheduling meetings. Asana is a business that makes software to increase team productivity. It found it worthwhile to declare a policy of "No Meeting Wednesdays," noting that managers often have schedule-driven days and find it easy to disrupt the calendars of other people. "Makers," including coders and designers, can't work effectively when their time is being allocated by others.[47]

While any number of other companies have initiated a "no meeting day" requirement, few go as far as Southwestern Consulting. This firm's people have varying work schedules and locations and are often traveling to client offices. The firm adopted "Mad Meeting Mondays," one day when their people are expected to come into the office to meet, talk, and make decisions.[48]

Limiting meetings to one day a week might seem extreme for organizations with established meeting cultures. But, doesn't it sound wonderful?

### FRICTION TAKEAWAY

Meetings have gone from being infrequent sessions to exchange information and make decisions to being a massive waste of time in many, if not most, organizations. While a discussion of how to make meetings productive is beyond our scope here, one small step would be to add some friction to the meeting scheduling process. Make it easy to set up a one-on-one meeting but more difficult to schedule groups. Perhaps the software could display the calculated cost of a meeting as people are added to it. Or, meetings with more than a specified number of participants would require approval by a higher-level manager. (Bureaucracy, for sure. But, in this case, it's bureaucracy for a good cause.) And, consider making at least one day off-limits for meetings.

## E-MAIL FRICTION

If meetings are the biggest waste of time in many organizations, e-mail is a close second. It wasn't always that way. The legendary founder of Intel, Andy Grove, once declared, "Businesses that have pervasive use of electronic mail operate differently." He said they are "much faster, much less hierarchical," and that e-mail "squeezes all the slack out of the system."

Grove did warn that being open to e-mail from anyone in the company had a downside, but that it was ultimately a way to democratize the company.[49]

Over time, the technology that revolutionized internal and external communication proved to have a dark side. Before e-mail, written communications were created on typewriters. This meant that the number of copies were limited by how many sheets of thin stationery and carbon paper a typewriter could accommodate and still produce legible copies. The advent of photocopying removed that limitation. It became far easier to distribute longer documents to more people. Soon, offices seemed to be drowning in paper. But the effort and cost of distributing individual copies did limit the number of recipients. A front-line manager would be unlikely to send a memo to everyone in the organization, at least more than once.

Digital technology promised to usher in the "paperless office." While that failed to materialize, there's no doubt that e-mail removed a lot of friction from business communication. A quick, one-line e-mail could ask or answer a question with just a few seconds of effort, far less than a phone call. And, this kind of exchange didn't require both parties to be available at the same time. They could be in different cities, or even countries.

## The Downside of Lowering Friction

This ease of creating and distributing e-mail resulted in an explosion in the total amount of communication. If you had a question, why not e-mail 10 people simultaneously instead of just phoning only the one most likely to have the answer? The odds of a quick and helpful reply are far better when the group is bigger. Keeping everyone informed about everything became nearly frictionless—e-mail lists for teams, departments, divisions, and even entire companies made it effortless to send an e-mail to dozens or even hundreds of people.

Individually, these e-mails no doubt served the sender's purpose. Even if the recipient had nothing to contribute, or didn't need the information contained in the e-mail, it wasn't a problem. The e-mail could be read quickly and deleted.

The problem, of course, is volume. One mildly off-target e-mail is no problem. But multiply that by 10, 100, or 1,000, and e-mail becomes almost unmanageable. Bain estimates that midlevel managers spend *11 hours per week* processing e-mail—that's more than two and a half hours per workday![50]

Like meetings, e-mails have become a case study in friction. The easier it became to create a communication, and the easier it became to add multiple recipients, the more people did both.

### Ferrari: High-Octane E-mail

While exotic sports car maker Ferrari doesn't seem like the most obvious candidate for e-mail overload, even they found that their people were spending too much time dealing with e-mails. And, as in most companies, not all those e-mails were important or even relevant.

As a company with a history of solving problems with creative engineering solutions, Ferrari attacked the problem in the most direct way possible—modifying their company e-mail software to limit senders to just three recipients. No more distribution lists. No more CCing everyone who might possibly have an interest. Every employee sending a message will have to select no more than three people to get the e-mail, including CCs and BCCs.[51]

#### FRICTION TAKEAWAY

E-mail is an indispensable tool in today's organizations, but it has also become a burden on individual productivity. Use technology to your advantage by identifying users who send too many e-mails or distribute messages too broadly. Use both cultural and technical means to limit e-mail distribution. Managers should model good e-mail etiquette by limiting the number of both e-mails they send and recipients they include. If a severe limit like Ferrari's isn't practical, at least limit access to team and department distribution lists. When it's easier to copy everyone than choosing recipients in a thoughtful way, that's exactly what people will do.

## YELLOW CARDS TO PROTECT GOOD IDEAS

The British Broadcasting Corporation (BBC) is renowned not only for its global reach and high-quality content but also its bureaucracy. Titles like "thematic adviser, governance" and "client solutions executive" have been found among the organizations 20,000+ employees and nine layers of hierarchical management.[52]

To their credit, BBC top brass has been aware of the problems created by complexity. The service is constantly under budget pressure, as their primary funding comes from government-imposed license fees. Expenditures must be controlled to fit the available funds.

One of the early initiatives to fight bureaucracy employed the metaphor of a football (or soccer, for Americans) yellow card. An official pauses play and holds up a yellow card to warn a player of an infraction. (A second infraction by that player would earn a red card and immediate removal from the game.)

In 2002, then BBC director general Greg Dyke issued staff yellow cards to hold up at meetings as part of a "cut the crap and make it happen" initiative. Dyke felt that a red tape culture existed at the BBC and that good ideas were being stifled by cynics or caught up in bureaucratic procedures. A staffer could wave the card to pause the discussion and highlight how a potentially good idea was being smothered by the bureaucracy.[53]

At the time, employees were skeptical of the yellow card initiative, calling it a gimmick that would never be taken seriously. One identified the BBC's meeting culture itself as the source of most of the "crap." Another anonymous skeptic said, "I could flash this card permanently at meetings, but I don't think I will. It will be brave person indeed who will pull this out of their back pocket to flash at their boss."[54]

A couple of years later, Dyke left the position after the BBC was criticized for problematic reporting and editorial judgment and was caught up in a government inquiry about a deceased biological warfare expert.[55]

## A Red Card for Red Tape

Years later, the BBC bureaucracy was apparently alive and well. In 2013, the organization's top brass launched a new effort focused on simplification. To drive the point home, they escalated Dyke's yellow card to a red. The new slogan was "Give red tape the red card!" Additional measures included a simplicity "hotline"—an e-mail address where staff could send suggestions for cutting red tape—and a goal of "60 fixes in 6 months." One of the suggestions was to make five buildings at one BBC location accessible with the same pass instead of requiring five different ones.[56]

While I'm quite certain nobody would agree that red tape is a thing of the past at the BBC, there seems to be progress. The 2016–2017 annual report from the BBC notes that the senior management ranks had been reduced by 172 "heads" in the preceding five years, with 47 decapitated in the last year alone. Senior leadership as a percentage of total staff had been reduced to 1.6 percent with an ultimate goal of 1 percent.[57]

While drastically thinning the executive ranks seems to be a grim approach to simplification, it is certainly one way of eliminating the friction that comes from too many layers of management and too many staff executives who are more likely to demand information from productive employees than make their jobs easier.

The same annual report notes that just 5 percent of the BBC's annual budget goes to administrative costs, with the remaining 95 percent to content creation and distribution.[58] While it seems likely that some of these costs are fungible and subject to being classified in various ways, the simplicity gospel is still being preached at the BBC.

### FRICTION TAKEAWAY

While it isn't clear that the yellow cards had much effect at the BBC, the idea of empowering even lower-level employees to call attention to bureaucratic stifling of ideas is sound. The later approach of setting measurable goals for simplification seems to have been more effective. To cut red tape in your own organization, empower the people who deal with it every day. Let them fix things on their own or, if higher-level approvals are needed (say, for legal or compliance reasons) provide a robust reporting and follow-up mechanism.

## RECEIPT MADNESS

After 25 years of being an entrepreneur, I did something I never expected to. I became an employee at a big company. I had no choice, really—this company, part of a diverse global corporation, had acquired my business. As part of the deal, I signed an employment agreement to facilitate the transition and to bring my experience in digital marketing to a group that had been mostly print focused in the past.

The experience wasn't nearly as bad as what some of my entrepreneurial colleagues feared. My new associates were honest, open, and eager to work on shared goals. It probably helped that I worked remotely most of the time, insulating me from any office drama and politics.

One quirky detail, though, was the expense reporting process. When I first joined the company, the workflow for getting travel expenses reimbursed was paper based. You filled in a standardized form, stapled your receipts to it, and gave the paper form to your boss to approve. Here's the part I found odd at the time: Internal Revenue Service guidelines generally don't require receipts for business travel expenses like meals unless they exceed $75. But, my new employer said *every* expense needed a receipt.

That meant that, for example, if you were rushing to catch a plane and grabbed a coffee at Austin Java and a breakfast taco at Maudie's (both Austin favorites with airport locations), you had better save both receipts, even if together they added up to $5 or $6. Even short trips created a blizzard of receipts.

I wondered if humans ever sifted through all the receipts to match them to the form, which seemed like a wasteful and time-consuming activity. I found out they actually did check every piece of paper when I somehow lost a $2 coffee receipt between filling out the form and stapling everything together. That expense report bounced back to me to be corrected if the proper receipt couldn't be found.

Was this "no expense too small for a receipt" policy that onerous? Not really. I know I never submitted a fair number of small expenses simply because I forgot to get a receipt or lost it, but those amounts weren't large. Accounting for every little expense down to the penny and attaching documentation did take more time on the employee's end. I'd guess even more time was spent by the accounting staff who had to match everything up and contact employees to resolve issues. There's no doubt that if you combined additional employee time (this office had hundreds of employees, many of whom incurred travel expenses) and accounting time, quite a few hours per month were devoted to dealing with low-value receipts.

## Making Inefficiency Efficient

The company eventually found a way to streamline the process by adopting an electronic workflow. Paper submissions were replaced by electronic forms that had standardized account numbers and could flow easily from employee to supervisor to accounting. Expense items could be transferred directly from a company credit card.

More time could have been saved by eliminating the receipt requirement for small expenses. That didn't happen. In a classic example of effort-shifting, the new system required the employee to take a photo of each receipt or capture images using a scanner. While the software was supposed to make this easy, taking a dozen photos or (arranging that number of receipts on a scanner) and associating each image with the expense line item was far more time-consuming than simply slamming a staple through a pile of paper receipts.

The accounting staff no doubt *did* save time. Now they could quickly glance at an image for each line item to be sure it was properly documented. No longer would they have to lay out a mosaic of little paper rectangles and play a matching game. Still, even this easier, more efficient process took longer than it would have with a higher documentation threshold and far fewer receipts.

All in all, the process was more efficient from an accounting workflow standpoint, but only because it shifted work to the employees reporting their expenses.

All too often, this is how organizations deal with time-consuming activities. Instead of questioning whether the activity could be eliminated completely, they look for ways to save time in performing the activity.

Long after we had both left the firm, I asked the former top financial person why the company insisted on far more documentation than legally required. He explained that there were two reasons. First, management thought some employees couldn't be trusted not to inflate their expenses if receipts weren't attached. Second, they thought people might spend less if they had to document everything. The company always seemed to be struggling to meet its profit goals, and this was one way, they thought, to control costs.

## FRICTION TAKEAWAY

This is another example of time-consuming processes established because of a lack of trust. It's also an example of automating a process in a way that seemed efficient but simply shifted the effort from one group to another. If your people are spending time on processes that aren't absolutely necessary, don't try to automate the processes, just eliminate them. If your procedures are driven by lack of trust and the amounts at risk are small, change or eliminate the wasteful steps. You'll save time and you'll let your people know that you trust them.

## KILLING STUPID RULES

*If following a "company rule" is obviously ridiculous in a particular situation, such that it would make for a great Dilbert cartoon, then the rule should change.*

—Elon Musk, Entrepreneur

One of the annoying aspects of working in many organizations are rules that seem to have no real benefit. At GE, work gloves had to be obtained in another building with a requisition form signed by a supervisor. In my expense report example, even a $2 expense needed a scanned receipt, account number, and project identification. It's likely that you can think of a rule or two in your own organization that doesn't make sense.

In her book *Why Simple Wins*,[59] author and consultant Lisa Bodell does a deep dive into organizational complexity and why simplicity is better. She offers many techniques to reduce complexity, and one of my favorites is an exercise she calls "Kill a Stupid Rule."

The concept is simple enough. People spend 15 minutes identifying rules they think are frustrating or slow down productivity. Then, the rules are quickly evaluated to be sure they aren't mandated by government regulations or aren't otherwise illegal to change. The remaining rules can be discussed, and, if possible, eliminated. If a rule can't be discarded completely, then it should be modified to reduce its complexity.

### Impact and Difficulty

In her book, Bodell offers a matrix to prioritize rule-killing efforts. Rules can be high or low in their impact on productivity, and easy or hard to kill. Rules that have a high impact and are easy to kill get attended to first.

This process can produce some surprises. Bodell describes a rule-busting session at Accenture where they found that many of the "rules" weren't even rules at all. People assumed that things had to be done in specific ways, either because they had always seen them done like that or because they misunderstood the rules. These nonrules were easy to kill simply by explaining that they need not be followed.

Other rules discussed in the session were killed on the spot. They weren't necessary, and no coordination with other departments or upper management was needed to put an end to them. By the end of the session, all but a few of the rules discussed had been eliminated. The few remaining ones were assigned to team members to follow up with the corporate office or whoever needed to be involved to change or eliminate the rule.

In her book, Bodell's suggestions for killing stupid rules include:

- Get input from everyone, not just managers.
- Set a numeric goal, like killing 10 rules in a defined time.
- Create a shared document for questionable rules to allow people to add new suggestions.

I chuckled when I saw one of Bodell's specific recommendations related to stupid rules: "Stop demanding receipts for items on expense reports that cost less than $75 (or specify the amount that's right for your business)."[60] Clearly, the corporate overlords demanding that I scan every $2 receipt hadn't read Bodell's book.

## FRICTION TAKEAWAY

If you want to declare war on organizational complexity, Bodell's *Why Simple Wins* is a great place to start. If you want to get quick results and engage your team, have a Kill a Stupid Rule meeting. If a frustrating, time-consuming rule serves no purpose, kill it immediately if at all possible. Swift action will demonstrate a willingness to help and spark further suggestions.

# CHAPTER 10

# A World of Friction

Friction doesn't just affect businesses. Regions and entire nations can trace success or failure to elements of friction. We saw that Rome dominated the ancient world in part by making communication and troop movement much faster and easier than its competitors, but there are far more recent examples.

## FROM HERO TO OUTCAST

In Holland, Esther Jacobs went from national hero to national outcast in a matter of weeks.

She didn't commit a heinous crime. She didn't have a profane meltdown on social media. She didn't do anything obviously wrong at all.

Rather, Jacobs got caught up in a web of regulations that even the highest levels of government couldn't, or wouldn't, fix.[1]

### Transforming Worthless Coins into Millions for Charity

Jacobs's signature accomplishment came at a relatively young age. In 2002, she was 28. She had no background in either fund-raising or nonprofit organizations. She did have a desire to help others, though. And she had a compelling idea.

As the European Union (EU) transitioned to a single currency for many of its members, many of the old national currencies were being phased out. Banks were able to exchange paper currency for euros, but coins could be converted only in their country of origin.

Even before the EU, Europeans were quite mobile. It was quite common to return from a trip with currency and coins from neighboring countries. These would be saved and used on the next visit to that country. Now, these small stockpiles of obsolete foreign coins would soon become worthless. Their holders would be unable to convert them to euros locally, and it would hardly be worth the effort to carry them to the other country and seek out a bank to exchange them.

Jacobs had a flash of insight and launched an effort she called Coins for Care. Her idea was to collect these soon-to-be-worthless coins for charity.

At first, she got little traction and almost no publicity. Then, Jacobs got a break. Her effort was featured in a major women's magazine, and the idea went viral. Coverage by other media exploded, and potential sponsors asked to become part of the effort.

Ultimately, Jacobs had more than a thousand volunteers helping her with thousands of collection boxes in the affected countries. She rejected any help that came with financial strings attached and did everything as cheaply as possible.

Coins for Care raised more than $25 million in coins while incurring little or no expense.[2]

### FRICTION TAKEAWAY

Jacobs's fund-raising was successful because she exploited a contrast in friction. On one hand, there was the impossibly high friction of converting these coins into useful currency—it could only be done by a bank in the country where the coins originated. On the other hand, there was the low-friction option of helping people in need by dropping them into a collection box. With the coins soon to become worthless, it's not surprising that so many citizens took the easy path and supported Jacobs's charity.

## Lady Esther

That story would be remarkable by itself, but Jacobs found a way to further improve the world of nonprofit management.

When it came time to distribute the funds, which she eventually donated to more than 140 charities, she asked for each recipient organization to account for how they would spend the money. While some were able to do this, others gave vague answers about using the funds "for their organization's purpose." EU laws, unlike those in the United States, required little in the way of disclosure of how nonprofits used their funds.

Jacobs's response was to publicize these nonspecific replies and launch a drive for transparency in the way nonprofits use their funds. She founded the first "donor organization" in the Netherlands with the objective of breaking through the wall of secrecy erected by many charities.

Her resourcefulness, level of success, and activism resulted in a unique honor. At 33, Esther Jacobs was officially knighted by the Dutch queen. She was one of the youngest people ever to receive this honor.[3]

## Rules Are Rules

*Bureaucracy is the art of making the possible impossible.*

—Javier Pascual Salcedo

As the Coins for Care effort wound down, Jacobs returned to her global nomad lifestyle and focused on her writing and speaking.

Then, the Dutch legal system upended Jacobs's life.

Jacobs was back in her hometown of Amstelveen, a small town near Amsterdam. She had owned a house there for almost 20 years and considered it her permanent home.

When she went to city hall to renew her passport, she was shocked to be told, "Sorry, you don't live here anymore."

Initially, she thought it was some bureaucratic mix-up. There was another Esther Jacobs, perhaps, or a clerk made a data entry error.

It proved to be no mistake. There's a Dutch law that says you must spend four months in a town to be registered there. She was, they said, in violation of this requirement.

It got worse. When she asked to see her records, the officials told her they couldn't show them to her for privacy reasons. She pointed out that it was her own privacy that she'd be violating, but they shrugged. Rules are rules.

When she asked what she had to do to fix the problem, she was told the "research committee" would investigate, as her case was now in the "fraud section."

Jacobs owned a house, paid taxes, and took no government assistance. She had been knighted by the queen.

Now, she had become a presumed fraud.

## We Know No Nomads

Jacobs's travel was curtailed, as her soon-to-expire passport was no longer valid for many countries. She immediately began writing letters and calling officials, to no avail.

Her only weapon to fight the bureaucracy was her own modest fame. With no other avenue open, Jacobs wrote a blog post about her dilemma. Within 24 hours, government ministers were meeting on her case. In any normal world, a phone call would be made, a memo would be sent, and Jacobs would get her passport renewed in short order. In the bizarre world of Dutch government rules and regulations, that didn't happen.

Instead, the ministers agreed that the law hadn't been written to disenfranchise frequent travelers like her, but that its requirements were clear. They gave the town permission to deregister her.

The frustrating situation turned into a nightmare. Once she was no longer legally a resident at the address where she was still living, the dominos of Jacobs's life began to fall.

Losing her parking permit wasn't a big problem, but then she lost her voting rights and her right to later claim a government pension. Her health insurance, partly sponsored by the government, was canceled. Her company no longer had a legal address, so it, too, was deregistered. Her bank account was closed and her telephone plan canceled since her business had no valid address. She couldn't bill clients or deposit checks.

Jacobs jokes that in the entire Dutch government, just one unit still was pleased to fully recognize her as a citizen of the Netherlands—the tax service!

Her lifelong hometown never recognized Jacobs as a legal resident again. After months of struggling with the bureaucracy to no avail, she changed her legal residence to Andorra, which ironically allowed her to resume most of her life as a Dutch citizen.

**FRICTION TAKEAWAY**

While Jacobs is an extreme example, it's significant that her ordeal took place in a prosperous, economically advanced nation. Around the globe millions of individuals are confounded daily by bureaucratic rules and regulations that make no sense. Laws remain on the books for decades, even as new and conflicting laws are layered on top of them. It's important for both citizens and legislators to identify laws and regulations that create friction without a corresponding benefit to society. Changing obsolete laws and eliminating pointless regulations is difficult but essential work; it benefits both citizens and the national economy.

## THE HIGH PRICE OF BUREAUCRACY

*You will never understand bureaucracies until you understand that for bureaucrats procedure is everything and outcomes are nothing.*

—Thomas Sowell, Economist

The story of Esther Jacobs is amusing today, at least for those of us who didn't have to live through it. Her life was disrupted, but she survived and adapted. She continued to build her business. A handful of other digital nomads may have been caught in the same trap, but most found simple workarounds to satisfy the bureaucratic box-checkers. The economy of The Netherlands wasn't affected in the least by the nonsensical application of the law. And, eventually the regulations will be changed if too many productive citizens are affected.

In some countries, though, a tangled bureaucracy and a plethora of regulations can have enormous implications for the prosperity of the nation and its people.

### Ajay Prasad's Story

Ajay Prasad is a successful California entrepreneur who traces his roots to Patna, India. Patna has brutally hot summers that are relieved only by the arrival of monsoon season. In Prasad's youth, Patna and its surrounding area were primarily agricultural, with government as the biggest employer.

In the past decade, it has become one of India's fastest-growing cities. But at the time that Prasad was finishing his degree in English literature at Patna University in 1978, the city and its environs were one of the least prosperous areas in India.[4]

Almost all of Prasad's classmates considered government jobs to be the best form of employment, both from a prestige and stability standpoint. Top graduates of elite schools aspired to work for the government, since a position there offered lifetime employment at a good salary. Prasad's own extended family held key positions in local government, making that path a logical choice for him.

But, the Indian bureaucracy in those days was legendary. Want to start a business? Simply getting a sales tax license, one of the many necessary government documents, took more than a year of chasing from office to office. It would likely require bribing functionaries from top to bottom as well.

When Prasad was accepted to study at the University of Georgia's Terry College of Business in 1980, he jumped at the chance. One of his early surprises was the difference in attitude about careers. None of his classmates were interested in government jobs, which they considered boring, low paying, and lacking in growth prospects. The American business students considered found careers in business to be vastly more appealing.

Prasad was even more surprised by an "entrepreneurship" class offered at Georgia. That, too, conflicted with his experience in India. While business jobs were not as desirable as government jobs, at least large, well-known companies offered some cachet and job security. Why would graduates of good universities want to start their own business instead of working for a large, well-established company?

He never did enroll in the entrepreneurship class, but Prasad's thinking about start-ups had changed by 1987. After finishing his MBA in 1982 and spending the next five years in the marketing department of Denny's Restaurants, Prasad identified a business opportunity that he knew could work.

## The Big Idea

A friend of his in Detroit had a vision care business that, among other products, sold eyeglasses with progressive lenses. These lenses are like bifocals or trifocals, but without the visible lines dividing the lenses. These progressive lenses are generally desirable for their wearers—nothing says you've hit middle age like obvious bifocals. But, these lenses pose a few challenges to eyeglass sellers. The lenses can't be inventoried since each one is unique to the customer's prescription, and special grinding techniques must be used to produce the unique curvature.

Prasad's friend was grinding the lenses in the United States, at the relatively high cost of $10 per pair. Prasad knew he could produce them at much lower cost in India. While other places in India might have better manufacturing infrastructure than Patna, Prasad was excited by the idea of bringing high-quality jobs to the relatively poor area. Beyond making a profit, he could help his hometown, in at least a small way.

The equipment to grind the lenses was available from a Dutch manufacturer and wasn't prohibitively expensive. Prasad calculated that he could produce the lenses for a mere $3 and split the profits with his friend. He devised a way to achieve quick delivery of the finished lenses to their American customers. This was before the days of universal e-mail, but Prasad saw that a US-based store could send the day's orders to the factory in India by fax or telex. Within 24 hours, the custom lenses would be ground, packed, and shipped by air to the United States. The turnaround time would be comparable to their current US-based grinding operation.

Eager to bring jobs to his struggling homeland by starting a business he knew would be profitable, Prasad immediately returned to India to set up manufacturing.

He knew he'd encounter bureaucratic challenges—this was India, after all. But the promise of good jobs for a depressed area and bringing hard currency to India made the project a potential win for everyone. Combining those benefits with his network of powerful family connections, Prasad was confident he could get his lens grinding business up and running reasonably quickly.

## An Unhappy Ending

Eighteen months later, Prasad still hadn't ground a single lens. His American partner couldn't wait forever, so he established a lens operation in Puerto Rico. The cost savings were similar to the planned operation in India, but Prasad had no stake in that venture. After spending a year and a half in Patna trying to get the business off the ground, Prasad had nothing to show for his effort. With his credit cards stretched to the breaking point, he returned to the United States to take a job working for someone else.

Why did what looked like a surefire winner of a project fail so miserably? Bureaucracy. Despite his familial connections, the new jobs, and the much-needed hard currency, government procedures and red tape proved to be an insurmountable obstacle.

The first blocker was zoning. India had no zoning laws covering the location Prasad wanted for his operation, which in many countries would make things easier. But in India, lack of specific zoning meant that Prasad had to get his use for the property approved by government officials with no guidance from an "industrial" or similar designation. In most places, if something isn't specifically prohibited, it's allowed. The perverse logic in India is that if something isn't specifically permitted, you can't do it. Prasad's zoning approval could be approved or denied at the whim of the bureaucrats.

The zoning process alone consumed nine months. At one point, officials told Prasad that the plant could be approved only in an area designated as an "export zone," which required another set of officials to give their stamp of approval.

When the location was finally approved, Prasad moved to import the specialized grinding machinery. Even though there was no local source for the equipment, the Indian government would collect an import tariff of 150 percent. The duty would more than double the price of the machinery, but Prasad and his partner were willing to pay it.

One might predict that with that much tariff income in the balance, Indian officials would be eager to authorize the importation of the equipment. This tariff payment would create yet another "winner" for the project. Yet, the officials who reviewed and approved import permits weren't moved by the various benefits offered by the project. They met just once a month to review a large stack of such requests, and never got to the bottom of the pile before retiring to their offices for another month.

Obviously, being at the top of the pile was a key advantage for anyone hoping to get approved. The order of the pile wasn't determined by anything as simple as how long the applicant had been waiting. Rather than using chronological order, lower-level bureaucrats arranged the applications as they wished. As was common then, those bureaucrats were willing to move applications to the top when applicants paid them to do so.

For whatever reason, Prasad's application never made it to the top. So, after nine long months, the machinery import approval still had not come through. Defeated by the bureaucracy, Prasad gave up and returned to work in the United States.

### The Biggest Loser

Prasad and his partner lost a considerable amount of money on a project that never produced a dime—or a rupee—of income. But India lost jobs in an area that needed them, not to mention hard currency payments for the exported products.

Perhaps India's greatest loss in this exercise was Prasad himself. He stayed in the United States and ended up being instrumental in the evolution of the GPS navigation systems we take for granted today. Later, he founded a successful transcription business with offices around the United States. If he had been able to get his business going in Patna, would Prasad have been an early driver of the development of the city as a center of commerce and manufacturing? We'll never know.[5]

**FRICTION TAKEAWAY**

> Sometimes, friction wins. If you are faced with an implacable bureaucracy that you can neither avoid nor co-opt in some way, cut your losses and move to a more hospitable climate. In a land controlled by bureaucrats, every corner you turn will reveal new obstacles. Your progress will be hindered as long as you remain in that environment.

## THE CURIOUS TALE OF CRABTREE'S CATS

*India is a land of irksome bureaucratic hurdles. They hit you soon after arrival and keep coming until the day you leave, which for me comes later this month. But, even after four years here, nothing prepared me for one final trial by paperwork: exporting a pair of cats.*

—James Crabtree, *Financial Times*, 2016[6]

James Crabtree is a journalist, author, and professor. Thirty years after Prasad's bureaucratic misadventures in India, Crabtree found that the nation's red tape culture was still alive and well.[7]

When he took an assignment in Mumbai, Crabtree decided to bring his two Maine Coon cats along. The Maine Coon seems like a less than optimal choice for Mumbai's stifling heat and humidity. The breed is one of the largest domestic cats and features distinctive long hair that looks better suited to, say, Maine in the winter.

Bringing the cats to India was surprisingly uneventful. They had pet passports (that's a thing!), microchips, and up-to-date vaccinations. Sometimes countries hold incoming pets in quarantine for extended periods, but, despite India's reputation for red tape, Crabtree's felines entered the country with no delay.

## Cat Export Woes

It wasn't until Crabtree prepared to relocate to Singapore that India's bureaucracy manifested itself. Getting the cats *out* of the country proved to require much more in the way of documentation and approvals.

Crabtree described his interaction with one agency that was part of the export approval process. He took a day off work and drove the two cats and his "feline export agent" to the agency's office in a suburb located a two-hour drive away. Arriving at the agency, the two humans and two cats had to sit in the hot parking lot to await an inspector.

When the inspector finally arrived, he barely glanced at the cats before stamping the document. Crabtree notes that nobody could explain what the document was or why the stamp was needed. The cursory inspection could have proven little more than that the animals in question looked like cats, albeit with more hair than most.

Crabtree spoke with Manish Sabharwal, the chief executive of recruitment outsourcing group TeamLease, about his experience. Sabharwal says much of India's sclerotic bureaucracy can be traced back to the British Raj. The attitude, he explains, is that things that aren't expressly allowed by regulation are forbidden. The red tape culture has created a thriving category of entrepreneurial "fixers" who can navigate the paperwork and bureaucracy, and (maybe) grease the palms of officials who might otherwise slow-walk or ignore even properly completed paperwork.

Crabtree wisely hired one of these fixers to facilitate the cat export process. Did some of the fee he paid end up in the hands of government officials? He doesn't know. But, after a convoluted multimonth process, the cats were declared ready to leave for their Singapore adventure.

In his article, Crabtree points out that some people think cats are "stubborn, capricious and indifferent to the concerns of those around them." Hence, he observes, cats have a lot in common with the Indian bureaucracy![8]

## Fixing Friction

*Bureaucracy is simultaneously the most crippling of Indian diseases and the highest of Indian art-forms.*
—Shashi Tharoor, Author, politician, and diplomat

While fixers, expediters, and similar roles can be friction-reducers, they rarely contribute to solving the friction problem. They make their living by dealing with friction so their clients don't have to. And, if they must make payments to speed up government processes, the officials involved likewise have no reason to make things easier. Indeed, the more onerous and time-consuming the process is, the more they can charge for shortcuts.

Even outside India, moving pets across national borders can be difficult. In Austin, entrepreneur Kevin O'Brien has built a thriving global business, PetRelocation, that helps businesses and individuals with the often-complex logistics and paperwork. Moving a family to a new country can be stressful, and O'Brien's firm takes much of the friction out of bringing a pet along.

### FRICTION TAKEAWAY

When you are confronted with a sea of red tape, sometimes the only way you can reduce friction is by getting help from a person or company who knows the system and the people who run it. Be aware, though, that while doing that may solve your individual friction problem, you are not improving the system. You may even be making it worse.

## CHINA AND INDIA

When friction is institutionalized within a nation, the effects can be devastating and long-lasting.

Perhaps the greatest economic story of the last few decades is the rise of China as an economic superpower. China's economy grew at an average annual rate of 9.4 percent between 1978 and 2012, a remarkable accomplishment considering the nation's earlier political turmoil and restrictions on foreign investment.[9] Even more amazing, perhaps, is that just a few years before, China had suffered a purge of intellectuals during the Cultural Revolution and a damaging industrial policy in the Great Leap Forward. Most industries were state-owned and China was only beginning to shift away from the failed Soviet model of centralized planning.

Entering the 1980s, India seemed to have all the advantages. The country had well-established legal and education systems. As a former British colony, English, the language of international business, was spoken by most professionals.

But, the very legal and administrative systems that gave India the appearance of a well-organized society were among its biggest obstacles. India was a difficult place to do business, both for its own people and for foreign companies.

Figure 10.1 tells the tale of comparative GDP growth.

Figure 10.1 **India vs. China Gross Domestic Product**
**(USD—Billions)**

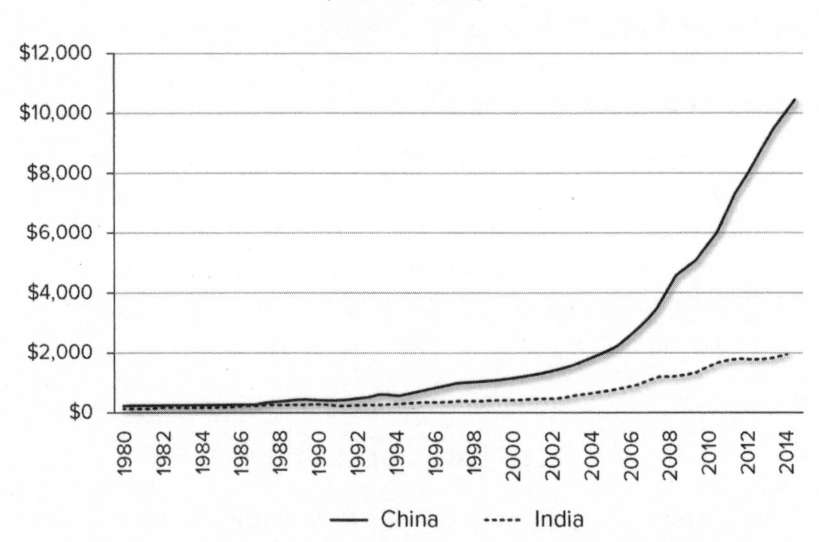


The World Bank produces an annual report on the ease of doing business in different countries. Their data only goes back to 2004, unfortunately. Both countries had seen economic growth by then, but the World

Bank Data shows how China remained an easier place to do business.[10] (See Table 10.1.)

Table 10.1 **India vs. China, Average Time for Business Processes**

| | China | India |
|---|---|---|
| Days to start a business | 46 | 88 |
| Flexibility of hiring Index | 17 | 33 |
| Days to enforce a contract | 180 | 365 |
| Years to close a business | 2.6 | 11.3 |

*Source:* Doing Business 2004, World Bank

Starting a new business in China took just about half as long as in India, as did enforcing a contract. Hiring was easier in China (higher numbers on the flexibility of hiring index mean more regulations). And, closing a business took more than 11 years in India compared to 2.6 years in China.

The 11-year process to go through the official bankruptcy process in India creates an incentive for the owners of a failing business to simply walk away, leaving behind unpaid employees, creditors, and taxes owed. A more efficient process might first explore saving the company in some form, and, if that isn't likely to work, then distributing the assets in an orderly and legally determined way.

## Middle-Class Differences

A robust entrepreneurial environment tends to diversify wealth distribution and add to the middle class. The different paths of India and China stand in stark contrast. Half of India's billion citizens live in poverty equivalent to the most impoverished African countries, and another 40 percent are on a par with India's poor neighbors, Bangladesh and Pakistan. Just 10 percent have annual earnings equivalent to those in central Europe.[11]

In the period between 1980 and 2014, well-off Indians became 10 times richer. Midrange earners didn't even double their income in the same period. An article in *The Economist* says one big reason for India's failure to follow China as a manufacturing center is that most people are employed in the informal economy and notes that "turning small businesses into productive large ones is made nigh-on impossible by bureaucracy."[12]

In 2008, the World Bank began ranking countries for ease of doing business. That data shows China initially ranked 86 in the world. (The World Bank ranks about 185 economies.) By 2016, they had improved to 78.[13] While those are not stunning numbers, India in those same years moved only from an abysmal 132 to 130.[14]

There was one bright spot in the most recent data—after spending nine years at 130 and higher, India's ranking in 2017 improved to 100. While that doesn't vault India into the "easy" category by any stretch of the imagination, it represents a remarkable improvement in one year. The report cites regulatory reforms in India as a primary driver of the improved ranking.[15]

*The more laws and restrictions there are, the poorer people become. . . .*
*The more rules and regulations, the more thieves and robbers.*

—Lao Tzu, Chinese philosopher

## FRICTION TAKEAWAY

There are many reasons for India's slower pace of economic growth compared to China, but bureaucratic stifling of business activity is one. China itself isn't the easiest place to do business, particularly for foreign companies. But the Chinese government has been less of an obstacle for domestic businesses and has shown it is able to move infrastructure projects forward far more rapidly than most nations, including the United States. The comparative growth rates of China and India, plus the building of a far larger middle-class population in China, demonstrate the importance of minimizing business friction as an important national priority.

# CHAPTER 11

# Bureaucrats and Red Tape Warriors

*The worst attributes of bureaucracy should much more often be treated like the cancers they so much resemble.*

—Charlie Munger, Investor and business philosopher

It may seem like the battle against red tape is hopeless. Just as entropy increases in our universe, it seems that rules, procedures, and wasteful practices inevitably get worse with time. But, human intervention can add order to a disordered universe. And, we'll see, that efforts by individuals, organizations, and sometimes even the bureaucrats themselves can take action to reduce friction.

## YINCHUAN, CHINA

City Hall in Yinchuan, China, is a modern building that bustles with activity. It's the hub for most of the city's social services and official activities, so it attracts an eclectic mix of citizens throughout the day. Few of the thousands of people who cross the expansive lobby in Yinchuan's City Hall pause to stop at a small glass display case that holds dozens of cylindrical objects. Those who do pause might be hard-pressed to say what the objects were without reading the case's label. But, these odd-looking cylinders are emblematic of the city's friction reduction crusade.

## Smart City

Yinchuan's population of three million would make it a large city in most countries, but the most recent data ranked it as the eighty-first most populous city in China. Located at the edge of the Gobi Desert and far from China's best-known attractions, the city doesn't attract many Western tourists. Yinchuan's main claim to fame is as a "smart city"—it has built an extensive digital infrastructure for traffic control, environmental monitoring, security, data sharing, and much more. In 2016, a CNN article suggested that Yinchuan might be the "smartest city on earth."[1]

Located in an area far less industrialized than others, Yinchuan has been targeted for development. The city is attracting nearly 50,000 new residents a year. China's aggressive approach to building infrastructure in advance of the need for it ensures that there will be housing and official services available for these new residents. But, one critical need that is harder to address is employment. These new residents need jobs.[2]

Yinchuan's city leaders knew they couldn't simply dial up tens of thousands of jobs annually. In conjunction with their smart city planning, they focused on making life easier for both citizens and businesses. They wanted to create an environment that would attract businesses seeking to expand or relocate. With a somewhat remote location and few natural advantages, Yinchuan would distinguish itself by being a better place to both do business and live.

## One Stamp to Rule Them All

Yinchuan vice mayor Guo Baichun explains that as they planned for the city's growth, they identified many convoluted processes that citizens had to endure if they wanted, say, to obtain a travel visa or open a restaurant. They would have to carry documents from one government office to another, each time collecting a stamp of approval. Often, these offices were in different parts of the city. Twenty-six different departments had approval responsibilities, and as many as four layers of management hierarchy might be involved in approving some documents. It could take days, weeks, and sometimes even months, to collect all the required stamps.

This high-friction approval process was hardly going to facilitate the start-up and expansion of new businesses to employ and service the new residents flooding into the city every day. As the newcomers filled the prebuilt housing complexes, they would need restaurants, shops, and more to make their neighborhoods livable.

The first simplification step was to centralize all the city services, as well as the departments responsible for document processing, in the new City Hall building. A citizen would be able to go to the same location for assistance with health insurance, travel visas, business permits, and any other need. The days of navigating to multiple offices around the city were over.

The more radical step, Guo explains, was the "One Stamp Rule." Documents that in the past needed three, five, or even more stamps would be approved by one office, with just one stamp. Processes that had taken weeks could be handled far more quickly, rarely taking more than a day or two.

Undoubtedly, these changes weren't appreciated by the bureaucrats previously in charge of departmental fiefdoms. No longer would they be the gatekeeper that every applicant had to placate. But from the standpoint of Guo and other city leaders, the benefits were enormous. Guo says the number of employees needed to process approval paperwork went from 600 to just 60—a 90 percent reduction in headcount.

Yinchuan is a textbook example of how eliminating pointless paperwork, collapsing layers of approvals, and streamlining processes can save money and, at the same time, unleash creativity and increase desirable outcomes.

## No Stamp?

The city of Yinchuan is still seeking ways to make it easier to start businesses and accomplish other tasks that require government registration or approval. One approach being considering is a sort of automatic approval that lets someone start a business first and then file the paperwork later. Since approval is a routine matter, why make the entrepreneur wait for even one stamp?

It's too soon to tell whether Yinchuan will become the business magnet it wants to be. But, Guo explains, they are getting increased interest from businesses in other cities and have scored a few wins. He expects the pace to pick up as word spreads about Yinchuan's business-friendly climate and overall quality of life.

And, what are those mysterious objects in the unobtrusive display case at City Hall? They are dozens of approval stamps that will never be used again by Yinchuan's more efficient administration.

### FRICTION TAKEAWAY

> Friction created by government regulations and procedures can seem impervious to change. But, as Yinchuan shows, motivated leaders can transform a red tape culture into one that is far more responsive to citizens and businesses. Not only does eliminating bureaucratic friction stimulate economic growth and create a happier population, it can even reduce government expenses.

## HOMEGROWN FRICTION

The United States may consider itself a model for demonstrating the rule of law, but our rules and laws can be as nonsensical as those of any other country.

In Indiana, for example, a liquor store can sell alcoholic beverages but is mysteriously prohibited from selling chilled soft drinks or water. Warm soft drinks are fine. Why is this? My only guess is that well-meaning legislators anticipated that some liquor buyers would start their party in the store's parking lot. That doesn't sound like that much fun, but, if you plan to do that in Indiana, bring your own ice.[3]

While this rule is hardly a game-changer for either the stores or their patrons, it's emblematic of how needless friction is regulated into existence. Liquor stores would sell more soft drinks if chilling them was an option. Last-minute party shoppers might even pay a premium to avoid stopping at another store to buy their chilled mixers. And, from the consumers' viewpoint, it's hard to argue that they are better served when offered only warm beverages.

Parenthetically, I'd note that Indiana supermarkets that are licensed to sell liquor do indeed sell their normal range of chilled beverages. So, it seems, a law-abiding liquor store owner is at a competitive disadvantage for no good reason.

West Virginia, one of the many US states where hunting is popular, apparently wants to give their game a sporting chance. So, using ferrets to hunt is illegal.[4]

Of course, after I learned about this law I had to find out why someone would even consider hunting with ferrets. It turns out that in some places, notably the United Kingdom, ferrets are sometimes used to flush rabbits out of their holes. Ferret goes in, startled rabbit comes out, hunter catches rabbit. It seems like a practical solution that is unlikely to have a big impact on the rabbit population. After all, rabbits reproduce like, well, rabbits.

Nevertheless, you should keep your ferret on a leash and away from rabbit holes if you are in West Virginia lest you face the consequences of violating the ferret hunting rule.

No doubt when the law was passed it was written to prevent a perceived problem. Did a particularly nasty ferret terrorize too many rabbits? Are rabbits simply cuter? After all, rabbits have the Easter Bunny, Peter Cottontail, and other positive role models.

Even when they aren't enforced or have no practical impact on daily life, regulations like these make up the haystack that one must sift through to find the important and relevant needles.

## Friction Without End

It would be fun to stay focused on crazy examples of laws that make no sense, but these rules aren't the problem. Rather, they illustrate the real problem—the almost incomprehensible volume of laws, rules, and regulations that individuals and businesses are expected to follow.

The US Congress has enacted about 200 laws a year since 2000.[5] These laws, often highly complex and lengthy documents themselves, are usually then turned into even more detailed and specific regulations by the relevant government agencies.

In 1925, US laws fit into a single, albeit far from skinny, book. Today, it seems, nobody really knows how many laws there are nor how much space they take up. The tax code alone has been said to run 70,000 pages, although a more reasonable estimate is 2,600 pages.[6]

Even when one can quantify the number of laws, one also must consider what's known as "case law." In the United States and some other countries, laws that are on the books are interpreted by courts. Particularly when the wording of the law is ambiguous or could have multiple interpretations, the way a court rules becomes the correct interpretation. Of course, different courts may rule on the same issue in different ways, there are various levels of court authority, and so on. The text of the law or regulation may not be the whole story.

## FRICTION TAKEAWAY

The sheer volume of laws and regulations that exist in an environment can dramatically increase friction in the form of effort and expense devoted to compliance. This complexity can also lead to unintentional noncompliance, resulting in still more effort and expense to rectify the problem. The onus is on regulators to make their rules as simple and easy to understand as possible, eliminate obsolete or unnecessary requirements, and streamline processes.

## NEW YORK, NEW YORK

Businesses in New York City don't love the bureaucrats they have to deal with. In a recent survey, business owners were asked to rate various city agencies on a scale of 1 to 5, where 1 represented "very unsatisfied" and 5 was "very satisfied." Most agencies were scored at 2. These findings were part of the work of the city's "Red Tape Commission."[7]

Ironically, perhaps, the commission itself was an exercise in complexity. Its 31 members included lawyers, politicians, business advocacy groups, and even a representative from the Caribbean American Chamber of Commerce and Industry.

The commission released a 61-page report detailing their findings. One example described the process that a business must go through to open a sidewalk cafe, that is, place tables immediately outside its business where patrons can sit and be served.

Although permits are issued by the city's Department of Consumer Affairs (DCA), each sidewalk café permit must be reviewed by a "local community board." Every local community board has its own website and its own unique application, making it difficult for businesses to identify the correct form.

Sidewalk cafe applicants must send a letter notifying nearby building owners of the application, and also are required to provide DCA with both the certified or registered mail receipts and a notarized affidavit stating that the notification letter was sent.

One business owner reported that the process takes four to six months and costs thousands of dollars in architect fees to properly complete the forms. The commission suggested that the DCA standardize the local community board application form and eliminate the redundant requirement for both mail receipts and a notarized affidavit.

The lengthy report details similar red tape issues affecting many types of businesses wanting to operate in New York City. Unfortunately, the most this commission could do was identify a few of the issues and suggest solutions. The commission had no authority to change procedures, eliminate approvals, or otherwise cut red tape.[8]

**FRICTION TAKEAWAY**

> Identifying conflicting requirements, redundancies, and unnecessarily slow processes is a good and necessary start to reducing government-caused friction. But, big committees with no authority won't finish the job. Unless leaders and decision-makers are themselves strongly committed to cutting red tape, progress will be slow.

## AN INCONVENIENT BODY

*Every revolution evaporates and leaves behind*
*only the slime of a new bureaucracy.*
—Franz Kafka

I really like Holland and its people. But, they seem to provide no end of amusing examples of government red tape . . .

If you are a Dutch citizen, be careful where you die. A couple from Holland went on vacation to the Dominican Republic. Unfortunately, the husband unexpectedly died there. His wife, Ilse, flew back to Holland in a daze. The body was shipped back on another plane. Ilse chose a funeral home to collect her husband's remains and bury them. This is where things got complicated.

The funeral home couldn't bury the body without a death certificate from the Dutch Department of Civil Affairs. So, the morticians contacted officials in the Dominican Republic, who then faxed copies of their death certificate and autopsy report. They even included a statement from the Dominican mortuary that confirmed the gentleman was indeed deceased.

Ilse's son-in-law submitted the Dominican paperwork to get the necessary Dutch death certificate issued. First, the agency demanded that the documents be translated from Spanish to Dutch. After the family paid for the translations, the agency still refused to issue a certificate because a third agency had not certified the documents as correct.

Weeks were passing while Ilse's husband remained in cold storage. Finally, one civil servant had an idea—issue a temporary cremation permit. It's unclear what would happen when the time was up. Cremation tends to be an irreversible process. And, if there was any doubt as to whether Ilse's husband was actually dead, cremation would put the nail in that particular coffin.

This solved Ilse's problem, but did nothing to fix the dysfunctional procedures that caused her and her family so much difficulty in their time of grief.

Four months later, a Dutch death certificate was issued.

Ilse's tale is just one of many where an unlikely group called the Kafka Brigade helped a citizen take on an uncaring bureaucracy.[9]

## Arre Zuurmond

Arre Zuurmond had an unlikely start as a foe of bureaucracy.[10] He majored in public administration at the University of Amsterdam. Then, he earned a PhD from the Erasmus University of Rotterdam in the same field. The focus of his PhD thesis was the work of Max Weber, an influential and sometimes controversial social theorist. In the late 1800s, Weber advanced the idea that bureaucracies were the best way to run businesses.[11]

At a time when many firms were run as family ventures, Weber proposed an "impersonal" management system based on a hierarchical structure. His ideas, along with those of his contemporary, scientific management innovator Frederick Winslow Taylor, were highly influential as industry and businesses grew during the twentieth century. While the bureaucratic structures Weber advocated allowed business to achieve large scale and still maintain control, they also hindered the flow of information and reduced agility.

As he studied Weber's thinking, Zuurmond explored the concept that new forms of communication and data collection would strengthen the power of bureaucrats and make management controls more effective. Would technology enable the ultimate realization of Weber's impersonal, rational management theory?

By the time Zuurmond completed his thesis in 1994, he concluded the opposite. Zuurmond instead proposed that information and communication technology would break down bureaucratic hierarchies by enabling horizontal power structures. He called the new structure an "infocracy."

After completing his doctorate, Zuurmond stayed in academia as a researcher and theorist focused on public administration with an emphasis on technology. He cofounded a consulting business, Zenc, with a similar orientation.

## Holland vs. Belgium in the Red Tape Cup

In 2009, an argument about the quality of government and public policy in Holland provoked Zuurmond and fellow academic Jorrit de Jong to publish an embarrassing study. At that point, both were professors who wrote not only academic criticisms of the state of Dutch government but occasionally more public critiques in newspapers.

After one acrimonious disagreement with public officials (who thought that Holland's administrative procedures were just fine), Zuurmond and de Jong decided to stage a competition between Holland and Belgium. "Normally you wouldn't do that, it's like England versus Ireland," chuckles Zuurmond.[12]

Zuurmond and de Jong published a case study comparing the time to open a restaurant in the two countries. In Belgium, obtaining the necessary approvals took just three days. In Holland, it was an amazing two years. Their comparison garnered far more attention than a typical academic paper, but didn't lead to immediate reforms.

### FRICTION TAKEAWAY

Sometimes, to expose the negative effects of bureaucratic procedures it helps to get creative. By staging a "competition" between Holland and archrival Belgium, Zuurmond and de Jong created a sharp contrast and showed how Dutch processes could hinder business growth.

## The Kafka Brigade

As early as 2004, Zuurmond and de Jong decided that while publishing academic papers about government dysfunction was important, they were tired of nothing being done to solve real problems. On the spot, Zuurmond says, they decided to found the Kafka Brigade.[13]

Named for Franz Kafka, the author whose name has become a synonym for mindless bureaucracy and byzantine procedures, the group's driving purpose would be to help citizens caught up in government red tape. Since 2010, the group has both helped individual citizens and counseled government agencies.

The Kafka Brigade helped launch initiatives like home delivery of travel documents in Holland. By enabling passports and visas to be delivered directly to residences, the delivery program avoids citizens having to visit government offices during business hours, take time off work, deal with traffic, and so on.

The group also created the concept of "the Kafka Button." (The opposite of Staples's "Easy Button," one might say.) It's a digital reporting system that allows anyone within an organization to report rules and situations that are overly complex or demanding. It's not a functional button but rather "an internal procedure that can be activated where there is a complex procedure that cannot be managed at a lower level of bureaucracy."[14] The idea is to empower employees of all levels to bring unnecessary bureaucracy to the attention of those in the organization with the power to solve problems and make changes. The group encourages business and governmental organizations to place visible Kafka buttons in their offices as a constant reminder to simplify procedures and cut red tape.

## FRICTION TAKEAWAY

If you want to cut red tape and reduce waste in your organization, create your own version of a Kafka button. It could be a telephone hotline, an e-mail address, a form on a company's intranet, and more. The technology, if any, is less important than the message that *anyone* can report a rule or procedure that wastes time and effort. Also important is that the communication is reviewed by someone who has been trained to investigate these issues and propose (or impose) solutions. All reports should be reviewed and acted on in a timely manner—this can't be a suggestion box where ideas go to die.

## How Bureaucratic Are You?

The Brigade has also created a "Kafka Thermometer"—a system for assessing the level of bureaucracy in an organization. First, everyone in the organization completes a questionnaire. Members of the Kafka Brigade staff then analyze the responses and prepare a report on the level of bureaucracy in the organization. The data is graphed on a "radar chart" (these look a bit like a spider web) to illustrate which areas are the most problematic.

While hardly a global movement, the Kafka Brigade has continued its fight against red tape for nearly a decade. Zuurmond estimates that of 60 or so cases taken up by the Kafka Brigade, about 80 percent of the problems were solved at the individual level, and 60–70 percent resulted in structural fixes.[15]

Kafka Brigade chapters have formed in the United Kingdom and Mexico. Want to start a chapter in your region? Or perhaps train an internal Kafka team? Visit kafkabrigade.org for information and resources.

## The Fight Continues

Today, Zuurmond's Kafka Brigade cofounder, de Jong, is continuing to fight friction in government by other means. He's a lecturer at Harvard and heads the Bloomberg Harvard City Leadership Initiative, a joint program of Harvard Kennedy School and Harvard Business School with $32 million in funding from Bloomberg Philanthropies.[16]

In 2016, de Jong wrote *Dealing with Dysfunction: Innovative Problem Solving in the Public Sector*.[17] The book combines academic theories of bureaucracy with de Jong's hands-on experience at the Kafka Brigade. Among other things, de Jong's book explains why conventional approaches to bureaucratic reform are so often ineffective. The Bloomberg project and other initiatives enable de Jong to train city mayors and other leaders on how to deliver important services with less red tape.

Zuurmond is also no longer associated with the Kafka Brigade. But, he told me, he is in a position where he can directly impact the lives of his fellow citizens. He's now the ombudsman for the city of Amsterdam and six surrounding municipalities. In this position, although he has no direct authority over other departments, he can demand answers and action. Civil servants are required to respond promptly to his inquiries, and they must come to his office if requested in writing.[18]

His most potent tool is exposure. Zuurmond can take unresolved issues to the city council and discuss the problem in a public meeting. "That's what people really don't like," he says dryly. Usually, the bureaucrats find a way to solve problems before they reach the council floor.

In his ombudsman role, Zuurmond was finally able to solve the "body with no death certificate" problem in a more permanent way. Another incident involved a person who died on the border between two municipalities in the United Kingdom. Since it wasn't clear which jurisdiction the death occurred in, neither would issue a death certificate. The surviving partner was unable to get the deceased's parking permit (in Amsterdam, the government issues those, too) transferred without a Dutch death certificate.

Zuurmond intervened to resolve this case. Later, he worked with a few other municipalities and submitted a proposal to the Department of the Interior for a standard method of handling cases where there is a body but the foreign paperwork doesn't match local requirements. Today, citizens of any of Holland's 400 municipalities can venture abroad with the confidence of knowing that should they die while away, Dutch authorities will make their demise official with a death certificate.

Zuurmond has a budget he terms "agreeable," and has complete autonomy. "I'm in a position to more or less force organizations to improve their quality of service," he says—an enviable situation for any friction-fighter.

## FRICTION TAKEAWAY

Dealing with government agencies can be frustrating, but change is possible. The Kafka Brigade had no political power or leverage, but the pointing out of the absurdity of rules and processes has helped individuals and sometimes has achieved structural change. Sunshine, they say, is the best disinfectant. Zuurmond found that officials would scramble to fix problems to avoid appearing in a public city council meeting. Whether you have political leverage or not, challenge and expose bad procedures when you encounter them. You won't always succeed, but you'll at least draw attention to the problem.

## FRICTION AT A GLOBAL SCALE

For years, the World Bank has collected and published data showing that easing registration requirements for new businesses increases business activity. For example, Portugal implemented business reform, and business formations increased 17 percent. More importantly, job formation went up to an average of seven new jobs per 100,000 residents every month.[19] While that may not sound like many jobs, over a period of years those monthly numbers become a significant total.

The World Bank considers the ease of starting a business to be a key indicator of the health of a nation's economy. The more difficult it is to start a business, the easier it is for inefficient firms to stay in business. And, because of that difficulty, more businesses will stay in the informal sector where they pay no tax and may not follow employment and other laws.

Overall, the World Bank evaluates a host of factors to gauge how easy it is to do business in each country. Registration requirements, labor laws, credit availability, registering property, taxes, and other factors all go into their calculations. Aggregating their data, they have shown that countries that are easier to do business in have higher growth rates and lower unemployment.[20]

### 13 Panama Canals of Wasted Effort

Laws and regulations may constitute friction, but they aren't always bad. The World Bank constantly emphasizes that there is an optimal level of regulation. Laws protect property rights, they make contracts more enforceable, they help prevent fraud, and they have a variety of other benefits to businesses and individuals.

Unfortunately, laws and regulations can also add tremendous friction when they are poorly written, implemented, or enforced. World Bank researchers compared the time needed to comply with government regulations and procedures in nations globally. Comparing best practices to actual numbers in each nation, they calculated that businesses waste 4.3 million years of working days annually to comply with inefficient regulations and processes—*the equivalent of building 13 Panama Canals each year*![21]

We've seen the effect of too many regulations and bureaucrats in India, but doing business in a country with no central government, no laws, and no enforcement could be just as high in friction. Imagine if a business had to provide all its own security, could trust no other business not to cheat them, and so on. A great deal of time, money, and effort would have to be devoted to these areas that wouldn't be required in a well-organized society.

The best kind of laws and regulations are those sufficient to protect the population and discourage bad behavior while not creating onerous compliance requirements.

## FRICTION TAKEAWAY

If you can influence laws and regulations, strive for just enough government involvement to ensure fair play and to protect citizens and businesses. The World Bank's DoingBusiness.com website has extensive research and data on what works and what doesn't. If, like most of us, you aren't in a position to directly influence government, support those who are and have good ideas. If all else fails, you can control your own venue—choose a place to live and do business with lower government-induced friction. It's likely to be a higher-growth climate than the alternative.

# CHAPTER 12

# Taxes and Beyond

*Any tax is a discouragement and therefore a regulation so far as it goes.*
—Oliver Wendell Holmes, Jr., American jurist

While onerous regulations and bureaucratic procedures are easily identified as friction, other acts by governing bodies, like imposing taxes, can have similar effects on behavior.

## TAXES AS FRICTION

Taxes and fees are friction in the purest sense. While we think of them as a source of revenue for the governments that impose them, they are also behavior modification tools.

The most obvious examples of taxes deliberately intended to alter taxpayer behavior are "sin" taxes like those on tobacco. Today, tobacco is viewed as a dangerous product with negative effects on public health and medical expenditures.

While lawmakers could simply make tobacco products illegal, doing so would create both political headaches and enforcement issues. Legislators tried this with alcohol once in the United States, and Prohibition failed.

Another approach is education about the dangers of tobacco—a good idea, but not entirely effective. For those smokers who don't change their behavior after repeated messages about health risks, adding friction to the practice of smoking is the best option. Today, office workers can't light up at their desks. Instead, they must take a break and go to a designated smoking area. Sometimes, this is an unpleasant spot that's freezing in winter and stifling in summer. Similarly, smoking is banned in public buildings and many other indoor and outdoor spaces. The act of smoking takes more time and effort now than it used to, and even among smokers tobacco consumption has decreased.

Another way to add friction is to increase taxes. Fees and taxes are a perfect friction tool. Legislators can, in essence, dial up whatever level of friction they want. While political and revenue considerations may place some limits on their ability to levy ever-higher taxes, it's clear that at least some politicians understand that taxes modify behavior. Former New York mayor Michael Bloomberg famously said, "If it were totally up to me, I would raise the cigarette tax so high the revenues from it would go to zero."[1]

A widely cited study by the World Health Organization found that a price rise of 10 percent on cigarettes would reduce demand by about 4 percent in high-income countries and by about 8 percent in less affluent nations.[2]

In 2013, the Congressional Budget Office looked at the effect of a 50-cent tax increase on a pack of cigarettes, which would have been about a 10 percent increase in total cost. Based on both consumption trends and the effects of previous tax changes, they estimated as much as a 4.5 percent drop in youth smoking rates with a smaller effect on older smokers.[3]

Ever sticklers for detail, the CBO researchers noted that while the tax would generate revenue for the federal government and that there would be indirect savings from lower health care expenditures. Those savings, though, would be offset by higher levels of Social Security spending for longer-lived citizens.[4] Staying healthy in your golden years, it seems, may be as costly to the government as tobacco-driven health problems.

## Fill 'er Up!

The CBO also examined gasoline, another market that can be affected by excise taxes. The data is a bit noisy because of fluctuations in gas pricing unrelated to federal or other taxes. The behavior of drivers doesn't respond immediately to gas price changes, but over time the quantity of miles driven goes down when prices are higher. Vehicle purchasing behavior is also affected. When gas prices are historically high, more-efficient vehicles sell better and the demand for gas-guzzling trucks goes down.[5]

So, if a government wants to encourage greater fuel economy, raising the tax on gasoline will have that effect. Consumers will change a variety of behaviors to reduce gas consumption. Weirdly, according to the CBO report, the price sensitivity of gas among consumers is about the same as for smokers. The report estimates that in the long run, a 10 percent increase in gas prices results in a 4 percent drop in consumption.[6]

Perhaps fearing a backlash from voters enraged by artificially higher pump prices, US lawmakers have not employed this simple tool to conserve energy and reduce fossil fuel emissions. The federal excise tax on gas is a minimal $0.184 per gallon, a level unchanged for decades.[7]

Other countries have shown far less reluctance to add financial friction for their drivers. As of early 2019, the average gas tax for the Organization for Economic Co-operation and Development (OECD) nations is more than 10 times higher: $2.62 per gallon. Germany is at $3.29, France at $3.07, and the United Kingdom at $3.44. The total difference between these countries and the United States is even larger because they levy a value-added tax (a kind of super sales tax) as well.[8]

In April 2018, for example, UK consumers paid $6.57 per gallon of gas compared with $2.99 for US drivers.[9] Needless to say, drivers in the two countries exhibit different behaviors.

We won't try to disentangle other effects related to geography, suburbanization, and so on, but the average UK driver drives a mere 7,900 miles per year compared to an average of 13,476 miles for US drivers.[10,11] And, UK consumers buy far more efficient cars. In 2017, UK autos averaged 43 miles per gallon[12] compared to 25 in the United States.[13] It's reasonable to conclude that the British consumer burns just a fraction of the petrol used by their gas-guzzling American cousins in large part due to the tax-induced fuel price difference.

## Encouraging Desirable Behavior

The other way legislators employ tax policy as a tool to change behavior is to reduce taxes on activities they want to encourage. Charitable donations are good behavior, so they are deductible from one's income in the United States, reducing the taxes due. Similarly, US politicians have wanted to encourage home ownership. So, mortgage interest is usually deductible while rent and other kinds of interest are not.

When the government wants companies to spend more money on research and development, they offer tax credits. There are many such tweaks for individuals and businesses, all designed to selectively reduce friction and alter behavior.

Of course, unintended consequences often ensue. Taxpayers inflate the value of charitable donations to maximize their savings. People buy more expensive homes because the government is footing part of the bill. And companies comb through current expenditures to find items that might be reclassified as research and development (R&D).

While the efficiency of these tax incentives can be debated, their overall effect is to steer behavior in the desired direction.

## Unintended Behavior Change

While using tax friction as a behavior modification tool may represent enlightened and forward-thinking policy, more often taxation is primarily about revenue. Politicians routinely enact new taxes or raise existing ones blithely assuming that the behavior being taxed won't change.

Legislators who enact tobacco taxes and corporate R&D credits are always certain that behavior will be changed by their action. But, oddly, it's rare to hear a politician predict that people will work less or hide earnings if income taxes are raised.

In fact, taxes levied to raise revenue change behavior just as any other tax would.

## Follow the Money

Florida has five times more professional athletes than the average US state. In fact, "professional athlete" is the unique occupation that stands out for the Sunshine State when compared with the other 49.[14] While the warm climate may be one factor in the state's popularity with sports pros, it is likely the lack of a state income tax that drives many to claim the state as their residence. Another sunny state, California, is one of the highest tax states and is well *below* average in its athlete density. Athletes, who often compete only for part of the year, take advantage of their location flexibility to minimize taxes.

Another example of tax-driven behavior change is the border between Washington and Oregon. Washington has a sales tax that can run as high as 9.9 percent, while Oregon has none. So, those residents close enough to the border shop in Oregon to avoid the tax. Reportedly, Washington loses $80 million a year in revenue from this border-hopping.[15]

It's a good bet that most Washingtonians won't move to Oregon despite the cheaper shopping. Oregon has a substantial income tax while Washington has none. So, it's likely this tax arbitrage will continue in areas close to the border—live in Washington for no income tax, shop in Oregon for no sales tax.

The behavior of corporations, even at the highest levels, is affected by tax policy. Until the recent tax reform, corporate tax rates in the United States were higher than those in most other developed countries. As a result, large companies kept trillions of dollars in offshore accounts. If they repatriated that money, they would have had to pay taxes on it. One pre-reform compilation suggests that US companies had $3.1 trillion overseas and were avoiding hundreds of billions in taxes.[16]

Keeping this money offshore meant that it could not be used to build facilities, create products, hire people, or even reward shareholders in the United States. It remained offshore for years because it could not be repatriated without a major reduction in its value. Tax reform advocates feared that eventually the money would be put to use elsewhere in the world.

Any significant tax alters behavior over time. Either the taxed behavior will become less attractive or those involved will seek ways to avoid or evade the tax.

## COMPLIANCE FRICTION

*I love America, but I can't spend the whole year here.*
*I can't afford the taxes.*
—Mick Jagger

While the friction imposed by the monetary value of taxes is significant, that isn't always the only friction payload.

Some taxes are large in monetary impact but easy to comply with. The sales tax in my home state of Texas varies by city but is typically around 8 percent. The somewhat similar value added tax (VAT) in European countries is typically around 20 percent but can run as high as 27 percent. Both of these taxes are paid by consumers but collected by businesses. Calculation and compliance are simple and automated. The consumers who pay the tax don't have to keep records or file returns. The average sales tax collected for the 27 million residents of Texas is nearly $1,200 per capita, but remarkably little paperwork is involved.[17]

That kind of low-friction compliance is not the case for other kinds of taxes, particularly US personal and corporate income taxes.

As one measure of complexity, the US tax code and regulations broke the *10-million-word* barrier in 2015.[18]

This complexity comes at a high price. The National Taxpayers Union Foundation (NTUF) claims the US economy lost a total of $234 billion in value, including 6.1 billion hours of lost productivity, attempting to comply with the tax code.[19]

Individual taxpayers in the United States are so befuddled by the tax code that 94 percent either use tax preparation software or engage professional help.[20]

It's important to note these costs are merely for *complying* with the tax code, not the amount of the taxes themselves.

If the approach to taxation in the United States was magically simplified so that, say individual taxes were collected and tax returns generated automatically, the entire individual tax preparation industry would go away. Companies like H&R Block (the tax preparer) and Intuit (makers of TurboTax software) would experience hard times and have to reduce staff. Ultimately, I'm sure, these displaced people would find work that actually created value for the economy. The same applies to the legions of corporate tax experts, accountants, and attorneys. They serve a valuable purpose now by preventing legal problems and minimizing the taxes of the businesses that pay them, but their work isn't really adding value to the economy.

It's likely, too, that the complexity of the tax system reduces compliance and collections. Individuals and companies trying to minimize taxes can hire experts to find and exploit loopholes in the complex maze of rules. And, since these taxes are often paid later rather than being collected automatically like sales taxes, avoiding payment is an order of magnitude easier.

*The art of taxation consists in so plucking the goose as to obtain the largest possible amount of feathers with the smallest possible amount of hissing.*

—Jean-Baptiste Colbert, French Minister of Finance

### FRICTION TAKEAWAY

Taxes are an essential part of every economy. Governments need to provide essential services, and this is possible only because of tax revenue. But, friction must be a key consideration in developing tax policy. Tax decisions can ease or increase friction to steer the behavior of individuals and companies. Compliance friction can cost all parties—government and taxpayer alike—enormous amounts of time and money. To minimize unintended friction, rules should be simple and collection automatic whenever possible. The level of taxation should be high enough to meet the needs of the taxing entity but not so high as to discourage desirable behavior and promote avoidance.

## WHY SILICON VALLEY IS SILICON VALLEY

Laws, regulations, and taxes can have a big impact on the ease of doing business. But, when it comes to the comparative success of nations, states, or regions, they aren't the only differentiator. Sometimes, it's culture.

Boston should have been, or could have been, the epicenter of the technology revolution. In early era of semiconductors and computing, the Boston area had multiple world-renowned universities, including what was (and still is) one of the truly elite technology schools, Massachusetts Institute of Technology (MIT).

Beyond that, Boston's Route 128 was home to technology pioneers like Data General, Digital Equipment Corporation (DEC), and others.

The San Jose, California, area, meanwhile, was mostly agricultural. Stanford University wasn't on the same level as the Cambridge and Boston schools. The area did host a few tech companies, notably Hewlett-Packard and a transistor firm founded by William Shockley.

So what happened? Why did Silicon Valley see explosive growth while Boston lagged behind?

Friction happened in New England.

## Culturally Advantaged

Author and Berkeley Dean AnnaLee Saxenian researched the phenomenon and wrote a book about it, *Regional Advantage: Culture and Competition in Silicon Valley and Route 128.*[21] Her book was published in 1996, well before the Internet and mobile revolutions had built Silicon Valley into an even more dominant center of technology and venture capital.

According to Saxenian, cultural differences and ecosystems created a very different dynamic. In the greater Boston area, the successful computer businesses evolved in a traditional, bureaucratic way. They were focused on the company, and typically tried to vertically integrate as much as possible. Companies like DEC saw making their own chips, monitors, and hard drives as a key advantage. Nobel Prize–winning economist Ronald Coase would no doubt have endorsed their strategy.

Silicon Valley engineers and entrepreneurs, Saxenian says, created "a more flexible industrial system, one organized around the region and its professional and technical networks rather than around the individual firm."[22] A mix of "individual competition and social solidarity" emerged in the region.

The relationships in the early years of Silicon Valley were almost familial. Many in the industry knew one another from Stanford. Many others had worked at Fairchild and, like alumni of an elite school, thought of themselves as "Fairchilders." They ate lunch at the same places, and their families socialized together. These ties didn't reduce the vigorous, even brutal, competition between their businesses, but they did create a very different environment.

The compact geography of early Silicon Valley helped, too. A common joke was that one could change jobs without changing car pools. Since changing employers had minimal impact on family life—there was no need to sell the house or change the kids' schools—job-hopping was commonplace. While highly mobile employees aren't necessarily a good thing for a business, the job-hoppers did develop friends and connections across a range of firms. Everyone knew and socialized with people from other companies.

In contrast, the Boston firms had far less personal interaction. In those days, it was not uncommon for an engineer to spend his or her entire career at one firm. The idea of meeting an engineer from a competitor for lunch would have seemed strange, perhaps even treasonous. The East Coast technology firms were fiercely protective of their intellectual property.

They sought to do as much in-house as they could and were willing to enforce noncompete agreements in their employment contracts.

## Trust vs. Distrust

A concept that kept popping up as I was doing my research for this book is that distrust inevitably leads to more friction. If you don't trust somebody, you will create more detailed contracts to ensure there is no way for your counterpart to take advantage of you. You will implement rules, procedures, and checks and balances for the same reason. In some cases this is prudent, but often it wastes time and money.

Saxenian contrasts the rigid approach to legal and contractual issues by Boston firms with a far more relaxed approach in Silicon Valley. She quotes one report that says the style of law in that region was "informal, practical, result-oriented, flexible, and innovative, keyed to high-trust business relationships—that matches the business culture of Silicon Valley."[23]

In Palo Alto, an employee leaving a firm to start a new venture might have received support and funding. In Boston, that same departing employee might have been hit with a lawsuit, either to enforce a noncompete agreement or to defend intellectual property.

The way people viewed business failure differed as well. In the more traditional East, if you started a business and failed, you became a pariah. In Silicon Valley, being part of a failure was a rite of passage and, if anything, added to one's employability. This evolved into a "fail fast" philosophy that enabled unsuccessful ventures to quickly recycle their talent and any assets back into the overall pool. (Contrast that with India's legal system where dissolving a business takes more than 10 years!)

A higher trust environment changed the entire ecosystem in Silicon Valley. Firms were far more willing to go outside their own walls for both expertise and components. By not having to develop everything internally, they were able to move more quickly and benefitted from a broader range of ideas. This willingness to go outside the firm had a broader impact: an entire network of capable suppliers developed. The existence of outside expertise and support was particularly valuable to new start-ups—they required less funding and could get to market more quickly.

In contrast, Boston-area firms were more likely to view suppliers as potential weak points. Information about new products might leak out. In the worst case, a partner might end up being a competitor. So, they emphasized vertical integration. By designing and making as much of their finished product as possible, they retained control of the elements of production and kept their intellectual property to themselves.

While there's nothing inherently wrong with a vertically integrated business, historically they have proven to be less flexible and slower to adapt to changes. If you own a steel plant, are you likely to lead the switch to aluminum or plastic in your product if that's the way the market is headed?

As personal computers began to take over the market, DEC and its brethren followed the same model that had worked well in minicomputers. They designed and built the product and most of the components within the firm. With the slow rate of product evolution in the minicomputer space, this approach had enabled them to build large, secure businesses. But in the nascent PC market, it worked to their disadvantage. New products were being launched every few months. The Route 128 firms weren't part of the Silicon Valley ecosystem that was churning with new ideas, new technology, and better products.

## High Tech, High Friction

When DEC belatedly realized the importance of microcomputers, as they were commonly known, they moved quickly to design their own. Following the path that had worked in the past, they decided the way to win was to build a better mousetrap—actually, *mousetraps*. By 1982, they had introduced several models that had superior performance but were incompatible both with each other and with those of other manufacturers.[24]

There were issues beyond mere incompatibility, which was rife in the early days of PCs. To prevent piracy (remember, you can't trust anyone), DEC required software be uniquely keyed to the individual machine it would be installed on. In an era when software was mostly sold with the hardware or even customized by the hardware maker, that was common practice. But, in the fast-growing PC market, third-party software makers didn't want to deal with this complex distribution scheme and mostly ignored DEC.

For one of its new models, DEC built a better floppy disk drive. At the time, 5¼-inch drives were the standard solution for software distribution and data storage. DEC's floppy drive could store more data than the competition but encoded it differently. Hence, the DEC drives and disks were incompatible with everything else on the market. To make it worse,

DEC copyrighted its disk format and demanded licenses from anyone who wanted to use it. This made the disks hard to buy compared with standard media and required software makers to use nonstandard disks to distribute their product.[25]

Reliance on in-house development may have produced reasonable products, but the long development cycle and use of incompatible technology prevented DEC from getting any traction. It's worth noting that the focus seems to have been more on creating barriers to competition than offering customers a better experience. Certainly, customers were not clamoring for high-friction features like uniquely keyed software that could only run on DEC equipment and proprietary floppy disks that were more expensive and harder to buy.

Like the dinosaurs, the Route 128 minicomputer makers either died or survived only as small, unrecognizable versions of their former selves.

Saxenian's data shows the big picture story. Boston's Route 128 entered the 1960s with nearly two and a half times as many tech firms as Silicon Valley. By 1975, Silicon Valley had caught up. By 1992, they had earned a 60 percent advantage.[26] To look at it another way, in that period Route 128 multiplied its number of tech firms by more than nine times. That seems like enviable growth, but pales by comparison with Silicon Valley's multiple of 37. (See Figure 12.1.)

Figure 12.1 **High-Tech Firms in Silicon Valley vs. Boston's Route 128**

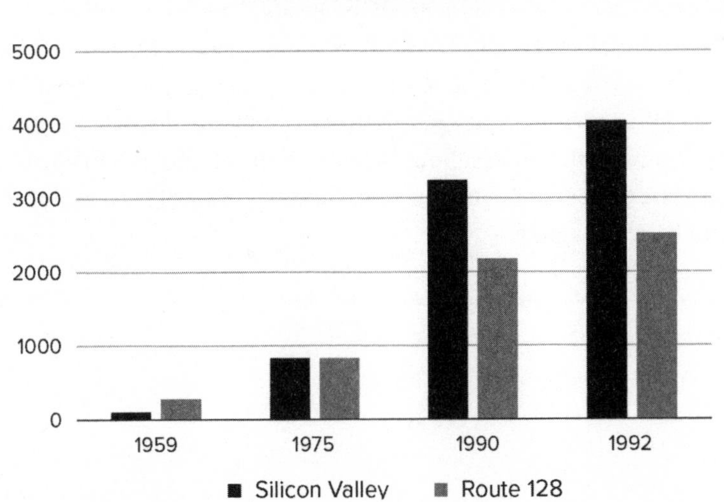

## The Internet Era

Saxenian's research focuses on the hardware years: first chips and then personal computers. In the early 1990s, the Internet hadn't had much impact. But the ecosystem of Silicon Valley proved ideally suited to the nascent Internet explosion. Plenty of venture capital, an environment friendly to start-ups, fluid employment expectations, and, of course, the newly ascendant Stanford University, set the area up for the next big boom.

Despite the setback of the dot-com bust in 2000, the Valley saw massive wealth creation and employment in high-tech companies. No location on the planet is as closely linked to the digital revolution. The only challenge to Silicon Valley's dominant role is its own success. The explosive growth of tech firms has led to a housing crisis, burdensome traffic, and an overall exorbitant cost of living.

Ironically, in a 2015 interview Saxenian admitted that in 1980 she predicted that Silicon Valley's growth had likely peaked. Transportation congestion, high housing costs, and rising salaries would force tech firms to expand into lower-cost areas.[27] She wasn't entirely wrong—Santa Clara–based Advanced Micro Devices set up a large operation in Austin in 1979. Other chipmakers like Motorola, Samsung, and even Silicon Valley stalwart Intel set up major operations in the comparatively low-cost, tech-friendly Texas city.

But, any loss of chip facilities in Silicon Valley was more than offset by explosive growth in other tech sectors. Apple just opened a new $5 billion headquarters campus in Cupertino. Google and Facebook continue to expand in Mountain View and Menlo Park, respectively. Entrepreneurs still flock to the area like would-be starlets making a beeline for Hollywood.

That Silicon Valley continues to thrive despite inadequate infrastructure and some of the highest housing costs in the country shows just how valuable the tech ecosystem and rich, fluid talent pool is to established firms and start-ups alike.

## FRICTION TAKEAWAY

While there are multiple lessons here, including prioritizing smooth customer experience over corporate advantage, the big one is that ecosystems built on trust can be giant killers. In Silicon Valley, smaller, more nimble firms trusted each other enough to work together freely, share ideas, and move technology forward quickly. Because companies treated departing employees as graduates rather than as traitors, a web of personal connections strengthened the trust. The Silicon Valley ecosystem trumped the monolithic market leaders on Boston's Route 128 that didn't trust outside suppliers, their customers, or even their own employees.

# CHAPTER 13

# Habits and Productivity

*Don't focus your motivation on doing Behavior X.*
*Instead, focus on making Behavior X easier to do.*
—BJ Fogg, Stanford University researcher

At this point, we all agree that adding or reducing friction can guide the behavior of others. More than one habit-formation expert recommends doing the same to change your own behavior in ways that will make you healthier and more productive.

## BJ FOGG

The first time I encountered BJ Fogg, we were both speaking at a digital marketing conference. He was onstage, wearing a magician's robe. Despite his unconventional keynote attire, Fogg conveyed a serious message. He described his Fogg Behavior Model, a simple but powerful framework that describes how human behavior works. His model applies to one-time behaviors, like placing an order on a website, and longer-term behaviors, like forming an exercise habit. Fogg's Behavior Model has been the basis for any number of high-growth programs and services.[1]

## Behavior Design

A researcher at Stanford University, Fogg leads the university's Behavior Design Lab. Some digital industry players have called him the "millionaire-maker," since more than a few of his students have gone on to become wealthy by applying his ideas. But, Fogg says, making money has never been the purpose of his research.

As a doctoral student in 1993, Fogg ran the first series of scientific experiments to learn about computers as persuasive technologies. Over time his experiments consistently showed that computers could indeed influence people's attitudes and behaviors. Fogg's natural inclination was to see the positive potential of technology to promote health, financial security, and even world peace. However, Fogg also thought deeply about the pitfalls—what could go wrong.[2]

In 1998 Microsoft released a computerized plush toy for kids, ActiMates Barney, that grabbed Fogg's attention. He thought that digital toys interacting with children as friends could be a dangerous path. Fogg's early efforts to shine a spotlight on this worrisome direction included an elite conference panel, academic publications, and even a dedicated conference at Stanford.[3,4] His warnings were mostly ignored by the growth-focused digital industry.

In 2006, Fogg presented testimony to the FTC about his concerns (and predictions) around the dangers of persuasive technology. In that testimony, he predicted that in the future technology companies would sell information about their users to influence political campaigns. He also warned about how video will be manipulated (we won't be able to "believe our eyes" in the future), and he explained some specific ways video games could do serious harm, especially to young people.[5]

His prescient advice to the FTC went unheeded. In fact, not a single person followed up with Fogg to learn more.[6]

## Theory Meets Real World

In 2007, when Facebook launched Platform (their solution for hosting apps), Fogg wanted to understand the potential and pitfalls of this new ecosystem. He created a new Stanford course that attracted more than 75 students. Fogg gave them assignments to create simple apps to test in Platform. He urged them to use metrics to evaluate impact and then to iterate quickly. In 10 weeks, the student apps collectively attracted *16 million users*.[7]

By the end of the course, unbeknownst to Fogg, some students were monetizing their digital creations. In fact, one app was generating $3,000 per day in revenue and turned into a company that later sold for a six-figure price. Another student dropped out of Stanford to focus on turning his app into a business; it later raised $6 million in venture capital.[8]

Fogg didn't design his Facebook app course to help students make money. Instead, he wanted to demonstrate the potential for social networks to influence behavior. As his students engaged millions of people with their creations, Fogg saw how this power could be harnessed for the most ambitious of dreams: world peace.

Ultimately, he created a Stanford course and then a dedicated Peace Innovation Lab. To some, achieving global peace through behavioral science might seem quixotic at best, but one must admire this novel approach to a seemingly intractable problem.

## THE DARK SIDE

Critics of behavior design find it potentially manipulative if used primarily to achieve commercial goals. Some worry that game and app developers create products that are too distracting and even so engaging as to be considered addictive.

The dilemma faced by game makers and other digital product designers isn't unlike that faced by fast-food companies, also accused of creating addictive products. One can argue these firms are creating what their customers want—tastier food, more exciting games. Should a game maker make the game more boring so that people play less? But what is their responsibility if many customers use it far too much for their own good? It's a question with no facile answer.

## THE FOGG BEHAVIOR MODEL

The Fogg Behavior Model is the core of what he taught his students who attracted millions of Facebook users in just a couple of months. The model says you need three things to get someone (or yourself) to do something: motivation, ability, and a prompt.[9]

**Motivation** is how much you want to do something or want the result of doing something. You may be motivated to alter your diet by a desire to look better and live longer. Unless you are independently wealthy, I could increase your motivation to stick to your diet by offering you, say, $10,000 to lose 10 pounds.

**Ability** is the level of difficulty, or, more precisely, the absence of difficulty. Walking five steps is easy. Running a marathon is hard. In the context of this book, ability is more or less a synonym for lack of friction.

If motivation and ability are present in the right combination, Fogg says, a **prompt** will cause the desired behavior. The prompt could be anything: an e-mail, an advertisement, a call to action in an app, or anything else that gets the individual's attention. For habits, the prompt can be an association with an existing behavior.

## Motivation vs. Ability

Motivation and ability have a distinct relationship. Easy behaviors can be prompted with modest motivation. Hard behaviors require high levels of motivation. You might walk 10 steps simply because I asked you to. If I wanted you to walk for a mile, I might have to increase your motivation with a reward of some kind, like buying you dinner. If I asked you to run a marathon, your lack of ability (unless you happen to be a distance runner) would make the behavior impossible, even if I used powerful incentives like a trip to Paris or large sum of money.

When he teaches his Behavior Model, Fogg emphasizes a key point: it is almost always easier (and less expensive) to increase ability than motivation.[10] In an e-commerce business, increasing customer motivation often requires the use of bonus products, limited-time offers, exclusive access, and other costly incentives. Increasing ability can be as simple as taking steps out of the checkout process, keeping forms short, remembering users' information, and doing other things to reduce effort.

### FRICTION TAKEAWAY

Fogg's years of behavior design research show that you can change behavior or cause an action by increasing motivation and/or reducing friction. In business and other contexts, it's usually easier and less expensive to start by reducing friction. A one-time process change costs less than ongoing discounts or incentives.

## TINY HABITS

One of the practical outcomes from Fogg's extensive study of behavior change is his "Tiny Habits" method.[11] Many believe that changing important behaviors is hard. Desirable activities, like exercising more, flossing daily, reading more books, and so on, require effort and can be difficult. The more effortful an activity, the harder it is to turn into a long-term habit. Health clubs are packed in January when people are excited about their New Year resolutions, but are far less busy in February when motivation has faded.

In the same way, after a visit to the dentist's office you may be highly motivated to floss your teeth daily. One dentist I visited posted grisly images of diseased gums in direct view of the patient's chair. It would be hard not to leave the office motivated to floss frequently!

But, after a few days, motivation wanes. First, you skip a day. Then, a couple of days. You eventually abandon the practice. At least, until just before your next appointment—that's when your motivation rises again, driven by fear of getting a stern lecture from your dentist!

Fogg's solution for this common experience is the Tiny Habits method. To use it, you take any behavior you want to do (flossing, exercising, eating more fruits and vegetables, etc.) and you reduce it to its simplest, quickest variation. This hack makes the behavior easy. Instead of vowing to floss your teeth daily, he suggests *flossing a single tooth*. Incorporating this trivially simple action into your bedtime routine can form a new habit quickly and easily.

In terms of the Fogg Behavior Model, here's what's happening. Flossing is low "ability" (or high-friction) behavior, meaning it takes time and effort, and, for most of us, isn't inherently pleasant. Our motivation to floss is high immediately after or just before a dental visit but is too low in between to overcome our preference for the far easier choice of doing nothing. Remember the Law of Least Effort. . . .

Although flossing one tooth seems pointless, Fogg's Tiny Habit method lays the groundwork for a habit. He's defining a high-ability, low-friction behavior that takes just a few seconds. This behavior requires less motivation because of its ease of execution. So, even as your motivation declines as your memory of your last dentist appointment fades, it will still be enough to get you to spend a few seconds flossing one tooth. Fogg is also tying the flossing action to an existing habit, brushing your teeth before bed—he calls the prompting behavior an "anchor."

Fogg has found that using this approach is an effective way to form a habit that lasts. People fall into the routine and maintain it without thinking. Over time, the habit can be expanded . . . say, flossing two teeth, which only takes a second or two more. The more established the habit becomes, the more it can be extended to the desired behavior—flossing all your teeth.

## Gimme Two!

Regular exercise is one of the most challenging habits to form. Thousands of studies show that exercise improves longevity, brain function, cardiovascular function, and just about every other human health metric. But many people find it difficult to build daily exercise, even walking, into their routine.

Walking can be a pleasant activity, but few people would say that about push-ups. A few fitness fanatics may revel in dropping to the ground and demonstrating their push-up prowess, but the rest of us are more likely to associate push-ups with a sadistic drill sergeant punishing a hapless boot camp recruit by screaming, "Get down and gimme 20!"

Fogg chose the push-up as the exercise of choice for a self-experiment in habit formation. Rather than vowing to spend, say, 20 or 30 minutes doing calisthenics every day, he decided to go tiny—just two push-ups. And, for the trigger, he chose an activity he knew he would engage in multiple times per day—using the bathroom. "After I pee in my home toilet, I will do two push-ups" was his initial commitment.[12] It wasn't a big commitment, and soon he found it easy to increase to three. Over a period of weeks, Fogg increased his commitment to 7 push-ups each time, and often did 10 or 12.[13] He increased the number of push-ups only when it became easy to do—pushing to barely squeeze out a few more difficult repetitions might work for a drill sergeant but would defeat the Tiny Habits concept.

Other behavior scripts for Tiny Habits include:

- "After I pour my morning coffee, I will open my journal."
- "After I sit down on the train, I will take three deep breaths."
- "After I put my head on the pillow, I will think of one good thing from my day."[14]

Fogg's point is that you maximize your chance of success when you reduce your desired habit to its simplest, easiest element and anchor it to something you are already doing. The easier the new habit, the more likely that you'll actually keep doing it. As the habit gets to be routine, it's easier to expand it without abandoning it.

### FRICTION TAKEAWAY

If you want to adopt a habit, particularly one that will require some effort, use Fogg's Tiny Habit method. Find a tiny version of the habit that is very easy and very fast to perform—meditating for three breaths, doing three sit-ups, and so on. Attach new tiny behaviors to something you already do on a routine basis. Only expand when the behavior is habitual and increasing the behavior will be nearly effortless.

## HABIT STACKING

While I was in the early stages of writing this book, I had a couple of habits I wanted to form. After seeing studies touting the positive effects of meditation, I decided to try meditating daily. So many successful people, from unicorn CEOs to Navy SEALs, talked about their meditation habit that it seemed worth a try. I also wanted to work on recovering my much-deteriorated Spanish. I was never highly fluent, but after decades of nonuse I had lost a lot of vocabulary and grammatical details.

So, I signed up for meditation app Headspace and language app Duolingo. Both were easy to start up, well-reviewed, and relatively pleasant to use. But, I found it difficult to execute this habit on a regular basis. I'd start the day with good intentions, get busy, respond to e-mails, prepare for a speech, write a blog post . . . and, before I knew it, the day was over. It simply had never occurred to me that I wasn't performing the two daily behaviors that I wanted to.

Setting a calendar item to remind me helped a little. If I hadn't done my meditation or Spanish practice by 9 a.m., my phone and laptop would remind me. If I was scanning e-mail or checking social media, I'd drop what I was doing and heed the reminder. But, as was more often the case, if I was in the middle of something, I'm mentally say, "As soon as I finish writing this section, I'll do it. . . ." You can guess how often I remembered to do it.

*The problem with making mental notes is that they are written in disappearing ink.*

I settled on a different approach, one derived from BJ Fogg, that some call "habit stacking." Habit stacking suggests combining multiple habits in a chain builds a stronger overall habit and is a great way to introduce a new habit on top of existing habits. As you can see, this approach comes from Fogg's Tiny Habits method.

I know that one thing I do every morning, without fail, is eat breakfast. The time might vary, but breakfast is my favorite meal. Whether I eat one of the breakfast tacos Austin is famous for or fix breakfast myself, there is zero chance that I'll get to midday and find I've forgotten to eat breakfast—it is my ingrained habit.

So, I decided to meditate for 20 minutes as soon as I finished breakfast and then do 25 minutes or so of Duolingo drills and listening to Spanish news. Neither of these was difficult—if anything, these activities were relaxing and fun.

Stacking these habits worked well, for a while. With breakfast as my anchor/prompt, the next two activities flowed naturally. For a period of weeks, I was a diligent meditator and language student. Then, life intervened. I had to finish my slide deck for an important keynote speech, and the organizers needed it the next day. Or, I had to respond to an urgent request for consulting. In the moment, these activities had a higher priority than my daily routine—you have to pay the bills if you want to engage in the luxury of meditation, right? As Fogg might say, these business activities had a higher motivation level.

Sometimes, I went for a week or two this way. I couldn't afford to devote the better part of an hour to habits that were desirable but, one could say, optional. Or so it seemed. Eventually, I gave up on that approach to building a habit.

What did I do wrong? In retrospect, committing that much time during my prime working period was destined to fail.

Habit stacking got me through the initial phase of habit formation but failed when the amount of time and effort conflicted with other priorities.

Had I asked Fogg, he no doubt would have suggested a smaller commitment—say, 5 or 10 minutes total instead of my original 45. The duration at the start would have to be small enough that it would be easy to do and difficult to blow off even when there were other pressing commitments. Once I had formed a true habit, I could increase the time when I wanted to do more. (But doing more should never be a requirement, Fogg says.) I made the mistake of going for my end-goal habit instead of starting tiny.

**FRICTION TAKEAWAY**

To adopt a new habit, combine it with existing ones. Make it as low friction as possible at the beginning so that it can be integrated into your routine without seeming onerous or conflicting with other priorities. Keep the behaviors locked together—as soon as you say, "I'll do it right after I return that phone call," you are on the road to abandoning the habit.

## SMART HABITS

Art Markman's encounter with popular culture stardom came when, as a guest on the *Dr. Phil* television show, he explained why people like kitten videos. Markman explained that our brains find all kinds of babies adorable. Real human babies intersperse moments of adorability with longer periods of demanding attention by crying, needing to be fed and changed, and otherwise being annoying. Kitten videos, Markman told Dr. Phil, are edited to be a continuous dose of adorability. Nothing annoying, just maximum cuteness—our brains love them.[15]

In reality, Markman doesn't spend all day watching kitten videos. (At least we assume not.) He is a professor of psychology and marketing at the University of Texas, Austin, campus and heads up both their Human Dimensions of Organizations (HDO) unit and IC$^2$ Institute. The HDO is a unique, interdisciplinary liberal arts program designed to teach and study how humans and organizations interact. The IC$^2$ Institute fosters innovation, technology, and entrepreneurship. Markman has written more than 125 scholarly articles and is the author of multiple books, including *Smart Thinking* and *Smart Change*.

In person, Markman is trim, bespectacled, and sports a shock of tousled, prematurely white hair. He's what Central Casting might deliver if you ask for a smart, credible academic. But Markman wasn't always slender. For years, he struggled with his weight. The bane of his existence, he explains, was the pint container of Ben & Jerry's ice cream.

If you like ice cream, you probably know that Ben & Jerry's is delicious, if not physically addictive. Flavors like Cherry Garcia, Chunky Monkey, and Chocolate Chip Cookie Dough draw ice cream lovers to the supermarket freezer case like a magnet draws iron filings. And, best of all, you don't have to commit to a huge container—the brand offers pint containers that let you take home an assortment of flavors without feeling like a glutton.

Markman explains that it was easy to grab a pint from the freezer and eat the ice cream directly from the container. I've been there, too—no sense getting a bowl out if you are going to have a few spoons of ice cream from your personal pint, right?

Halfway through the container, he might start feeling full. But, looking at the small amount left, it was easy to keep going. The amount remaining seemed too small to put back in the freezer, and besides, it was delicious.

Needless to say, consuming a pint of Ben & Jerry's every evening is not a great plan for weight loss. The company says the pint contains four servings—one-half cup each. If you eat just the recommended serving of Chocolate Chip Cookie Dough, you'll take in a modest 270 calories. But, I'm in Markman's corner on this issue—the idea that most people would limit themselves to a half cup is laughable. I can identify with his experience—you start eating out of the pint container and, before you know it, you have reached the point of no return. Yes, you *could* return the few remaining spoonfuls to the freezer, but it just seems . . . wrong. And, your brain is urging you to keep going.

By the time you finish the container, you've added a thousand calories to your daily total.

How did Markman break his pint habit? He jokes that he made a remarkable discovery: Trying to stop yourself from eating ice cream that's a few steps away in the freezer requires tremendous force of will if you really crave it. But, if satisfying that craving requires getting in the car and driving to the store, you are much less likely to act on it. "It's actually impossible to eat ice cream that isn't in your freezer."[16]

His simple strategy is to make an undesirable behavior hard to perform. He's adding friction.

The difficulty you add doesn't have to be as extreme as requiring a drive to another location. Markman says that a company that wants its employees to walk more could make using the elevator a little more difficult. They could slow the elevator's speed a little or make the pause before opening the door longer. Employees who only have to go up or down one or two floors might find it more convenient to take the stairs, while those who need to transit 20 floors wouldn't be overly inconvenienced.

## The Netflix Effect

Another point Markman makes is that the time to add that difficulty is when the undesirable action is in the future. So, deciding not to buy the ice cream in the supermarket is comparatively easy because you know you want to consume less and your decision won't affect you in that moment. Markman calls this the "Netflix effect."[17] When Netflix delivered movies in the form of physical DVDs, they found an interesting phenomenon. People would order movies they "should" watch, like well-reviewed documentaries, but took longer to return them. They consumed "want to" watch movies like romantic comedies and action thrillers much more quickly. They were making future decisions based on "should" but in-the-moment decisions based on "want."

One other piece of Markman advice: if you are trying to change the behavior of others, take advantage of laziness. Make it easy for people to take desired actions. To cut down on dog waste from owners walking their dogs, he notes, the City of Austin installed "dog hygiene stations" along common walking routes. The stations have receptacles, liners, and disposable plastic mitts that make it much easier and more convenient to dispose of their dog's waste. This didn't entirely eliminate the elimination problem, but the amount of visible waste was reduced.[18]

Similarly, Markman says, the Cleveland Clinic reduced staff smoking by making it more difficult.[19] The only permitted smoking locations were a long walk away. I employed a slightly different strategy at a company I co-owned in northern Indiana. We built a new building and, before moving in, decided it would be nonsmoking. (At the time, that was far from typical.) We didn't want smoke smells and cigarette butts near the entrance to our shiny new offices, so we built a bare concrete pad behind the warehouse with its own little door. (Some joker printed out a "Smoking Lounge" sign and taped it to the door. New employees were always surprised when they opened it and found themselves outside.) The walk wasn't all that far, but frequent subfreezing weather and occasional blistering heat ensured that only the most motivated smokers would indulge their craving.

## FRICTION TAKEAWAY

Adding difficulty reduces undesirable behaviors. So, if you eat too many potato chips and want to quit, the best time to act is when you are shopping. If you don't bring them home, to satisfy a craving later the only option will be a trip to the store. If the chips are already in the house, putting them on a hard-to-reach shelf won't prevent you from eating them but might help resist the temptation. Even making them harder to see can help.

## MR. DISCIPLINE

*Too often, we try to start habits in a high friction environment. . . . Instead, we should find ways to reduce the friction associated with our good habits and increase the friction associated with our bad ones.*
—James Clear, Author of *Atomic Habits*[20]

James Clear doesn't look like a person who has difficulty controlling his own behavior. His shaved head and muscular build suggest a serious guy. He can bench-press more than 300 pounds, squat more than 400, and deadlift more than 500. To put this another way, I'm not a small guy, but Clear could do squats with one of me on each shoulder and not break a sweat.

Clear's discipline in other areas is equally impressive. By adopting a regular blogging habit, he developed an enormous following—cracking 450,000 subscribers.[21] He's also the author of the excellent book *Atomic Habits.*[22]

How did Clear become an expert on habits and habit formation? He traces his interest to his high school days. On the last day of his sophomore year, he suffered a devastating injury that was nearly fatal. A classmate lost control of a bat while swinging and it struck Clear in the face with horrific force. Transported to the hospital by helicopter, he was unable to breathe on his own and was put into a medically induced coma. For days, the outcome was uncertain. Fortunately, Clear improved and was eventually released to begin a lengthy rehabilitation process.

He didn't make his high school baseball team the next year and played just a few innings his senior year. When he showed up at Denison University the following year, the baseball coach saw enough in Clear to offer him a place on their team. At that point, Clear decided that to take advantage of this opportunity he'd need to build habits that led to success.

These habits were simple things, like keeping a tidy room and getting to bed early every night. He adopted good study habits and got straight As his first year. By his second year, he was getting playing time. He began regular strength training sessions. In his third year, he was voted Team Captain and, at year-end, selected for the All-Conference team.

Clear's senior year achievements capped his comeback from his near-death experience six years earlier. He was named the Top Male Athlete at Denison and made the ESPN Academic All-America Team. He graduated holding eight school records and with the university's highest honor, the President's Medal.

## Small Wins

Adopting good habits allowed him to fulfill his potential as an athlete, says Clear. He suffered an injury that might have sidelined most athletes, but instead he persevered and ultimately succeeded. Today, Clear combines his own experience with behavioral science to teach others how to build desirable habits and break undesirable ones.

Clear, like other experts on habit change, recommends starting small. He recommends a "small win" strategy, noting that incremental improvements ultimately lead to major change. Clear's small wins approach resembles Fogg's in some ways. Both think that if you start off with a habit that's too ambitious and too much of a stretch from your current habits, you'll likely fail. Smaller steps that are easier to accomplish will eventually lead you to your goal.

Making the small steps part of your "identity" reinforces the behavior. For example, Fogg suggests flossing just one tooth to begin with. Clear would also make flossing part of your identity. Instead of thinking of yourself as someone who is bad at keeping up with flossing, think of yourself as someone who values dental hygiene and overall health. Use that tiny flossing habit to underscore that identity. If you internalize the belief, you will find it easier to floss more teeth over time and to maintain the habit in the long term.

Clear identifies Four Laws of Behavior Change. To create a habit, he says, one must:

**Cue—The 1st Law:** Make it obvious.

**Craving—The 2nd Law:** Make it attractive.

**Response—The 3rd Law:** Make it easy.

**Reward—The 4th Law:** Make it satisfying.

To reduce a behavior, he alters the list:

**Cue—The 1st Law:** Make it invisible.

**Craving—The 2nd Law:** Make it unattractive.

**Response—The 3rd Law:** Make it difficult.

**Reward—The 4th Law:** Make it unsatisfying.[23]

Clear's first law, arguably, is about visual friction—an easy-to-see cue is more likely to spark a behavior than one that is hard to see. His third law is all about adding and subtracting friction. Making it easier to perform a behavior makes it more likely that you will do it. Making it more difficult has the opposite effect.

## Play It Again

Making an action easy increases the likelihood of repetition. If you are doing just one push-up, you won't come up with a lot of reasons to skip it, like, "It will take too long," or, "I don't want to tire myself out, I've got important work to do."

Repetition is an essential ingredient for habit formation, Clear says. He cites Hebb's law: "Neurons that fire together, wire together."[24] That long-established principle says that when you perform an activity repeatedly, your brain undergoes changes that make it easier to do. The first time you got behind the wheel of the car, it no doubt seemed impossibly complex. Pedals, levers, traffic signs, and other vehicles made it a confusing experience that required your full attention. But, it soon got easier. Today, you can drive almost automatically, adjusting for the flow of traffic, traffic lights, pedestrians, and so on, while carrying on a conversation with a passenger.

Sometimes these changes in your brain are profound. A concert violinist must play the notes of a composition without conscious thought as to what the next note is or what finger positions it will require. Some call this "muscle memory," but scientists have observed physical brain changes from specialized behaviors. Concert violinists have larger brain structures for controlling their fingers and hands than the rest of us.

Most habits won't change our brain's observable physical characteristics, but they will change it in small ways that make it easier to perform the action the habit involves. That's why starting with a very easy action is important. It will get repeated over and over again, becoming automatic. Famed cellist Yo Yo Ma didn't pick up an instrument for the first time and try to play Shostakovich concertos. Like every other string player, he began with single notes, scales, and eventually the simplest of melodies.

Learning to play an instrument well is a high-friction experience because it requires lots of time, lots of effort. It's difficult, and, at the beginning, there are few rewards, including the fact that what's coming from the instrument doesn't sound much like music. The good news is that you don't need the dedication of Yo Yo Ma to develop your own habit. Starting with trivially simple actions that take minimal time and effort—flossing one tooth, doing one push-up—can make the behavior instinctive and automatic.

What you are striving for is "automaticity," and making the behavior easy to do will help you repeat it often. It's the number of repetitions, not the period of time over which you perform them, that builds automaticity.

## Prime the Environment

Like Fogg, Clear emphasizes that while motivation is important for behavior change, it's better to make things easier rather than trying to stay highly motivated. Motivation fluctuates. The easier something is to do, the less motivation it takes.

Clear recommends reducing even small elements of friction. If your gym isn't on the route of your daily commute, even by a few blocks, it will seem like you are going out of your way. The smaller a new habit makes you deviate from your existing habits, the more likely it is you'll make it permanent. So, go to a gym that is either on or close to your daily commute.

Reducing friction even worked in the Clear household. Have you ever had a friend experience a life event, like having a baby, and think, "I should send a card!" only to remember months later that you never bought the card, much less sent it? Clear had the same problem, but his wife didn't. She bought a variety of cards for different occasions and kept them at home. Whenever a friend has an event worth noting, she has a card ready and can send it immediately.

That's what Clear calls "priming the environment."[25] If you want to work out in the morning, lay out your exercise clothes, shoes, gym bag, and water bottle. (Others suggest that you should sleep in your workout clothes to reduce morning friction even more.) If you want to eat healthy food, set out any necessary pans, dishes, utensils, cooking spray, and so on, before you go to bed. If you want to practice guitar more, put the instrument and stand in the middle of the living room. The good habit, Clear says, should be the path of least resistance. (Remember the Law of Least Effort?)

## Add Friction to Bad Habits

Friction can be used to reduce bad habits, too. Adding difficulty makes it less likely that you'll give in to the impulse to engage in the undesirable activity. Want to watch less television? Clear suggests unplugging the television and taking the batteries out of the remote control when you finish watching something. Even though reversing those steps adds only a few seconds, that might be enough friction to stop you from idly turning on the TV when you are bored.

Want to add more friction? Unplug the television and carry it to the closet, Clear says. Then again, that's advice from a guy who can bench-press 300 pounds. (For me, the high-friction part of that process would be plugging umpteen cables back into the right connectors on the TV. The show I intended to watch would be over by the time I got it right.)

Even small increases in friction can help. Clear found that putting beer in the back of the refrigerator where he couldn't see it and it took a little effort to reach was enough to cut his suds intake. He also relates a story of how Fogg cut down his popcorn consumption—he moved the bag from a convenient cupboard to a high shelf in the garage. It would only take a minute to retrieve it, but Fogg was, to use his own term, "designing for laziness."[26]

### FRICTION TAKEAWAY

Your environment can change your behavior and help you develop or rid yourself of habits. Change your environment to make desirable habits and behaviors easy and to make bad ones more difficult.

# CHAPTER 14

# Friction Design

Almost everything we've discussed shows the negative effects of friction. But, since we know friction affects behavior, in some cases it can be used to steer people toward positive or desired outcomes. I call this "friction design" or "friction engineering" to distinguish it from the much more common process of reducing or eliminating friction.

*Betcha can't eat just one!*
—1963 slogan for Lay's Potato Chips

Eating too much snack food is a problem for many people. Some experts, like former FDA commissioner David Kessler, claim that the manufacturers optimize these foods for overconsumption and addiction.[1] A more benign interpretation is that the products are the result of both taste tests and delivering what consumers buy most of.

Lay's Potato Chips introduced their famous slogan, "Betcha can't eat just one," in the early 1960s, long before modern neuroscience and tools like fMRI. And, in 1993, they changed it to "Too good to eat just one."[2] Both demonstrate the simple fact that people consume and buy snacks that taste good (and reward the brain) at the moment of consumption, usually disregarding the long-term health aspects.

## YOU PROBABLY SUFFER FROM HEDONIC HYPERPHAGIA

Some of these foods taste so good, or so appeal to our brains, that we eat them even when we aren't hungry. I may be quite full after dinner, but put a dish of homemade chocolate chip cookies in front of me and I'll find them hard to resist. And, remember how difficult it is to stop eating a Ben & Jerry's pint halfway through? As with most things, there's an impressive scientific name for this: "hedonic hyperphagia."

But, there is good news for those of us who find it difficult to resist the lure of unhealthy snacks. Even the smallest changes can affect the quantity of those snacks that we consume. Simply moving them a little farther away reduces the propensity to indulge.

## CHOCOLATE? POTATO CHIPS? OVER THERE

It's no surprise that adding a lot of friction will reduce the consumption of unhealthy foods. A cafeteria experiment conducted by researcher Herb Meiselman moved chocolate candy and potato chips out of the main service line at different times. To purchase these items under the "effort" condition, the patrons would have to pick them up at a different station and pay separately. With this added friction, chocolate purchases dropped by 92 percent and chips by 87 percent. As appealing as these snacks can be, the diners stopped buying them almost completely when more effort was needed to obtain them.[3]

While this kind of strategy can be effective, in typical commercial settings it would be unlikely to work. Customers would complain, and no matter how laudable the goal, a change of this sort has a negative impact on customer experience. The same would be true of an even more effective measure: not stocking the items at all. Realistically, the challenge would be to reduce consumption in a way that doesn't cause customers or employees to rebel.

### Friction vs. Chocolate

Not all food interventions are as extreme as the cafeteria example. Cornell scientist Brian Wansink conducted an experiment with 40 female administrative staff members in their everyday office environment. Over a period of weeks, Wansink and his team varied the placement and visibility of a candy bowl filled with tempting chocolates for each subject. In the "near" condition, the bowls were placed on the subject's desk. The "far" condition had the bowls about six feet away, just far enough that the subject would have to stand up to get a candy. The bowls were always covered with lids, but some were clear ("visible") and others opaque ("less visible").

Figure 14.1 **Distance vs. Candies Eaten**

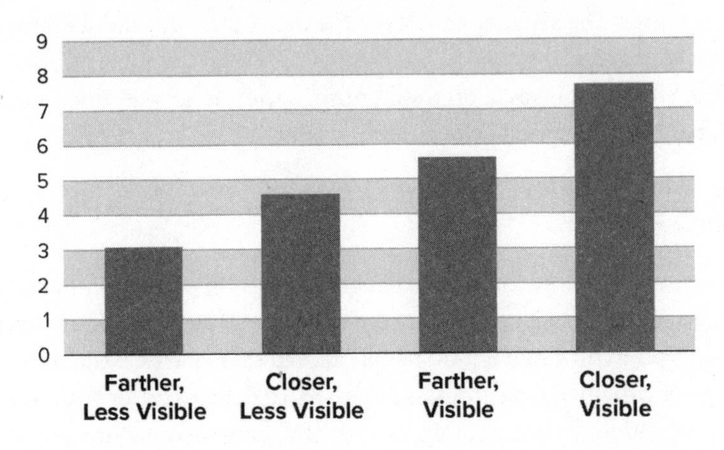


The results confirmed the effect of adding a little friction to accessing the candy bowl (see Figure 14.1). When the bowl was close at hand instead of a few feet away, the subjects ate almost 50 percent more candy from the opaque bowls and 37 percent more from the clear bowls. Contrasting "close and visible" with "farther and less visible," the number of candies eaten more than doubled.[4]

## A Mere 20 Inches

In the real world, if a candy bowl was placed just out of reach so that one had to stand up to get it, the logical response would be to move the bowl closer. Wansink's subjects didn't know their consumption was being measured, but they were instructed to leave the bowl where it was placed.

An experiment at the University of Cambridge tried a more modest intervention.

In a lab setting, subjects sat at a table that had some magazines and a large bowl of M&M chocolate candies. First, they completed a few tests on a laptop stationed next to the table. Then, they were given 10 minutes to "relax" and were invited to read the magazines and help themselves to the candy. Randomly, the bowl was positioned about 8 or 28 inches away from their arms—a difference of just 20 inches.

In different variations of the test, candy consumption increased by as much as 60 percent in the closer condition. The extra effort to reach just 20 inches farther made a big difference. And, before you ask, the answer is "yes," some clever (or hungry) subjects did grab the bowl and move it closer. The scientists analyzed the data both with and without the motivated movers.[5]

The effect of distance on food consumption is so well documented that it has its own name—"the proximity effect."

## Utensil Friction

Another study showed that small changes in position (as little as 10 inches) and the type of utensil provided could effect small but statistically significant changes in how much food people served themselves. Notably, when tongs were provided, consumption was 8 to 16 percent lower than when a spoon was offered.[6] Presumably, mechanical factors come into play—it's easier to shovel more of a small or granular item onto your plate with a spoon. Tongs are great for bigger items, but imagine trying to get more than one or two M&Ms at a time with them. It's so slow and difficult that most people would give up prematurely. Providing mismatched utensils can be annoying, but it's a minor nudge that won't be perceived as an obvious intervention.

## Nudging at Google

Google consistently ranks as one of the best places to work, and part of its appeal to employees is the constant availability of free food and drinks. Beyond being a means of attracting and retaining good employees, this practice is itself a friction strategy aimed at its employees. It makes food and beverages easy. Mike Harm, an engineer in the New York office, commented on the espresso machine in the kitchen: "What I love is that I don't have to ever think twice about the coffee beans in this machine being stocked. It's removing the obstacles of my day to just let me focus on what I want to do."[7] Less friction, more lines of code.

And, Harm has a real point. A small study in the United Kingdom found that employees spent less than three hours a day doing actual work. They cited checking social media, reading news websites, chatting about nonwork matters with coworkers, and . . . preparing hot beverages! Overall, the study found that the respondents spent *25 minutes per day* preparing and consuming snacks and beverages.[8] Almost certainly, time spent in the breakroom or kitchen leads to more lost time socializing. Google's free food and drinks cost the company money, but if providing them gets employees back to their desks quickly and avoids trips outside the office, the freebees likely pay for themselves in increased productivity.

Of course, there's a downside to this benefit—people sometimes make unhealthy choices. In most office environments, there are elements that discourage consuming large amounts of unhealthy food. For example, if you crave a candy bar, you'll have to go to a vending machine in the breakroom and buy one. Some offices may not even have easy access to such snacks. After you return to your desk and enjoy your snack, it's unlikely that you'll get up a few minutes later and feed more money into the vending machine. But, what if the candy was there on the counter, free for the taking? What if every time you got slightly bored or restless, you could walk a few steps and light up your brain with a dose of sugar and chocolate?

This was the problem faced by Google. The continuous availability of free food and drink for employees was a desirable benefit, but it also led to overconsumption of unhealthy foods. Google wasn't about to take away the benefit, though. Instead, Google partnered with a team from the Yale School of Management to use behavioral science to encourage healthy eating habits. The team observed employee behavior, measured consumption, and tested various interventions.

## A Pound of Fat in a Cup of Coffee?

One observation the Yale team made was that moving the snacks farther from the beverages reduced consumption. When the snack station was 6.5 feet away from the coffee and other drinks, employees were 50 percent more likely to get a snack than when they were 17.5 feet away. The researchers calculated that the difference in snack consumption for male employees would add up to *a pound of fat per year for every cup of coffee consumed each day.*[9] With many employees consuming multiple coffees or other beverages during the course of the day, adding the extra effort to retrieve snacks could deliver important health benefits.

Another intervention the Yale scientists tested was intended to reduce candy, specifically chocolate M&M, consumption. Based on some of the lab research we've already discussed, they designed the intervention to add a little friction. They placed the colorful M&Ms in an opaque container and put them behind healthier snacks like dried figs and pistachios that were displayed in clear glass jars. It worked—in the ensuing seven weeks, employees consumed 3.1 million fewer calories of M&Ms. That translates to about nine vending machine–size packages of M&Ms for every employee in the office.[10] Assuming that not all employees indulged in the candy equally, the consumption reduction (and calorie savings) was likely far higher for some individuals.

Reflecting on this and earlier experiments, I have to wonder what Mars, Inc., the maker of M&Ms, thinks about behavioral scientists around the world trying to find ways to reduce consumption their branded product. Perhaps they appreciate the fact that scientists think that M&Ms are among the more difficult snacks to resist.

### FRICTION TAKEAWAY

Increases in friction that are small or not even noticed by people can change their behaviors in significant ways. Making tasty chocolate candies a little harder to see and/or reach reduced consumption in every case. Whether you are trying to change your own behavior or that of a larger group, make undesirable behaviors a little harder to perform.

## DIGITAL FRICTION ENGINEERING

*Friction engineering ought to be taught in computer-science and design schools everywhere.*

—Clive Thompson, Journalist, WIRED

Digital designers are usually far more interested in reducing friction than increasing it. They want people to take actions like placing orders or requesting information, and reducing effort usually maximizes results. But occasionally adding some friction produces desirable outcomes.

Journalist Clive Thompson describes one such example. Nextdoor is an online community tool for neighborhoods. Users can discuss neighborhood events, seek help in finding lost pets, and so on. Nextdoor also has a crime reporting feature that lets neighbors report suspicious activity. While this was a useful feature, it seemed to encourage racist posts in which people reported minority neighbors simply because of their skin color.[11]

The solution employed by Nextdoor was to add in some friction to its crime reporting feature. The redesigned form asked users to describe details like clothing, age, and specific actions of the individuals they were reporting. This process required more user effort (and perhaps reflection). Thompson reports that the number of racist reports dropped dramatically.[12]

### FRICTION TAKEAWAY

> Nextdoor could have tried to reduce racist posts by asking its users to avoid such behavior. Or, they could have eliminated the crime reporting feature completely. Instead, they preserved the feature but reduced problem posts by adding friction. If your website or app users are doing too much of something, try a little friction engineering.

## THE BIG UGLY FORM

My friend Brian Massey bills himself as a conversion scientist and lab wear model. The latter comes from his unique approach to branding himself. When speaking at conferences, he's the guy who dons a white lab coat for his presentation. This makes him stand out because everyone remembers "the lab coat guy." It also conveys an image of scientific authenticity. Why else would so many commercials for health-related products use an actor in a lab coat? And, as Massey himself occasionally points out, research shows that a lab coat makes its wearer smarter, at least as measured by attention tests.[13] It's science!

Conversion optimization specialists like Massey use testing to improve business results on websites and mobile apps. Many websites, for example, convert a percentage of visitors into customers or leads. Increasing the conversion rate from, say, 5 to 8 percent might seem like a modest improvement but could make a huge difference in a company's profitability.

Typically conversion practitioners will analyze the current design and content and propose changes based on experience and best practices. Conversion specialists often employ psychological concepts like scientist Robert Cialdini's principles of influence and cognitive biases like loss aversion. These improvements are treated as hypotheses and tested using A/B and other testing. After multiple rounds of testing, dramatic improvements in conversion can be achieved if the original website or app was poorly optimized.

Friction is well known to conversion experts like Massey. Testing almost always shows that reducing friction increases the conversion rate. Reduce the number of form fields that a visitor must complete? More completed forms. Require fewer steps to place an order? More orders. Frictional elements are the low-hanging fruit for conversion optimizers.

Sometimes, though, adding friction can produce a surprising and positive result.

## Nudging Customers to Call

One client that hired Massey's firm used its website to generate sales leads. The original site design included both a web form and a toll-free phone number so that visitors could connect with the company in whichever way they found most convenient.

Over time, though, the firm found that leads that came in via telephone were far more valuable, generating 5 to 10 times more revenue per lead than the web form. The reason for this wasn't clear. Were the visitors who picked up the phone more motivated? Did they have a more immediate need? Or, more likely, is it that humans were better at closing sales than websites?

Whatever the reason, phone leads dramatically outperformed web form leads and the client wanted more of them.

The first thing Massey tested was eliminating the web form completely. Instead, the phone number was made very prominent and repeated at various points on the page. The hypothesis was that phone leads would increase since a portion of those visitors who would have completed the form would decide to call. The visitors who preferred calling to begin with would, presumably, be unaffected by the missing form. While some visitors might not inquire at all without the web form, the larger number of higher-performing phone leads should have more than offset this decline.

The results were surprising, even to a seasoned optimizer like Massey. The number of web form leads dropped to zero, of course, since the web form was gone. Shockingly, phone leads also dropped—by a stunning 56 percent!

This was clearly an undesirable result, so the next test added the web form back to the page. But, there was a twist this time—the new variation used what Massey calls a "big ugly form." This time, the form had lots of fields to complete. It was the kind of form that most people hate to fill out. A new headline told visitors, "If you really want to take action now, you'll call us. But if you want to, fill out this form."

As illogical as it seems, the version with the difficult form produced the *most* phone leads of any variation. Massey has since employed this with other clients who find telephone leads more valuable.[14]

## Friction Contrast

What's going on here? I think the reason for the surprising increase in phone leads is what I call "friction contrast." A phone call seems easy and simple but has potential drawbacks. Will there be an annoying and time-consuming automated menu system? Will there be a pushy salesperson? Will I have to offer up a lot of personal information? To a person interested in the company's products, filling out a short web form might seem quicker and easier. On the other hand, a long and complicated web form would tilt the balance in favor of a phone call.

But why did phone leads drop so much when there was no form? We can't be certain, but one possibility is that visitors felt they were being *forced* to call. Perhaps making the telephone number the only way to contact the firm made visitors anticipate a high-pressure sales pitch. Whatever the reason, taking away choice hurt results.

**FRICTION TAKEAWAY**

> If you want someone to do something, consider offering a much more difficult alternative. It will make the action you want seem easier.

## CONVERTING FREE USERS

The freemium model for digital products is well established. Give away a simple or limited version of your product for free to get lots of people to use it, and offer a paid version with more features, better performance that will convert free users to paid customers.

One tool I used in writing this book was Evernote, discussed in Chapter 4. This flexible way to store information of all types is easy to use and the free version is powerful enough for the vast majority of its users. I was one of those free users for years. Finally, I had saved so much stuff that I hit my storage limit. So, I happily signed up as a paying customer. It's very likely that I wouldn't have begun using Evernote initially had it demanded payment. But, the freemium approach worked as Evernote intended in my case, as it did for millions of other customers.

Unlike Evernote, some app creators place severe limits on the free product. The free product works just well enough to evaluate but isn't powerful enough for real use. This may make business sense where offering a fully functional free product might satisfy the needs of so many users that almost nobody would ever pay.

Sometimes, users might get the full product but with a hard cutoff. I wrote this book using a program called Scrivener, and that's the approach it uses. Any user can download the app and use it for 30 days, free of charge. It's fully functional, but at the 30-day point users have to purchase a license to keep using it.

## FRICTION AS MOTIVATION

A different strategy also employs friction as a motivator to pay. Another application I used while writing was a citation generator. a web page that, when you enter a web address or book title, creates a properly formatted citation for footnotes or endnotes. The one I used was Citation Machine (citationmachine.net). Their strategy is to give the free user access to most of the app's functionality but to show ads on the page.

Showing ads on free products isn't a bad thing. I've used the free version of Pandora, the music app, for years. The app airs an ad occasionally but not so often as to be an experience-killer. The ad load is tolerable, and I assume the ads pay at least some of Pandora's cost of delivering me music.

Citation Machine is far, far more aggressive with ads. When you load a new page or submit a form, the content jumps around like a bucking bronco as more and more ads load. Ads appear above the content, below the content, and on both sides. In free mode, the site is almost unusable because of the slow page loading and erratic content motion. It takes many seconds to load a page because of the ads.

I turned on an ad blocker, and it told me that the page tried to load 39 ads! I never use ad blocking—I don't mind and even appreciate relevant ads. Here, though that seemed to be the only way to fix the awful user experience. But, the site was one step ahead of me. It detected my ad blocker and forced me to either turn it off or pay to subscribe.

## Crazy Like a Fox

After seeing how bad the site's user experience was, my first thought was that Citation Machine had a really inexperienced developer. There are long-established, well-known ways to build a web page that keeps the content stable and the page usable while slower external content, like images and ads, load. Obviously, the coder didn't use those techniques.

After a bit of reflection, I decided that Citation Machine actually had a very *skilled* developer. The number of ads and the way the page was coded added massive friction for users who didn't subscribe. Those free users could see that the app produced good results, but would be frustrated by the slow process of loading each page. Any user planning on making regular use of the app, say, an academic frequently writing content with citations, would find paying the modest monthly fee to be well worth it. I decided that the odds that the site had arrived at such an awful interface for free users by accident were slim to none—rather, it was a friction design strategy.

And, the added friction worked in my case. I paid up.

### FRICTION TAKEAWAY

We all want to do the best job possible for our users. But, if you employ a freemium model and the free product is so good that nobody would need to upgrade to a paid version, adding friction is one way to help convert users from free to paid. It's annoying, but perhaps not as annoying as making the free product so feature-poor as to be worthless.

CHAPTER

# 15

# Nonprofit Friction

*Too often, nonprofits are viewed as rigid and bureaucratic—less nimble and capable of adapting in this fluid environment than our corporate counterparts. I don't agree.*

—Anna Maria Chavez, former Girl Scouts CEO

Perhaps it's not surprising that we'd find examples of friction in nonprofit institutions like colleges and universities. Nonprofits are more focused on their mission than performance metrics and organizational efficiency. But, the news isn't all bad—in some cases, institutions are recognizing the effects of friction and taking direct action to eliminate it.

## UNIVERSITY OF CHICAGO

For the past century, the University of Chicago has been one of the top educational institutions in the world. Researchers affiliated with the university have won more Nobel Prizes than all but a few other schools.[1] But, in the early years of this century, Chicago administrators identified a problem.

Despite its storied history and excellent reputation, the university was receiving far fewer undergraduate applications than its peer institutions like Harvard, Yale, Columbia, and Stanford. This was a disadvantage in several ways. First, a much smaller applicant pool meant that the school was probably missing out on highly desirable applicants. The students they accepted had superb scores and grades, but these weren't quite as high as the schools that had far larger applicant pools.

Second, and perhaps more significantly, the smaller applicant pool meant that Chicago had to offer acceptance to a much higher percentage of those applicants to fill its class each year. While those admitted were still excellent students, the numbers made the school appear to be much less selective than its peers. This, in turn, caused a lower ranking in the US News Best Colleges lists.

While most academics dismiss the US News rankings as arbitrary and irrelevant, there's little doubt that these rankings have an impact on both domestic and international applications. With more than 3,000 institutions of higher education in the United States, students and parents need ways to help choose a short list of schools to apply to. The US News rankings can be both a starting point for ideas on where to apply as well as a filter to select the most desirable schools. Hence, even school officials who are highly skeptical of the rankings may take steps to achieve a better number for their institution.

## The Uncommon App

Why did Chicago attract far fewer undergraduate applicants than comparable universities? The school's reputation as a haven for serious academics and hard work is no doubt one reason. The school has been described by students as "the level of hell Dante forgot" and "the place where fun comes to die."[2]

Perhaps the most important cause of low applicant volume was the application itself. Chicago had long prided itself on what it called the Uncommon App. The nickname was a play on words referencing the Common App, a straightforward universal application accepted by hundreds of colleges. The Common App made applying to each additional school as simple as checking a box.

*What would you do with a foot and a half tall jar of mustard?*

—University of Chicago Essay Prompt

The Chicago application, meanwhile, was famous for challenging, quirky essay questions like asking applicants what they would do with a giant jar of mustard.

Here's another essay prompt from the 2005 application:

> In a book entitled *The Mind's I*, by Douglas Hofstadter, philosopher Daniel C. Dennett posed the following problem: Suppose you are an astronaut stranded on Mars whose spaceship had broken down beyond repair. In your disabled craft there is a Teleclone Mark IV teleporter that can swiftly and painlessly dismantle your body, producing a molecule-by-molecule blueprint to be beamed to Earth. There, a Teleclone receiver stocked with the requisite atoms will produce, from the beamed instructions, you—complete with all your memories, thoughts, feelings, and opinions. If you activate the Teleclone Mark IV, which astronaut are you—the one dismantled on Mars or the one produced from a blueprint on Earth? Suppose further that an improved Teleclone Mark V is developed that can obtain its blueprint without destroying the original. Are you then two astronauts at once? If not, which one are you?

Just *reading* that essay prompt is high friction. It's easy to see why applicants might say, "Ummm, OK, skip Chicago!"

The application was not only daunting in its length and scope, its essays could not be repurposed for other applications. More common essay topics used by other colleges, like "Describe a person who had a great impact on your life," could often be used on multiple applications with only minor adjustments.

By the early 2000s, most elite schools were accepting the Common App, further exacerbating the difference in effort in applying to Chicago compared to its peers.

## Friction Isn't All Bad

The high-friction aspect of the University of Chicago's application may have caused it to have far fewer applicants, but it offered benefits, too. One challenge faced by admissions officers is that many applicants may not be all that serious about attending. The school may be a backup choice, only to be considered if the student isn't admitted to their preferred school or schools. Or, an undecided student might simply apply to a large number of schools to see where he or she gets in. Chicago's brutal application screened out most of these casual applicants. Chicago's admissions officers could be fairly certain that most applicants were quite serious about attending the school.

For a university interested in admitting students who were serious, hardworking, and focused on academics, the Uncommon App was perfect. Its challenging nature discouraged less intellectual applicants, and the content of the application highlighted the most creative and thoughtful ones. Admissions officers at Chicago had fewer applications to read than those at other schools, and they could spend more time on each one.

## Uncommon No More

In 2007, a new provost at Chicago decided to take much of the friction out of the application process by accepting the Common App. Applicants could still answer their choice of a quirky essay question, but the humdrum process of completing a lengthy, unique form would be eliminated.

This decision wasn't without critics. Students protested, pointing out that the Uncommon App was part of the culture at Chicago. Nevertheless, the university moved forward with the plan. The results were dramatic. The far easier application process enabled Chicago's applicant count to rise from 9,542 in 2010[3] to 32,283 in 2018.[4]

In 2005, Chicago accepted more than 40 percent of its applicants. In 2007, just before switching to the Common App, the number was 35 percent. By 2013, that rate dropped to 8.8 percent.[5] By 2018, it was 7.2 percent.[6] For better or worse, Chicago was now rejecting applicants at a rate comparable to the most elite schools in the country.

The big increase in applications enabled the Chicago enrollment staff to be more selective and offer admission to more statistically strong applicants.

The increase in apparent selectivity (lower acceptance rate combined with a statistically stronger freshman class) improved Chicago's US News Best Colleges ranking. This created a sort of virtuous cycle, as a higher ranking produces more applicants and increases the probability that an accepted student will enroll. ("Yield"—the percent of accepted students who enroll—was used as a ranking metric until 2017, with higher yield being better.) In successive years, Chicago was able to ride this wave of increased selectivity and higher rankings. The school rose from a not-too-shabby #15 in 2006 to a remarkable #3 (tied) in the 2019 US News Best Colleges rankings.[7]

Was the University of Chicago a vastly better school in 2019? Of course not. It was a great school a dozen years earlier, and it remains a great school. But, a focus on reducing application friction was the most important factor in achieving the US News rank that they no doubt felt they deserved all along.

### FRICTION TAKEAWAY

Getting rid of Chicago's Uncommon App was not an easy step, as many stakeholders felt it reflected the university's core values and differentiated Chicago from other elite schools. I won't attempt to make a value judgment on whether the change was a good one. I found the older application admirable for its uniqueness and intellectual challenge. But, there is no way that applicant counts would have hit their current levels with the old system. Eliminating friction in the application process achieved the quantitative results administrators were seeking. Sometimes, "sacred cows" must be sacrificed to achieve important goals.

## ONLINE DEGREE CHALLENGES

Online education represents a very different challenge than traditional undergraduate programs. The latter has a well-defined applicant pipeline—students complete high school and move on to a college or university. The market has clear boundaries, and the application process has become highly standardized.

Online education, in contrast, serves a wide range of students, most of them nontraditional. They are harder to identify and market to, and are more challenging to enroll.

### Indiana University

Chris Foley is Associate Vice President & Director of Online Education at Indiana University (IU). In that role, he and his team have worked to identify barriers to converting potentially interested students into applicants, starting with competing for their attention.

Foley and his team first looked into the nature of his group's potential students and found that they bore little resemblance to the stereotypical college applicant. They weren't seamlessly transitioning from high school to college, and they didn't have support from parents or school counselors. Their research found that fully three-fourths of his school's potential applicants were currently employed, while nearly as many had a spouse and/or children. Almost half were accessing information about the IU program on a mobile device with no conventional keyboard.

Even the time of day when these potential students were working on their applications was a surprise. Lunchtime was the busiest time, implying that applicants were utilizing a few moments of downtime when they had a break from both work and family responsibilities.

In short, IU's potential online degree applicants are consumed by nonacademic life priorities and are frequently multitasking. They are often viewing program information on a tiny screen, navigating and typing with thumbs, and squeezing their college search and application effort into whatever free time they could find in the course of a busy day.

Reflecting on all this, Foley and his team realized that IU's competition didn't come as much from other academic institutions as from the myriad activities demanding the attention of potential students. The battleground was *time*.[8]

## Enabling Easy Action

Traditionally, the college application has been the center of the admissions and enrollment process. It was, Foley notes, "the gateway to the ivory tower."[9] While few universities used an application as daunting as the University of Chicago's "Uncommon App," most of them did use the application to garner as much information as possible about the background, capabilities, and interests of prospective students. The application wasn't designed to be easy; it was designed to be thorough.

For adult learners, though, the application process isn't a rite of passage—it's a market transaction. It's an inconvenience that must be dealt with, often while distracted and pressed for time. There's no support from family, teachers, or guidance counselors. The application will be sandwiched in between work and family responsibilities.

This realization led Foley to conclude the application process needed to be changed. First, the application had to be integrated with the school's marketing. Beginning the application had to flow seamlessly from engaging the learner with an advertisement, an e-mail, or website.

Most important was the idea of "enabling easy action." Simplifying a normally high-friction application process was essential to converting interested individuals into enrolled students.

The streamlined application paid off quickly in a pilot project. The application totals doubled, and IU enrolled 46 percent more online students. (See Figure 15.1.)

Figure 15.1 **"Easy Action" Pilot Project, Spring 2018**

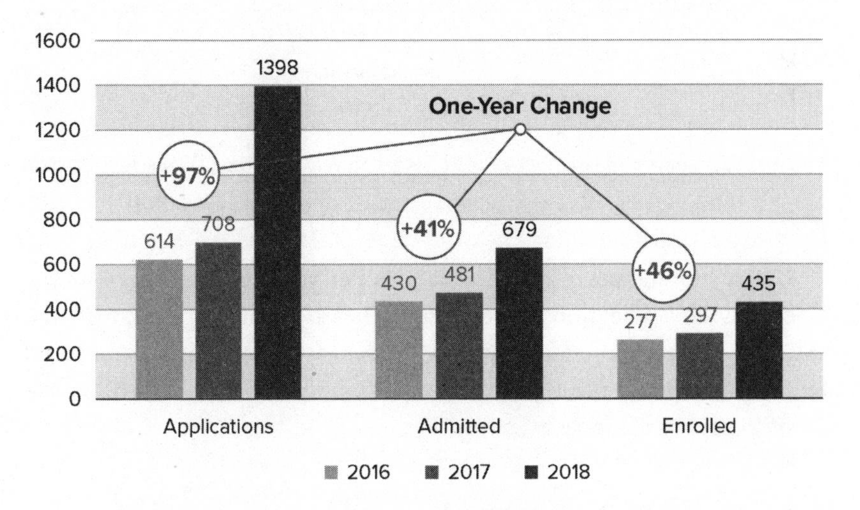


*Source:* Chart and data reprinted with permission from Chris Foley, Sharon Wavle, Chelsie Deatrick, Abby Kaufman, and Rebecca Deasy (all of Indiana University).

A further test with undergrad applicants and an even easier application process boosted applications a remarkable 250 percent compared with the old process. (See Figure 15.2.)

Figure 15.2 **Second "Easy Action" Pilot Project, Fall 2018**

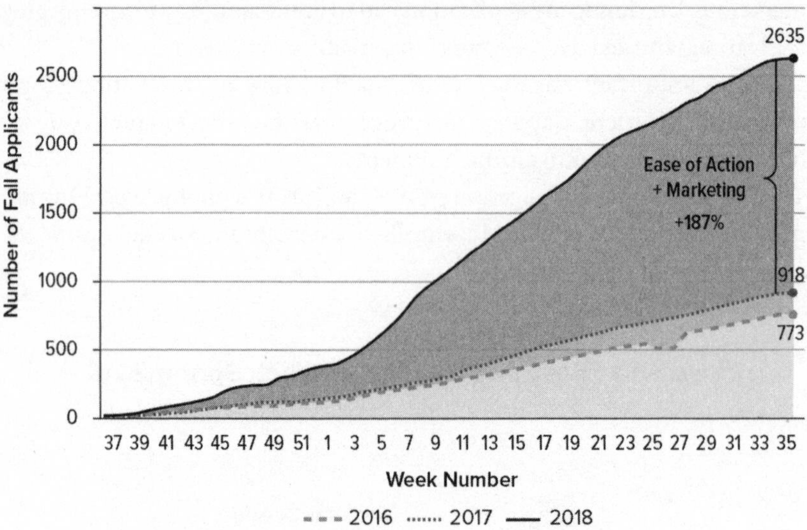

*Source:* Chart and data reprinted with permission from Chris Foley, Sharon Wavle, Chelsie Deatrick, Abby Kaufman, and Rebecca Deasy (all of Indiana University).

Foley summarizes by pointing out, "When you are competing with the clock and life's obligations, saving time generates more applications." The increase in conversion rate that the simplified application afforded caused IU's marketing cost per application to drop by as much as two-thirds. He terms the approach "ease of action."

## Smart Defaults Save Effort

The friction-reducing application process begins simply—the applicant's first and last name, and two quick choices reflecting the type of program and timing. To reduce effort even more, the program may be preselected based on the advertisement. So, if someone clicks on an ad for "Language Programs," that person's program choice will be set to that value with the option to select "other." The timing choice will be preselected to the next term, with the option to change to one further in the future.

A key step in making the application process as easy as possible is to avoid the typical "account setup" step. Foley thinks setting up passwords can be complicated and confusing to applicants. Instead, they can resume a session automatically when they return to the site via a saved "cookie" on their device or when prompted by an e-mail reminder. Many applications, Foley notes, can be completed in a single sitting—the ultimate in "ease of action."

## Cutting Campus Confusion

A point of friction at some universities is that an applicant for online programs must choose programs by campus or the academic unit that offers the program. While different online programs may originate in different IU units, these distinctions are not intuitive and are largely meaningless for potential students. These distinctions are irrelevant from the applicant's standpoint, so that the "easy action" application is uniform for all units and all programs are offered under the single IU brand. Applicants do not have to specify either a campus or an academic unit.

The last element of friction eliminated in the optimized application was the application fee. Since multiple types of fee waivers were already available, the modest revenue loss from simply getting rid of the fee is more than offset by increased enrollment revenue.

The online education market can be brutal—for-profit colleges have turned the online environment into a costly exercise in lead generation and high-pressure sales. Traditional colleges and universities, meanwhile, are learning to cope with the concept at varying speeds. Indiana University with its statewide uniform branding and low-friction application process is coping better than most.

### FRICTION TAKEAWAY

The first step in optimizing the IU application was to study the applicants and their challenges. The finding that they were distracted and completing the application in bits of time between other priorities led to a focus on making it very fast and very easy. Eliminating the fee was justified by the numbers. Know your customer and their pain points to take the friction out of your own processes.

CHAPTER

# 16

# Friction Everywhere

*The pessimist sees an obstacle in every opportunity;*
*the optimist sees an opportunity in every obstacle.*
—Apocryphal

## IF IT'S NOT BROKEN . . .

Elevators (or lifts, if you are a Brit) have a very low friction user interface. The user merely pushes the up or down button, and a door opens with an indicator light confirming the direction of travel. Then, the user pushes a floor button, the door closes, and eventually it opens on the desired floor.

Most of us can manage that process with no attention at all. Sometimes, that lack of attention has amusing results. I've occasionally been in autopilot mode, exited the car when the door opened, and then found that the elevator had stopped at a floor before my destination. Naturally, I emerge from my fog and realize this just as the door closes behind me.

The reason we can operate elevators almost entirely without conscious thought is because the user interface is simple and unchanging. The way you call an elevator is pretty much the same at a historic hotel in London or a sleek office building in Manhattan.

Frankfurt, on the other hand, is a different story.

### Elevator Operation 101

My first public presentation of my Persuasion Slide framework (and its key element, friction) was at a conference in Frankfurt, Germany. The host had arranged rooms for speakers in a sleek high-rise hotel. Check-in was simple enough, but I was surprised when the young woman who gave me my key card came out from behind her counter and walked with me to the elevators.

"I'll show you how to work the elevators," she said. I wondered if she thought Americans were so clueless that they couldn't operate an elevator. Or, if it was just *me* that appeared to be clueless.

Soon, I saw why elevator training was mandatory in this hotel. The elevators were arranged in a partial circle around a pleasant, glass-enclosed lobby. At one side of the lobby there was a stainless-steel pedestal that had an LCD display and a keypad. There was nothing anywhere that resembled an up-down button.

The clerk took my key and waved it near the pedestal. That woke up the display and allowed her to enter my floor number on the keypad. The display then changed to "B." The clerk explained, "It's simple—now just wait for elevator B." Each of the five elevators did indeed have a letter identifying it.

She then recited the steps needed to call an elevator, and how to do that from the floor where my room was located. (Despite the training, I had apparently not accurately recalled exactly where to wave my room card to activate the pedestal. Several attempts failed to find the magic spot, and it wasn't until I watched someone else do it that I realized it was unmarked and well below the display.)

When the doors to elevator B opened, I entered and was surprised to see not a single floor button in the car. A tiny LED showed that my floor was on that car's itinerary. The door closed, the elevator went up, and I arrived at my floor.

Oddly, I had to use my key card to get out of the elevator lobby. I imagined a few scenarios where someone lacking a key card (a guest of a guest, for example) could get trapped with the elevators until someone else chose their floor.

This procedure is fairly simple once you know the system, but there were multiple points of potential failure. I saw quite a few guests flummoxed, as I was initially, by their inability to wake up the controller and select a floor. Like me, they weren't paying close enough attention during Elevator Operation 101.

## Efficiency vs. Ease

So why would anyone take a user interface that has been working for a century and turn it into an inscrutable mess? The answer is efficiency. Humans, left to their own devices, will board the first available car. They might, for example, board the same car as their colleague and not the one with a stranger who is going to their floor.

The engineers at German elevator manufacturer Schindler found that by directing careless humans to specific cars, they could ensure everyone going to the twenty-third floor was on the same car. Never would two elevators travel to the same floor within seconds of each other, wasting time and capacity. Schindler says this "destination elevator" system not only provides individualized security but improves capacity by 30 percent.[1]

Boosting elevator capacity by a third is no small deal. If you've ever suffered a frustrating wait for a hotel elevator, you know that many buildings could use more elevators. The Schindler system adds the capacity without adding more costly shafts.

The friction in this system came from applying it in a setting where every day dozens or hundreds of new users had to cope with it. Many times per day, the hotel clerks had to go through the training process with new guests. And, for the first day or two, guests continued to struggle with getting to where they wanted to go.

When a system like this was installed in News Corporation's Manhattan headquarters building, Chairman Rupert Murdoch complained, "Somebody put these new elevators in, and nobody knows how to use them." Usability expert and Bentley College professor Tom Tullis encountered one of these installations and was inspired to deliver a presentation titled "You shouldn't have to read a user manual to ride an elevator!"[2]

## Elevators as Metaphors

This elevator example is no different than situations where a developer creates a checkout process whose steps and actions seem obvious when you know what they are but confuse first-time users.

After using the elevators for a day, most of the friction went away. And, if a guest had encountered one of these elevator interfaces before, using one in a new building would be easy enough. The problem here was twofold:

- In a hotel, many, if not most, guests are first-time visitors.
- Stays are short, and every day brings new guests.
- This elevator access system was uncommon in hotels, meaning that even frequent travelers were encountering it for the first time.

### FRICTION TAKEAWAY

To avoid confusing people and slowing them down, don't tinker with the way they are accustomed to doing things. On a website, for example, put features like the business name and navigation elements where users expect to see them. If you must create a new way of doing things, be sure the interface is intuitive enough that even a first-time user isn't befuddled.

## WRITTEN FRICTION

I never thought about writing as a source of friction until I read Josh Bernoff's excellent book *Writing Without Bullshit*.[3] Perhaps because my friction goggles are now engaged 24/7, his message about business writing hit home. Bernoff's cardinal rule is that writers should treat the reader's time as more valuable than their own. Unfortunately, few writers take that advice to heart. Their prose is too long, too vague, and too slow to get to the point. When readers have to fight their way through dense and confusing text, that's friction.

In a blog post, Bernoff analyzes and translates a press release from software maker Adobe. He deconstructs and comments on every part of the overblown, mostly meaningless, thousand-plus words in the press release. Here's just one example:

> Original text:
>
> Adobe is the leader in designing and delivering digital experiences through content and data. At the core of every great experience are content and data, which enable the consistent, personal, intuitive experiences consumers have come to expect. Commerce is also integral to the customer experience. Consumers

> and businesses now expect every interaction to be shoppable—whether on the web, mobile, social, in-product or in-store.

Bernoff comments that the statements here are so broad as to be meaningless, calling it "more of a dreamy musical theme with techie marketing words than a statement about actual digital experiences."

> Bernoff's translation:
>
> Marketers already use Adobe products for every customer interaction but shopping. After this acquisition, they can add shopping.[4]

Can you see how much less friction there is in the translated version? It's easy to read, and it takes no reader effort to grasp the one key idea that was buried in the original wordy paragraph.

Press releases are great examples of high-friction writing. I get many of them every week, almost never related to the topics I write about. These missives are filled with superlatives and describe a bright future. The releases then present more claims, superlatives, and optimistic commentary in the form of fabricated, stilted quotes from executives. Finally, they include a lengthy and even more complexly worded legal disclaimer that says all the preceding information might not be accurate. An *Adweek* article reported findings that showed reporters, if they opened a release at all, spent less than a minute on it.[5] Is that any wonder?

The smarter people want to sound, the more likely they are to pad their writing. Bernoff points out that reports, white papers, blog posts, and even e-mails can suffer from "bullshit overload."

## Editing Out Written Friction

Bernoff offers guidelines for eliminating friction (or, as he calls it, bullshit!) from your writing. A few from his book are:

- **Write short.** In school, long writing often got better grades. In business and life, long writing doesn't get read at all.
- **Put the important stuff first.** Journalists know that many readers never get past the first paragraph. So, get right to what people need to know.

- **Don't use the passive voice.** Responsibility for actions is ambiguous when passive verbs are used. "Alternative methods were tested" doesn't make it clear who tested them.

- **Don't use jargon.** Academics like jargon. Technical people like jargon. Why? Lots of people use specialized, uncommon words instead of simple ones because they think it makes them sound smarter or like they are "insiders." In reality, it just makes their writing hard to read and understand. Get rid of the jargon—your readers will thank you.

- **Don't use weasel words.** When we don't have a good source for a fact, the quick solution is to add qualifiers that muddy the waters. Bernoff identifies words like "most," "often," "deeply," and many others that seem to make a point but lack precision. "Most Americans own stocks" is less accurate and compelling than, "According to Gallup, 55 percent of Americans own stocks." When it comes to weasel words, Bernoff is ~~nearly always mostly probably often~~ right!

Bernoff's book *Writing Without Bullshit* has many more ways to eliminate communication friction, so I suggest you pick up a copy. He changed the way I looked at my writing, and he will change your style, too.

### FRICTION TAKEAWAY

> Writing can be high friction or low friction. The latter gets read, is easily understood, and spurs action. Strive for the shortest, clearest, most direct wording. Your readers will appreciate your clarity and brevity. (Caution: You are reading this advice in a book where the author was contractually obligated to provide 75,000 words of text!)

## THE SLIPPERY SLIDE

Joe Sugarman is one of the best-known and most successful copywriters and direct marketers of all time. He's best known for selling millions of pairs of BluBlocker sunglasses via print ads, television ads, and infomercials. Sugarman is credited with being the first major direct response marketer to give customers a toll-free number to call. His awards include the Maxwell Sackheim direct marketing award and being named Direct Marketing Man of the Year.

Sugarman's most productive years were before the e-commerce era, but his advice is as relevant today as it was in the days of print and traditional television.

In his 1999 book *Triggers*, Sugarman states:

> As a direct marketer, I have determined that the most important thing you can do to turn a prospect into a customer is to make it incredibly easy for that prospect to commit to a purchase . . . [6]

It sounds a bit like something Amazon's CEO Jeff Bezos would say, doesn't it?

## Low-Friction Copywriting

In his later title, *The Adweek Copywriting Handbook*, Sugarman explained how copy should flow by using the metaphor of a playground slide:

> Picture a steep slide at a playground. Now, picture somebody putting baby oil or grease along the entire length of the slide, including the side rails. Picture yourself now climbing up the ladder, sitting at the top of the slide, and then letting gravity force you down the slide.[7]

Sugarman says that every element in persuasive copy should flow into the next, forming a slippery slide that won't let you stop until the end. Headlines should be so compelling that you must read the subheadline. That element, in turn, must be so engaging that you read the first sentence.

The text of the ad should not only be compelling, but easy to read, Sugarman says in his book. Each sentence must lead inexorably to the next until the end.

**FRICTION TAKEAWAY**

When you are writing advertising or any persuasive copy, follow the legendary Joe Sugarman's advice. Make your copy so easy to read and so compelling that the reader can't stop. This means using fewer words and simple phrasing. Avoid jargon or anything likely to make the reader pause. Keep your slide slippery!

## TRUST SCIENCE

If you are introduced to Paul Zak, he'll almost certainly envelop you in a big hug. It's not a Hollywood affectation, even though Zak is known as Dr. Love and has his own IMDb page—he's appeared on television in shows ranging from "Stossel" to "Outrageous Acts of Psych."

In fact, Zak is a neuroscientist who has been studying the science of human connection for decades. He's the founding Director of the Center for Neuroeconomics Studies at Claremont Graduate University, where he's also a Professor of Economics, Psychology, and Management.

Zak is the world's leading expert on oxytocin, a hormone and neurotransmitter colloquially known as the "hug drug." Zak achieved prominence when he published research showing that oxytocin, even when administered by inhalation, created trust between humans. A more common way to increase oxytocin levels is a hug. Hugging increases oxytocin levels in both participants, hence Zak's penchant for embracing people. (It even works with dogs—snuggle with your pooch, and Zak's research shows that both you and your canine companion can get an oxytocin boost.)[8]

Oxytocin is a key driver of trust between humans.

### Vampire Economics

It would be easy to dismiss the relevance of Zak's work. His Claremont lab has been dubbed "The Love Lab," and Zak himself was nicknamed "Dr. Love" and "The Vampire Economist."[9] His approach is neither traditional nor mainstream. But, Zak's research has serious implications for businesses and organizations of all sizes and types.

Much of Zak's recent research has focused on why some organizations and teams perform far better than others. Unlike most business researchers who gather data via surveys and interviews, Zak and his team went a step beyond. In addition to using conventional research techniques, they collected and analyzed thousands of blood samples.

Zak found that employees at high-performing companies cause each other to release oxytocin in their blood samples more than those at other companies. What was the difference between the best and the worst? Zak concluded that it was trust. Conventional research methods confirmed the blood tests. People in the high-performing firms trusted each other more.

## High Trust, High Performance

In a *Harvard Business Review* article, Zak reports that employees at high-trust companies, when compared to those at low-trust companies, reported:

- 74 percent less stress
- 106 percent more energy at work
- 50 percent higher productivity
- 13 percent fewer sick days
- 76 percent more engagement
- 29 percent more satisfaction with their lives
- 40 percent less burnout[10]

In his book *Trust Factor,* Zak identifies eight practices that high-performing companies engage in to create trust. Recognizing excellent performance is one; another is sharing information broadly. A couple have to do with letting people choose how to do their work and choosing what to work on. Zak's research makes a persuasive argument for trust as the key factor in team and organization performance.[11]

## Distrust-Driven Friction

One common element in high-friction environments is a lack of trust. Nothing says "we don't trust you" like rules and procedures that assume people aren't honest.

Recall from an earlier chapter that General Electric managers thought its workers would steal gloves, so they created a control process that wasted hours of time every month. And Irv Refken's foreman thought that workers would steal tools, so they built a tool crib and hired a person to sign tools in and out. In both cases, the costly controls were later eliminated with no ill effects. Not only did these changes reduce friction, they also increased the atmosphere of trust in their organizations.

Amazon often reduces friction by refunding customers as soon as they drop off a product return at UPS or an Amazon Locker. Yes, it's possible that you might return an empty box and keep the item you purchased, but Amazon trusts you. An instant refund may not happen every time, but it's clear that Amazon trusts most of its customers, most of the time. This makes the company easier to do business with than competitors who might take a week or more to issue a refund.

## Culture-Based Trust

Amsterdam ombudsman and red tape foe Arre Zuurmond points out that trust differences can be cultural. Let's say one company orders 10,000 parts from another company for delivery at the end of the month at a total price of $500,000. In Holland and most other countries, there would be a series of steps necessary to initiate payment. When the shipment arrived, someone would count the items to be sure the shipment was correct. That person would forward that paperwork to accounting, who would eventually match it up with an invoice from the vendor. Assuming everything was in order, accounting would finally issue a check to the vendor.

In Japan, Zuurmond says, the payment might simply have been issued at the scheduled time. Both companies trust each other, so fewer bureaucratic processes are needed to verify that the other side is complying with their agreement. The buyer trusts that the seller will deliver the quantity promised at the agreed-upon time. The seller trusts the buyer to pay on time. Higher trust levels mean fewer steps and less paperwork. Zuurmond notes that some measures of economic activity and bureaucracy don't catch cultural nuances like this.[12]

## Get What You Give

Trust isn't just a matter of dollars and cents. Trust is reciprocated. When you show trust, you get trust in return. Lab experiments by Zak and his team used a procedure known as the "Trust Game" to gauge the extent to which people trusted each other. The game involves the experimenter giving one person an amount of money. That person can keep the money or send some to another person, knowing that the amount given will be tripled in value. The second person isn't obligated to return any money.

In a low-trust environment, the first person would just keep the money. Why risk any of it by expecting a stranger to behave in a trusting way? In fact, Zak found that 90 percent of the first players do send money, and a remarkable 95 percent of the second players who get money return some to the first player. The second player almost always reciprocates the show of trust by the first player.[13] Why? Because when we are trusted our brains produce oxytocin. Oxytocin motivates people to reciprocate nice with nice.

Zak did find that 5 percent of the subjects tested are "unconditional non-reciprocators"—or, as his lab team calls them, "bastards." These players didn't respond to trust, they simply kept the money. About one-half of these people had psychopathic traits. The other half were having really bad days—high stress inhibits the brain's release of oxytocin.[14]

## System-to-Human Trust

Even when trust is built into systems rather than human-to-human, it can create reciprocal trust. The first time I dropped off an Amazon return at UPS and found a refund notification in my e-mail 30 minutes later, my first reaction was, "Wow, they trust me!" The same thing happened the first time an Amazon e-mail told me to simply discard the defective item I had received; they would immediately send a replacement. They trusted me, whereas another company might have assumed that if they didn't demand I return the first product, I might be trying to get two for the price of one.

Another time, I inadvertently ordered an incorrect item. The item was fine, but I wanted to return it and get the one I needed. They told me to keep the wrong one and processed a credit immediately. Not only did they once again demonstrate trust, they also avoided a lot of friction. I would have had to repack the item and pay to ship it back; they would have to receive the item, inspect it, approve my credit, and perhaps return the item to stock. If the repeated handling had made it look less than new, they would have had to discard it anyway. All of that was avoided by their trust-based policy.

Amazon has earned the trust of its customers in many ways, but trusting them is one of the most powerful. And, think of the wasted effort the company saves when they tell a customer to keep an item that was incorrect. Likely, a friction calculation went into this policy—with the cost of shipping the item, inspecting the return, perhaps returning it to the vendor, and issuing a customer credit, it's cheaper just to issue the credit. Most companies could do the same thing with low-cost items, but they don't because they don't trust their customers.

### FRICTION TAKEAWAY

Are your systems designed assuming that your employees and customers might be less than truthful, or, even worse, outright liars and criminals? Sometimes, companies create rules after an incident of theft or fraud. Other times, an executive assumes that if employees or customers *can* steal from the company, they *will*. If your procedures are rooted in distrust of employees and/or customers, you may be imposing needless burdens on them. Weigh the cost and inconvenience of rules and processes that are based on distrust and compare them to the actual cost of bad behavior. When you eliminate distrust-based friction, you'll not only save time and money, you'll be one step closer to a high-trust, high-performance environment.

## IMAGINARY FRICTION

By now, we can agree that people usually avoid difficulty. It's human nature to take the path of least resistance, or, in the context of this book, of least friction. But what if there was a kind of friction that existed only in the person's head? That is, there is a perception of difficulty rather than real difficulty.

Surprisingly, science has shown there is indeed a sort of "imaginary" difficulty, and it's related to what scientists call "cognitive fluency." Things that are fluent are easy for our brains to process, while disfluent things are more difficult.

### Deadly Disfluency

Fluency is no trivial matter of scientific curiosity either.

In the United States, it's estimated that 125,000 people die each year from nonadherence to medication instructions. This costs the U.S. healthcare system as much as $300 billion annually.[15]

One might expect that patients lucky enough to get a kidney transplant would be rigorous about taking antirejection drugs. In fact, about a third of the recipients stop taking them.[16] Another study showed that typically patients with chronic illnesses take only half their prescribed doses.[17]

There are many reasons why patients don't take their medications as instructed, including high cost, mental illness, and so on. One less obvious reason is "imaginary" friction—difficulty that isn't real, but which is perceived because of the way information is presented.

A study at the University of Manchester and Leeds Beckett University found that the type font used to present medical information actually affected how patients viewed risks and complied with those instructions. In one experiment, the researchers found that the easier the description of a proposed medical intervention was to read, the lower the complexity of the procedure appeared to patients. In another experiment, a more difficult to read font reduced compliance with instructions.[18]

What if a few of those 125,000 deaths could be prevented just by making instructions easy to read?

## Hard to Read, Hard to Do

Fluency issues go far beyond medical instructions. Here's a quick question: look at the two sentences below, and estimate how long it would take to do those simple exercises.

> Tuck your chin into your chest, and then lift your chin upward as far as possible. 6–10 repetitions
>
> Lower your left ear toward your left shoulder and then your right ear toward your right shoulder. 6–10 repetitions

When University of Minnesota researchers asked a group of subjects that question, they estimated 8.2 minutes on average. Then, they asked a second group of subjects to read the exact same text, but printed in a "brush" font:

> *Tuck your chin into your chest, and then lift your chin upward as far as possible. 6–10 repetitions*
>
> *Lower your left ear toward your left shoulder and then your right ear toward your right shoulder. 6–10 repetitions*

The results were shocking. The second group estimated the exercises would take 15.1 minutes—almost *twice as long*. The text was identical, the size was identical... but although the brush text was quite legible, it was a bit more difficult to read.[19]

The scientists concluded that difficulty in reading translated into *difficulty in doing*. The less fluent font made the exercises seem more difficult and time-consuming.[20] Unfortunately, the scientists didn't take the experiment to the next phase and ask the subjects to perform the exercise voluntarily. I think it's likely that, just like prescription drug takers, compliance with the request would have been much higher in the simple-font group.

## More Fluency Friction

Another effect of fluency friction is that people delay or simply don't make decisions. In one experiment, people were asked to choose between two similar cordless phones. When subjects read the descriptions in an easy-to-read font, just 17 percent couldn't decide which phone they preferred. When the descriptions were printed in a more difficult font, the percentage shot up to 41 percent.[21]

Fluency affects more than just perceived effort—it can also change perception of risk and danger. One set of experiments had people estimate the side effects of two drugs, Magnalroxate and Hnegripitrom. The first name is comparatively easy to read, and was judged to be safer. Another experiment in the series asked which amusement park ride would be more likely to make you sick, Chunta or Vaiveahtoishi. The ride with the unpronounceable name was thought to be riskier, but there was a bright spot: it was also rated higher for excitement.[22]

## Financial Fluency

Weirdly, even stock prices have been found to be affected by fluency issues. A study at Princeton University found that stocks with fluent ticker symbols like KAR outperformed unpronounceable stocks like RDO in short-term fluctuations. The scientists found that the easy-to-say stock tickers gained 10 percent more in one-day measurements, and attributed the difference to fluency.[23]

### FRICTION TAKEAWAY

Hundreds of experiments show that the friction from disfluency has a very real effect on people's perceptions and behavior. When things are hard for our brains to process—fine print, fancy fonts, hard-to-say names—they seem more difficult or more dangerous. People will be less likely to follow instructions or make decisions. So, unless your objective is to slow down others' thinking, avoid this "imaginary" friction. Keep it simple: easy to read, easy to say. Text should be short and with simple language.

# CONCLUSION

# Go Forth and Find Friction

## EVERYBODY KNOWS ABOUT FRICTION

Not long before I began writing this book, I was a speaker at a private mastermind for entrepreneurs. I was recording an interview with the organizer, who asked for my best secret to increase sales. I began to talk about reducing friction for customers, and he cut me off. "Everybody knows about friction . . . give me something they don't know."

This was an advanced group of marketers, and perhaps they *did* all know about friction. But considering the amount of friction I encounter every day, online and offline, there are quite a few people in the world who do *not* know about friction. Or, if they do, they discount its importance.

Everyone may *know* about friction, but in too many cases they aren't *doing* anything about it.

## THE DEATH OF FRICTION

*The Internet will help achieve "friction free capitalism" by putting buyer and seller in direct contact and providing more information to both about each other.*

—Bill Gates, Cofounder, Microsoft

Bill Gates included a chapter in his 1995 book *The Road Ahead*, titled "Friction-Free Capitalism." Gates predicted that the Internet would eliminate friction by bringing buyers and sellers together directly and ensuring free access to information.[1]

Commenting on Gates's book, a *Los Angeles Times* article by Gary Chapman closed with a dire prediction:

> Beneath the celebratory rhetoric about the coming "friction-free" economy is a ticking time bomb: the explosive idea that tens of millions of workers can be summed up, and shunted aside, as mere friction.[2]

In 1997, author and professor T. G. Lewis wrote an entire book on the topic. In *The Friction-Free Economy*,[3] Lewis predicted an upending of traditional business models in the ensuing 20 years. He argued:

> The friction-free economy is (mostly) frictionless. That is, the cost of manufacturing, distribution, and support is much lower than in the old economy. This reduction in cost changes everything....
>
> For simplicity's sake, the friction-free economy can be thought of as a kind of frictionless capitalism. This is where the non-Newtonian part comes in. Frictionless capitalism assumes zero production and distribution costs, no competitors, and the availability of unlimited resources.[4]

The enthusiasm for friction-free business seemed to wane after the late 1990s. But, some of those early predictions have come to pass, at least in part. Today, shopping for any product you can imagine is far easier than when Gates and Lewis were predicting a friction-free world. The Internet, along with companies like Amazon and eBay, have indeed made it easier to find products, learn about them, and buy them.

The rise of companies like Instagram and WhatsApp, both acquired by Facebook for billions of dollars not long after they were founded, makes Lewis and Gates look prescient. Virtually all of today's "unicorns," start-ups with billion-dollar valuations, fit the model of using scalable, low-cost digital resources to dominate their space.

As the US economy hums along with record-low unemployment, Chapman's warnings about tens of millions of jobs being lost in a frictionless world seem flat-out wrong a couple of decades later. In specific industries, though, perhaps he had a point. The retail industry has seen a bigger reduction in friction than most, and there we do have an epidemic of retail chains struggling and shopping malls closing. To date, the jobs lost by stores closing or cutting back have been offset by new jobs added in e-commerce, warehousing, and transportation. We can hope that, as has happened in past disruptions, new jobs will absorb those that are going away.

## Ecosystems as Friction-Killers

The latest prediction of a friction-free world comes from Thomas Koulopoulos, founder of the Delphi Group think tank. In his book *Revealing the Invisible,*[5] he and coauthor George Achillias include a chapter "The End of Friction and the Industrial Age." While the pundits of the 1990s saw the Internet as the friction-killer, Koulopoulos sees a combination of artificial intelligence and individual behavioral data as change agents. He predicts powerful digital ecosystems will emerge to disrupt traditional businesses, citing the Apple App Store and Uber as examples.

Koulopoulos has an interesting concept about friction elimination. He thinks it's nearly impossible to eliminate it from inside a company or even inside an industry. People tend to assume that the way things are done currently is natural and necessary, and are motivated to make only small, incremental improvements. Koulopoulos proposes that friction is almost always eliminated only when there is some sort of existential threat, and that usually comes from outside the company or industry.

When Napster burst on the music scene, it offered a nearly frictionless way for consumers to get the music they wanted. Of course, along with consumer convenience came copyright violations and the fact that artists weren't being compensated for their work.

The music industry's reaction wasn't to applaud Napster's technology and try to integrate it into a business model that would be profitable for both labels and artists. Instead, the industry sued Napster. It even sued individual consumers. Even when a demonstrably friction-free (or almost so) customer experience was staring it in the face, the music industry tried to preserve its traditional business model of selling plastic discs.

Eventually, Koulopoulos notes, Steve Jobs and Apple convinced the record labels to list their music in the iTunes store. This took all the friction associated with distributing physical media away and gave consumers an easy way to purchase just the songs they wanted. Jobs took even more friction out of the process by licensing 1-Click ordering from Amazon.

Koulopoulos predicts that every business will have its Napster moment, and in most cases the innovation will come from outside the company or industry.[6]

## Friction Lives On

As much as I'd love to drive a stake in the heart of friction, instead I'll paraphrase writer and entrepreneur Mark Twain: the reports of the death of friction have been greatly exaggerated. It's true that in specific areas, notably shopping, there has been progress. But, in many areas that progress has been slow. Take ride-hailing services. Uber, Lyft, and the rest showed that there was a low-friction solution to personal transportation. But, just as the record companies responded when faced with the Napster threat, many cities around the world have moved to protect a high-friction business model instead of welcoming innovation.

Eventually, low-friction solutions will win. But, in the meantime, we can expect incumbent players to resist progress rather than adapting their business model to minimize customer friction.

### FRICTION TAKEAWAY

Finding a better, lower friction way to serve your customers isn't easy, particularly if it requires major changes in your business model. But, if you don't do it, someone else will. What if instead of fighting Napster and its users, the music industry had created a digital music store before Apple did? All that the industry's resistance to change accomplished was to encourage a formidable competitor to create a service and claim a big share of the profit pie.

## PUT ON YOUR GOGGLES

*Blessed are they that take away attritions, that remove friction, that make the courses of life smooth, and the intercourse of men gentle!*

—Henry Ward Beecher, American clergyman and social reformer

I'll make a bold prediction. If you've read this far, or if you've even read part of this book and skipped ahead, you have begun to see friction everywhere.

You see it in the supermarket. You see it when you try to get help from a company. You see it in your own organization.

Most of the time, you already knew something was wrong. Maybe an activity was more complex or time-consuming than it needed to be. The procedure didn't seem to make sense. But, now, you have a name for it—*friction.*

I hope you will use that name, often and loudly—and eliminate it at every chance you get.

## Pushback

Just as I was finishing this book, I ran across a new book by Nigel Travis, *The Challenge Culture*. Travis is the former Chairman and CEO of Dunkin' Brands, and the thesis of his book is that organizations need "pushback" to survive and thrive. Travis says the most successful organizations are those where people at all levels—from the newest recruit to the CEO—have the freedom to question the status quo. He emphasizes that the pushback should be positive and the discussion civil.[7]

I'm asking you to follow through. When you see friction, fight it. If you can fix it yourself, do it. If someone else can, ask that person to do it. Don't organize large meetings, send out mass e-mails, or be a jerk. Instead, be a fighter, not a creator, of friction. And, as Travis recommends, don't be afraid to engage in a little pushback—it's good for everyone!

## Observe Behavior

There's no more potent tool for not just spotting friction but also showing others that it exists than measuring and/or observing behavior. A development team may argue that the website search function is just fine unless you can produce data showing that two-thirds of user searches produce no results, or that users have to reformulate their search multiple times to find what they want. Sometimes just watching people do things, or try to do things, will reveal a lot.

## Spread the Word

Nobody likes wasted time and effort. Nobody enjoys pointless meetings. Everybody hates burdensome red tape. The more you point out friction to the people around you, the more they will see themselves. And, the more likely they will try to become part of the solution.

• • •

**Now, put on your friction goggles, grab your can of (metaphorical) WD-40, and eliminate some friction!**

# APPENDIX

# The Persuasion Slide

My friction journey began in 2013. I was going to give a keynote at a conference focused on conversion optimization—that is, maximizing the revenue or lead-generation performance of websites and mobile apps. Driving traffic to your website can be expensive, so maximizing the value derived from that traffic is critical.

I decided to formalize a mental model I had created for any persuasion or behavior change process. Loosely inspired by BJ Fogg's Behavior Model[1] and designed to incorporate both conscious and nonconscious processing, I called it The Persuasion Slide™.

I received plenty of positive feedback from my fellow speakers and conference attendees, so I continued to work on it. I blogged about it, did a podcast that explained it, and published a short e-book, *The Persuasion Slide,*[2] that showed how to use the framework. What follows is a quick summary of the framework.

## THE PERSUASION SLIDE

A playground slide is a simple device. A child sits at the top, and either Mom or Dad gives the child a shove or she pushes herself forward with her arms. Once into the sloped section with a little momentum, the force of gravity takes over. The steeper the slope, the more quickly the child will get to the bottom. Opposing that motion is another invisible force, friction. The child's progress is slowed by friction. Occasionally, if friction is very high due to rust or poor slide maintenance, the child may stop before reaching the bottom.

Each of those elements becomes part of our slide framework, as shown in Figure A.1:

Figure A.1 **The Persuasion Slide**

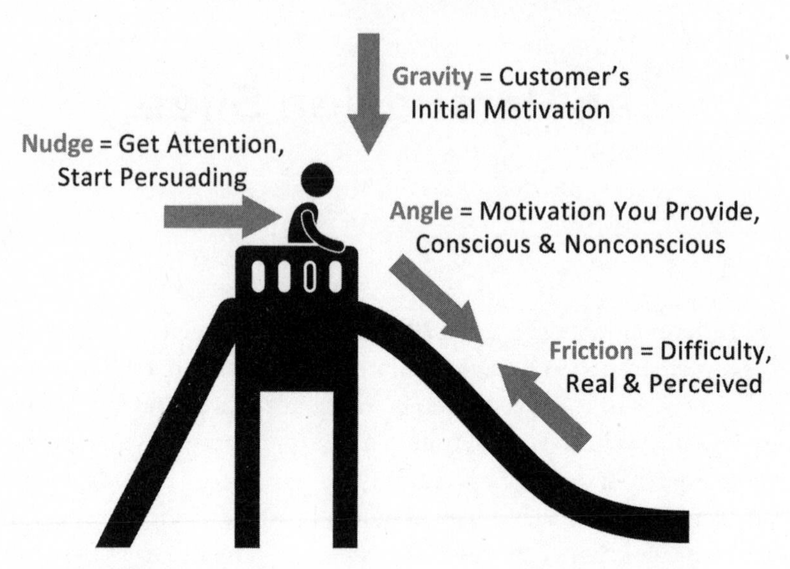


The parental push at the top becomes the **nudge**. In our framework, that means getting the customer's attention and starting the persuasion process. That can be an e-mail, a search ad, a visible call to action, a phone call, or any other tool that the customer notices. The nudge has to have a little motivation in it to get the customer moving to the next step. A banner ad, for example, has to (1) get the customer to look *and* (2) intrigue that customer enough to click.

**Gravity** is the force that moves the child down the slide, and in our framework it is the motivation that the customer starts with. Gravity has nothing to do with you or your offer—it's the customer's needs, wants, desires, pain points, and so on. Some are conscious—a car buyer needs transportation, affordability, and so on. But there is usually nonconscious motivation at work, too—a need for prestige or a desire to signal concern for the environment to others, for example.

The **angle** of the slide determines how effective gravity is in getting the child to the bottom. Steeper is faster. In our framework, the angle is the motivation *you* provide. It's how well your product and your marketing fit the customer's needs or relieves his or her pain points. Conscious motivators are product features and performance, sales and discounts, competitive comparisons, and more. Nonconscious motivators are appeals based on influence tools like scarcity and social proof, cognitive biases, and myriad other things that go beyond rational, logical behavior.

**Friction**, of course, is the other invisible force that opposes gravity and slows or stops the child. I won't belabor this element since the book is packed with examples. Most of the friction we encounter is conscious, but nonconscious friction creeps in via cognitive disfluency. When things are hard for our brains to process (e.g., instructions in a hard-to-read font), they *seem* more difficult than they really are. This friction may be imaginary, but its effects are very real.

This is a very abbreviated summary of The Persuasion Slide, but I hope you agree that it's quite intuitive. For a free Persuasion Slide Workbook, go to: https://www.rogerdooley.com/ps.

# Acknowledgments

This book was years in the making, and many people played a part in its creation.

The guests on my *Brainfluence Podcast,* now numbering more than 250, have immeasurably enriched my thinking of how the world works. Scientists, CEOs, authors, and lots of other smart people have brought amazingly diverse insights to my audience. I've tried to absorb as much as I could from these conversations and my guests' books and other content—a big thanks to all!

In the past year or two I've often raised the concept of friction with my guests, either on the show or in private conversations. I couldn't possibly name everyone who offered helpful advice here, but a few stand out. My friend Nir Eyal understands friction better than anyone. He was an early guest as I was getting my podcast off the ground, a South by Southwest (SXSW) co-panelist several times, and the first person with whom I discussed the idea of this book—on my patio after a long day at SXSW, if I remember correctly. Kintan Brahmbhatt helped convince me I was on the right track in multiple exchanges. BJ Fogg generously reviewed my description of his behavior design thinking and suggested improvements. Gary Hoover provided key insights into business history and the evolution of retail. Denise Lee Yohn suggested I dig into GE's history, which ultimately led to my Jack Welch section.

The legendary Tom Peters was kind enough to both record a podcast with me and provide some off-the-air suggestions that improved the book. Economics Nobelist Al Roth provided some early guidance on "frictions," the usage preferred by economists. So did my later guest, Ray Fisman. Entrepreneurs like Rammohan Malasani, Kevin O'Brien, Ajay Prasad, and Brian Massey told their stories, either on a podcast or in an interview. John Padgett gave me an inside perspective on two of the biggest tech-driven guest experience projects ever conceived. Art Markman and James Clear helped clarify my thinking on the effects of friction on habit formation. Paul Zak's work on the science of trust was instrumental in defining the links between trust, performance, and friction. Other helpful guests included Thomas Koulopolis and Nigel Travis.

Josh Bernoff and Ryan Holiday were unwitting but influential mentors via their books about writing and the creative process. Chris Foley and Ted O'Neill helped me with the higher education enrollment space. Arre Zuurmond explained the origins of the Kafka Brigade and his continuing battle against red tape.

Esther Jacobs shared her simultaneously sad and hilarious adventures with Dutch bureaucracy both on a podcast and privately. James Crabtree did the same for India. The World Bank provided a wealth of data on business and entrepreneurship around the globe. Most of my interviews were via phone, Skype, and other remote means, but Vice Mayor Guo Baichun met with me in Yinchuan to describe his city's effort to streamline procedures for citizens and businesses. Jennifer Kuperman, Erica Matthews, Liyan Chen, and Megan Tung of Alibaba Group helped me understand the firm's apps and ecosystem with in-person demos and conversation. Jason Montague interrupted his time aboard the *Regent Seven Seas Mariner* to discuss the cruise industry and passenger experience.

Perhaps the most common quote in author acknowledgments is Sir Isaac Newton's from 1608, "If I have seen further it is by standing on the shoulders of Giants." One can't write a book of this type without building on the earlier work of authors, scientists, and leaders. The insights of Daniel Kahneman, Richard Thaler, Robert Cialdini, Dan Ariely, the aforementioned BJ Fogg, and others are the foundation for many of the descriptions of human behavior here.

The process of taking a book from concept to physical reality can be complex. I'm indebted to my literary agent, Eric Lupfer, who helped refine my idea and found a publisher to back it. Cheryl Segura of McGraw-Hill Education, my editor, contributed greatly to the final form of this book. If you enjoyed reading the book, it was probably because of Cheryl's efforts. Amy Li, Mauna Eichner, Lee Fukui, Sharon Honaker, and the rest of the team all helped get it across the finish line. Bobette Gordon was supportive at key moments.

Being an author can be a lonely and frustrating pursuit at times, but the Write and Rant community built by Mitch Joel has been a source of support and practical advice from an amazing and unselfish group of authors. Mitch also gets a shout-out for introducing me to the world of podcasting eight years ago. Luckily, I was in the hands of a pro for my initial, halting "on-air" experience. This was the first of many guest appearances that ultimately led me to eventually start my own podcast.

And, there's no way I could have reached this point without my family. Both my children, Alicia and Brian, have careers in the digital marketing space and have often been sounding boards in discussions of technology, customer experience, and more. My patient and supportive wife, Carol, bears the brunt of my literary toils, more often than not seeing me only as a glowing face on the other side of my computer screen. The ideas in this book will help make people's lives easier, but getting here hasn't yet had that effect on *her* life.

# Notes

## Introduction

1. Bakker, E. (2016, November 15). Shopping Cart Abandonment: Merchants now leave $4.6 trillion on the table, and mobile is making the problem worse. Retrieved August 26, 2018, from http://www.businessinsider.com/shopping-cart-abandonment-merchants-now-leave-46-trillion-on-the-table-and-mobile-is-making-the-problem-worse-2016-11
2. Hamel, G., & Zanini, M. (2016, March). The $3 Trillion Prize for Busting Bureaucracy (and how to claim it). Retrieved August 26, 2018, from http://www.garyhamel.com/sites/default/files/uploads/three-trillion-dollars.pdf
3. World Economic Outlook Database April 2018. (2018, April). Retrieved February 14, 2019, from https://www.imf.org/external/pubs/ft/weo/2018/01/weodata/index.aspx

## Prologue

1. Matthews, R. (2018, April 2). Battle of Alesia. Retrieved August 6, 2018, from https://www.britannica.com/event/Battle-of-Alesia-52-BCE
2. Hickman, K. (2018, July 5). Gallic Wars: Battle of Alesia. Retrieved August 6, 2018, from https://www.thoughtco.com/gallic-wars-battle-of-alesia-2360869
3. Matthews, R. (2018, April 2). Battle of Alesia. Retrieved August 6, 2018, from https://www.britannica.com/event/Battle-of-Alesia-52-BCE
4. Speidel, M. P. (n.d.). Riding for Caesar. Retrieved August 6, 2018, from https://books.google.com/books/about/Riding_for_Caesar.html?id=4X1zUQsY36cC
5. 10 Incredible Roman Military Innovations You Should Know About. (2017, December 5). Retrieved August 6, 2018, from https://www.realmofhistory.com/2016/11/11/10-roman-military-innovations-facts/

## Chapter 1

1. The Kintan Brahmbhatt story comes from our time together when we were speakers at Nir Eyal's Habit Summit, Stanford Faculty Club, March 24, 2015; an additional interview on August 18, 2016; and other correspondence.
2. Judeh, N. (2016, September 22). How Much Does It Cost to Produce Your Favorite TV Show? On Stride Financial. Retrieved August 25, 2018, from https://www.onstride.co.uk/blog/much-cost-produce-favorite-tv-show/

3. Netflix is moving television beyond time-slots and national markets. (2018, June 30). Retrieved February 14, 2019, from https://www.economist.com/briefing/2018/06/30/netflix-is-moving-television-beyond-time-slots-and-national-markets
4. Ibid.
5. Walker, R. (2006, December 17). Ad Play. Retrieved August 7, 2018, from https://www.nytimes.com/2006/12/17/magazine/17wwln_consumed.t.html?_r=0
6. Bakker, E. (2016, November 15). Shopping Cart Abandonment: Merchants now leave $4.6 trillion on the table, and mobile is making the problem worse. Retrieved August 7, 2018, from https://www.businessinsider.com/shopping-cart-abandonment-merchants-now-leave-46-trillion-on-the-table-and-mobile-is-making-the-problem-worse-2016-11
7. Zaroban, S. (2017, July 12). Study: Home Depot and Macy's offer the easiest login, while Staples shines on security features. Retrieved August 7, 2018, from https://www.digitalcommerce360.com/2017/07/12/study-home-depot-and-macys-make-login-easiest-while-staples-shines-on-security-features/
8. Clifford, S. (2010, September 7). Packaging Is All the Rage, and Not in a Good Way. Retrieved November 16, 2018, from https://www.nytimes.com/2010/09/08/technology/08packaging.html
9. Ibid.
10. Bakker, E. (2016, November 15)
11. E-Commerce Checkout Usability. (2018). Retrieved August 26, 2018, from https://baymard.com/checkout-usability
12. Meola, A. (2016, March 16). E-Commerce retailers are losing their customers because of this one critical mistake. Retrieved August 7, 2018, from https://www.businessinsider.com/e-commerce-shoppers-abandon-carts-at-payment-stage-2016-3
13. Meola, A. (2016, March 16)
14. Company Overview—Alibaba. (n.d.). Retrieved February 6, 2019, from https://alibabagroup.com/en/about/overview
15. Alibaba: Mobile MAU 2018 | Statistic. (n.d.). Retrieved February 14, 2019, from https://www.statista.com/statistics/663464/alibaba-cumulative-active-mobile-users-taobao-tmall/
16. Alibaba. (2018, May 23). Here's how Alibaba helps US brands reach a half-billion consumers in China. Retrieved February 14, 2019, from https://qz.com/1269792/heres-how-alibaba-helps-us-brands-reach-a-half-billion-consumers-in-china/
17. Company Overview—Alibaba. (n.d.). Retrieved February 6, 2019, from https://alibabagroup.com/en/about/overview
18. Consumer Engagement Driving Growth for Mobile Taobao. (2016, June 28). Retrieved November 16, 2018, from https://www.alizila.com/consumer-engagement-driving-growth-on-mobile-taobao/
19. "Social Commerce" Blossoms on Mobile Taobao. (2016, July 26). Retrieved November 16, 2018, from https://www.alizila.com/social-commerce-blossoms-on-mobile-taobao/
20. Jacobs, H. (2018, May 21). Alibaba's futuristic supermarket in China is way ahead of the US, with 30-minute deliveries and facial-recognition payment—and it shows where

Amazon is likely to take Whole Foods. Retrieved February 14, 2019, from https://www.businessinsider.com/alibaba-hema-xiansheng-supermarket-whole-foods-amazon-future-2018-5

## Chapter 2

1. Much of the early history of Sears, Montgomery Wards, and the evolution of retail comes from my friend, entrepreneur, and business historian, Gary Hoover (https://www.linkedin.com/pulse/robert-brooker-unsung-warrior-one-greatest-battles-business-hoover/, much more at https://hooversworld.com/).
2. Popomaronis, T. (2016, July 13). Prime Day Gives Amazon Over 600 Reasons Per Second to Celebrate. Retrieved August 26, 2018, from https://www.inc.com/tom-popomaronis/amazon-just-eclipsed-records-selling-over-600-items-per-second.html
3. Kharpal, A. (2018, December 5). Alibaba sets new Singles Day record with more than $30.8 billion in sales in 24 hours. Retrieved February 6, 2019, from https://www.cnbc.com/2018/11/11/alibaba-singles-day-2018-record-sales-on-largest-shopping-event-day.html
4. Pruitt, S. (2018, October 16). An Ode to the Massive Sears Catalog, Which Even Delivered Houses by Mail. Retrieved February 14, 2019, from https://www.history.com/news/sears-catalog-houses-hubcaps
5. Much of the early history of Sears, Montgomery Wards, and the evolution of retail comes from my friend, entrepreneur, and business historian, Gary Hoover (https://www.linkedin.com/pulse/robert-brooker-unsung-warrior-one-greatest-battles-business-hoover/, much more at https://hooversworld.com/).
6. Walmart. (n.d.). Our Business. Retrieved February 14, 2019, from https://corporate.walmart.com/our-story/our-business

## Chapter 3

1. Blystone, D. (2018, July 9). The Story of Uber. Retrieved August 7, 2018, from https://www.investopedia.com/articles/personal-finance/111015/story-uber.asp
2. Dickey, M. R., & Lunden, I. (2018, May 23). Uber's raising up to $600M in a secondary round at $62B valuation, Q1 sales grew to $2.5B. Retrieved August 7, 2018, from https://techcrunch.com/2018/05/23/uber-q1-2018/
3. Michael, T. (2017, October 17). The Knowledge taxi test for black cabbies is renowned for being tough—but why? Retrieved August 26, 2018, from https://www.thesun.co.uk/news/3307245/the-knowledge-taxi-test-london-black-cab-drivers-exam/
4. Crudele, J. (2017, September 18). The challenges of driving a yellow cab in the age of Uber. Retrieved August 26, 2018, from https://nypost.com/2017/09/18/the-challenges-of-driving-a-taxi-in-the-age-of-uber/
5. Hawkins, A. J. (2018, April 19). How Uber is moving the "blue dot" and improving GPS accuracy in big cities. Retrieved August 26, 2018, from https://www.theverge.com/2018/4/19/17252680/uber-gps-blind-spot-shadow-maps
6. How Many Streets in Atlanta Are Named Peachtree? (2018, May 16). Retrieved February 6, 2019, from https://hotspotatl.com/3699042/atlanta-how-many-peachtree-streets/

7. CarMax, Inc. History. (n.d.). Retrieved February 7, 2019, from http://www.funding universe.com/company-histories/carmax-inc-history/
8. Ibid.
9. Ibid.
10. CarMax Celebrates 13 Years as One of FORTUNE Magazine's 100 Best Companies to Work For®. (2017, March 9). Retrieved August 26, 2018, from http://investors.carmax .com/news-releases/news-releases-details/2017/CarMax-Celebrates-13-Years-as -One-of-FORTUNE-Magazines-100-Best-Companies-to-Work-For/default.aspx
11. CarMax—Fortune 500 Listing. (n.d.). Retrieved February 7, 2019, from http://fortune .com/fortune500/2017/carmax/
12. McParland, T. (2018, May 30). Here's Why CarMax Makes More Money on Used Cars Than Anyone Else. Retrieved August 26, 2018, from https://jalopnik.com/heres-why -carmax-makes-more-money-on-used-cars-than-any-1826415410
13. Halberstam, D. (1994). *The Reckoning*. New York: Avon Books.
14. Womack, J. S., Jones, D. T., & Roos, D. (2007). *The Machine That Changed the World*. London: Simon & Schuster, p. 55
15. Fucini, J. J. (2008). *Working for the Japanese*. Riverside, NJ: Free Press,. p. 76
16. Ibid., p. 86
17. 2018 U.S. Initial Quality Study (IQS). (2018, June 19). Retrieved February 14, 2019, from https://www.jdpower.com/business/press-releases/2018-us-initial-quality -study-iqs
18. Car manufacturers by revenue. (n.d.). Retrieved February 14, 2019, from https:// www.statista.com/statistics/232958/revenue-of-the-leading-car-manufacturers -worldwide/

## Chapter 4

1. Google—Parisian Love. (2010, February 27). Retrieved August 8, 2018, from http:// adage.com/videos/google-parisian-love/413
2. Search Engine Market Share Worldwide. (n.d.). Retrieved September 1, 2018, from http://gs.statcounter.com/search-engine-market-share
3. Fishkin, R. (2018, August 1). The Future of SEO Has Never Been Clearer (nor more ignored). Retrieved August 10, 2018, from https://sparktoro.com/blog/the-future-of -seo-has-never-been-clearer-nor-more-ignored/
4. Ibid.
5. Contributor. (2012, April 09). Facebook Buys Instagram for $1 Billion, Turns Budding Rival Into Its Standalone Photo App. Retrieved February 14, 2019, from https://tech crunch.com/2012/04/09/facebook-to-acquire-instagram-for-1-billion/
6. Covert, A. (2014, February 19). Facebook buys WhatsApp for $19 billion. Retrieved February 14, 2019, from https://money.cnn.com/2014/02/19/technology/social /facebook-whatsapp/index.html
7. Eyal, N., & Hoover, R. (2014). *Hooked: How to Build Habit-Forming Products*. San Francisco: N. Eyal.
8. Dooley, R. (2017, July 18). The Power of FREE! Retrieved August 9, 2018, from https://www.neurosciencemarketing.com/blog/articles/the-power-of-free.htm

9. What can new start-ups learn from Evernote's failure? Evernote started as a very promising company with a $1 billion valuation in 2011. What went wrong? (n.d.). Retrieved August 26, 2018, from https://www.quora.com/What-can-new-startups-learn-from-Evernotes-failure-Evernote-started-as-a-very-promising-company-with-a-1-billion-valuation-in-2011-What-went-wrong
10. Kincaid, J. (2010, May 28). Video: Evernote CEO Phil Libin Shares Revenue Stats (And How to Make Freemium Work). Retrieved August 9, 2018, from https://techcrunch.com/2010/05/28/video-evernote-ceo-phil-libin-shares-revenue-stats-and-how-to-make-freemium-work/
11. Evernote: Number of users 2016 | Statistic. (2018). Retrieved August 9, 2018, from https://www.statista.com/statistics/446885/number-of-evernote-users/
12. Orlowski, A. (2018, July 12). Happy 10th birthday, Evernote: You have survived Google and Microsoft. For your next challenge . . . Retrieved August 9, 2018, from https://www.theregister.co.uk/2018/07/12/happy_10th_birthday_evernote/
13. Inside Twitter: An In-Depth Look Inside the Twitter World. (2009, March). Retrieved August 26, 2018, from https://sysomos.com/inside-twitter/
14. Knight, K. (2008, December 9). Brightkit offers twittering solution for marketers. Retrieved August 26, 2018, from http://www.bizreport.com/2008/12/brightkit_offers_twittering_solution_for_marketers.html
15. Olson, D. (2016, August 16). HootSuite Freemium Plans ~ Clarifications about teams, ads, stats & NPOs. Retrieved August 26, 2018, from https://blog.hootsuite.com/freemium-plans-clarifications/
16. HootSuite explains revenue generation strategy. (2010, June 03). Retrieved February 14, 2019, from https://biv.com/article/2010/06/hootsuite-explains-revenue-generation-strategy
17. Hootsuite Media Inc. (2018, September 13). Forbes Names Hootsuite Among "Best and Brightest" Private Cloud Companies in Cloud 100, Retrieved February 14, 2019, from https://hootsuite.com/newsroom/press-releases/forbes-names-hootsuite-among-best-and-brightest-private-cloud-companies-in-cloud-100
18. Taylor, C. (2011, December 20). Buffer gets $400K funding—and tells exactly how they did it. Retrieved February 14, 2019, from https://gigaom.com/2011/12/20/buffer-funding/
19. Eldon, E. (2011, December 20). Sharing Scheduler App Buffer Raises $400,000, Gets Kicked Out of US. Retrieved August 15, 2018, from https://techcrunch.com/2011/12/20/sharing-scheduler-app-buffer-raises-400000-gets-kicked-out-of-us/
20. Widrich, L. (2016, May 31). From 0 to 1,000,000 Users: The Journey and Statistics of Buffer—The Buffer Blog. Retrieved August 26, 2018, from https://blog.bufferapp.com/from-0-to-1000000-users-the-journey-and-statistics-of-buffer
21. Gascoigne, J. (2018, March 12). Why We're Changing the Buffer Free Plan. Retrieved February 14, 2019, from https://open.buffer.com/changing-buffer-free-plan/
22. Connell, A. (2018, May 10). Hootsuite Vs Buffer—The Heavyweight Social Media Showdown. Retrieved August 26, 2018, from https://www.uklinkology.co.uk/hootsuite-vs-buffer-comparison/

23. Ibid.
24. Kopprasch, C. (2016, June 1). The Power of Every Word: Why I Stopped Using "Actually" and "But" in My Customer Service Emails. Retrieved August 26, 2018, from https://open.buffer.com/customer-service-emails-words/
25. Miller, N. (2014, August 4). What Is a Community Champion? Inside the World of Buffer's Community Builder. Retrieved August 26, 2018, from https://open.buffer.com/community-champion/
26. Gascoigne, J. (2018, March 12). Why We're Changing the Buffer Free Plan. Retrieved February 14, 2019, from https://open.buffer.com/changing-buffer-free-plan/
27. Gartner acquires L2. (2016, March 6). Retrieved August 26, 2018, from https://www.crunchbase.com/acquisition/gartner-acquires-l2-inc--c8959034
28. Hansell, S. (2004, August 2). A Founder at RedEnvelope Tries to Take Back Control. Retrieved August 26, 2018, from https://www.nytimes.com/2004/08/02/business/a-founder-at-redenvelope-tries-to-take-back-control.html
29. Carter, A. (2014, February 19). World's Best B-School Professors: Scott Galloway. Retrieved February 14, 2019, from https://poetsandquants.com/2012/10/22/worlds-best-b-school-professors-scott-galloway/?pq-category=best-profs
30. Scott Galloway. (n.d.). Retrieved February 14, 2019, from https://www.penguin.co.uk/authors/1079576/scott-galloway.html?tab=penguin-biography
31. Galloway, S. (2017). *The Four: The Hidden DNA of Amazon, Apple, Facebook and Google.* New York: Random House.
32. Ibid., p. 187


## Chapter 5


1. Warsh, D. (2010). *Economic Principles: The Masters and Mavericks of Modern Economics.* Riverside, NJ: Free Press, p. 110
2. Fisman, R., & Sullivan, T. (2015). *The Org: The Underlying Logic of the Office.* Princeton: Princeton University Press, pp. 28–30
3. Citations for The Problem of Social Cost. (n.d.). Retrieved February 14, 2019, from https://scholar.google.com/scholar?cites=10739117159072125396&as_sdt=5,44&sciodt=0,44&hl=en
4. Most of the biographical information for Ronald Coase comes from his self-written biography that accompanied his Nobel Prize: Coase, R. H. (1991). Ronald H. Coase Biographical. Retrieved February 14, 2019, from https://www.nobelprize.org/prizes/economic-sciences/1991/coase/biographical/
5. Press Release. (1991, October 15). Retrieved July 30, 2018, from https://www.nobelprize.org/nobel_prizes/economic-sciences/laureates/1991/press.html
6. New Journal Launched. (n.d.). Retrieved February 14, 2019, from https://www.coase.org/otherevents.htm
7. Epstein, R. (2013, September 3). Ronald Coase: One of a Kind. Retrieved July 30, 2018, from https://ricochet.com/archives/ronald-coase-one-of-a-kind/
8. Warsh, D. (2010). *Economic Principles: The Masters and Mavericks of Modern Economics.* Riverside, NJ: Free Press, p. 110

9. Kahneman, D. (1990, December 1). Experimental Tests of the Endowment Effect and the Coase Theorem. Retrieved July 30, 2018, from https://www.jstor.org/stable/2937761
10. The Sveriges Riksbank Prize in Economic Sciences in Memory of Alfred Nobel. (2009). Nobel Media AB 2014. Retrieved June 10, 2018 from http://www.nobelprize.org/nobel_prizes/economic-sciences/laureates/2009/
11. Oliver E. Williamson—Prize Lecture. (2009, December 8). Retrieved July 30, 2018, from https://www.nobelprize.org/nobel_prizes/economic-sciences/laureates/2009/williamson-lecture.html
12. Grossman, R. (2017, May 15). Sears was the Amazon.com of the 20th century. Retrieved February 14, 2019, from https://www.chicagotribune.com/news/opinion/commentary/ct-sears-roebuck-homan-catalog-flashback-perspec-0514-jm-20170512-story.html
13. Why is there unemployment when jobs are available? (n.d.). Retrieved July 19, 2018, from https://www.ubs.com/microsites/together/en/nobel-perspectives/laureates/christopher-pissarides.html
14. Most of the biographical information for Christopher Pissarides comes from his Nobel biography: Christopher A. Pissarides Biographical. (2010). Retrieved February 14, 2019, from https://www.nobelprize.org/prizes/economic-sciences/2010/pissarides/biographical/, and a UBS Nobel profile, Why is there unemployment when jobs are available? (n.d.). Retrieved February 14, 2019, from https://www.ubs.com/microsites/nobel-perspectives/en/laureates/christopher-pissarides.html
15. Tim Harford on Christopher Pissarides. (2018, September 13). Retrieved February 14, 2019, from https://vimeo.com/151362446
16. Saeedi, T. A. (2017, December 12). Indeed to turn partly subscription-based in 2018. Retrieved July 19, 2018, from https://aimgroup.com/2017/12/12/indeed-turn-partly-subscription-based-2018/
17. The Bad News About the News. (2014, October 16). Retrieved July 19, 2018, from http://www.brookings.edu/research/essays/2014/bad-news#
18. Thaler, R. H. (2013, April 6). An Automatic Solution for the Retirement Savings Problem. Retrieved August 19, 2018, from https://www.nytimes.com/2013/04/07/business/an-automatic-solution-for-the-retirement-savings-problem.html
19. Resistance (n.). (n.d.). Retrieved July 24, 2018, from https://www.etymonline.com/word/resistance
20. Ferrero, G. (1894). L'INERTIE MENTALE ET LA LOI DU MOINDRE EFFORT. Revue Philosophique De La France Et De L'Étranger, 37, 169-182. Retrieved February 21, 2019, from http://www.jstor.org/stable/41075913
21. W. R. Boyce Gibson. (1900). The Principle of Least Action as a Psychological Principle. Mind, 9(36), new series, 469-495. Retrieved February 21, 2019, from http://www.jstor.org/stable/2247876
22. Zipf, G. K. (1949). *Human Behavior and the Principle of Least Effort: An Introduction to Human Ecology*. Cambridge, MA: Addison-Wesley Press.
23. Parsimony. (n.d.). Retrieved July 25, 2018, from https://www.merriam-webster.com/dictionary/parsimony

24. Kahneman, D. (2011). Thinking, Fast and Slow. United States of America: Farrar, Straus and Giroux, p. 35
25. Chopra, D. (2009). The Seven Spiritual Laws of Success: A Practical Guide to the Fulfillment of Your Dreams. London: Bantam.
26. Ibid.

### Chapter 6

1. Schwartz, B. (2006, June). More Isn't Always Better. Retrieved February 15, 2019, from https://hbr.org/2006/06/more-isnt-always-better
2. Kim, J., Novemsky, N., & Dhar, R. (2013). Adding Small Differences Can Increase Similarity and Choice. Psychological Science, 24(2), 225–229. https://doi.org/10.1177/0956797612457388
3. Vohs, K. D. (n.d.). Decision Fatigue Exhausts Self-Regulatory Resources. Retrieved August 26, 2018, from https://www.psychologytoday.com/files/attachments/584/decision200602-15vohs.pdf
4. Ibid.
5. Ibid.
6. Johnson, E. J., & Goldstein, D. (n.d.). Do Defaults Save Lives? Retrieved August 26, 2018, from http://www.dangoldstein.com/papers/DefaultsScience.pdf
7. Ibid.
8. Denmark lagging behind in organ donation. (2015, December 1). Retrieved November 16, 2018, from http://cphpost.dk/news/denmark-lagging-behind-in-organ-donation.html
9. Johnson, E. J., & Goldstein, D. (n.d.). Do Defaults Save Lives? Retrieved August 26, 2018, from http://www.dangoldstein.com/papers/DefaultsScience.pdf
10. Danziger, S., Levav, J., & Avnaim-Pesso, L. (2011, April 26). Extraneous factors in judicial decisions. Retrieved August 26, 2018, from https://www.ncbi.nlm.nih.gov/pmc/articles/PMC3084045/

### Chapter 7

1. Zdanowicz, C., & Grinberg, E. (2018, April 10). Passenger dragged off overbooked United flight. Retrieved February 8, 2019, from https://www.cnn.com/2017/04/10/travel/passenger-removed-united-flight-trnd/index.html
1. Powers, M. (2018, March 13). United flight attendant made a woman put her puppy in an overhead bin. He died. Retrieved February 8, 2019, from https://www.washingtonpost.com/news/dr-gridlock/wp/2018/03/13/united-flight-attendant-made-a-woman-put-her-puppy-in-an-overhead-bin-he-died/
3. Hanselman, A. (2012, May 18). Joshie The Giraffe—A Remarkable Story About Customer Delight! Retrieved July 28, 2018, from http://customerthink.com/joshie_the_giraffe_a_remarkable_story_about_customer_delight/
4. Dixon, M., Toman, N., & DeLisi, R. (2013). *The Effortless Experience: Conquering the New Battleground for Customer Loyalty*. London: Portfolio Penguin. p. 29
5. Bryan, J. (2018, July 12). What's Your Customer Effort Score? Retrieved February 5, 2019, from https://www.gartner.com/smarterwithgartner/unveiling-the-new-and-improved-customer-effort-score/

6. Ibid.
7. Here's Everything You Need to Know About Effortless Experience. (2018, April 2). Retrieved July 28, 2018, from https://www.cebglobal.com/blogs/heres-everything-you-need-to-know-about-effortless-experience/
8. Dixon, M., Toman, N., & DeLisi, R. (2013). *The Effortless Experience: Conquering the New Battleground for Customer Loyalty.* London: Portfolio Penguin. p. 153
9. Ibid., p. 54
10. Ibid., p. 24
11. Toman, N., Adamson, B., & Gomez, C. (2017, September 19). The New B2B Sales Imperative. Retrieved July 28, 2018, from https://hbr.org/2017/03/the-new-sales-imperative
12. Schwartz, B. (2009). *The Paradox of Choice: Why More Is Less,* Revised Edition. New York: HarperCollins.
13. Toman, N., Adamson, B., & Gomez, C. (2017, September 19). The New B2B Sales Imperative. Retrieved July 28, 2018, from https://hbr.org/2017/03/the-new-sales-imperative
14. Krasniewicz, L., & Blitz, M. (2010). *Walt Disney: A Biography.* Westport, CT: Greenwood Publishing Group, p. 130.
15. Mumpower, D. (2016, March 16). Disney's Ongoing Struggle to Eliminate Theme Park Queues. Retrieved February 5, 2019, from https://www.themeparktourist.com/features/20150725/30433/amazing-history-fastpass
16. Carr, A. (2017, December 2). The Messy Business of Reinventing Happiness. Retrieved August 26, 2018, from https://www.fastcompany.com/3044283/the-messy-business-of-reinventing-happiness
17. Ibid.
18. Ibid.
19. Interview, John Padgett & Roger Dooley, June 26, 2018
20. Carr, A. (2017, December 2). The Messy Business of Reinventing Happiness. Retrieved August 26, 2018, from https://www.fastcompany.com/3044283/the-messy-business-of-reinventing-happiness
21. Interview, John Padgett & Roger Dooley, June 26, 2018
22. Carr, A. (2017, December 2). The Messy Business of Reinventing Happiness. Retrieved August 26, 2018, from https://www.fastcompany.com/3044283/the-messy-business-of-reinventing-happiness
23. Schaal, D. (2013, August 24). Disney's $1 Billion Wristband Project Is Most Expensive in Theme Park History. Retrieved August 26, 2018, from https://skift.com/2013/08/18/disneys-1-billion-wristband-project-is-most-expensive-in-theme-park-history/
24. Nawijn, J., Marchand, M. A., & Veenhoven, R. (2010, February 10). Vacationers Happier, but Most Not Happier After a Holiday. Retrieved July 20, 2018, from https://link.springer.com/article/10.1007/s11482-009-9091-9
25. Carr, A. (2017, December 2). The Messy Business of Reinventing Happiness. Retrieved August 26, 2018, from https://www.fastcompany.com/3044283/the-messy-business-of-reinventing-happiness

26. Maeda, J. (2006). *The Laws of Simplicity: Design, Technology, Business, Life.* Cambridge, MA: MIT Press.
27. Market Share. (2018). Retrieved August 26, 2018, from https://www.cruisemarket watch.com/market-share/
28. Nawijn, J., De Bloom, J., & Geurts, S. (2013). "Pre-vacation time: Blessing or burden?" *Leisure Sciences*, 35(1): 33-44
29. Dooley, R. (2018, February 1). Why Sushi Pricing Is Painful, and How to Fix It. Retrieved July 20, 2018, from https://www.neurosciencemarketing.com/blog/articles /sushi-pricing.htm
30. Interview, Jason Montague & Roger Dooley, April 4, 2018
31. Ibid.
32. Interview, John Padgett & Roger Dooley, June 26, 2018 (A podcast based on this conversation can be found here: https://www.rogerdooley.com/john-padgett-carnival)
33. Ibid.
34. Ibid.
35. Ibid.
36. Ibid.
37. Ibid.
38. Maeda, J. (2006). *The Laws of Simplicity*. Cambridge, MA: MIT Press.
39. Maeda, J. (2007, March). Designing for simplicity. Retrieved February 8, 2019, from https://www.ted.com/talks/john_maeda_on_the_simple_life
40. Ibid.
41. Maeda, J. (2006). *The Laws of Simplicity.* Cambridge, MA: MIT Press.
42. Crook, J. (2011, October 4). Apple Has Sold 300 Million iPods In Ten Years, 45 Million Just Last Year. Retrieved August 26, 2018, from https://techcrunch.com/2011 /10/04/apple-has-sold-300-million-ipods-in-ten-years-45-million-just-last-year/

## Chapter 8

1. The Editors. (2011, October 14). To Indian Students, Harvard's Admission Rate May Appear Almost Welcoming. Retrieved February 9, 2019, from https://thechoice.blogs. nytimes.com/2011/10/14/indian-admissions/
2. Inside. (2012, June 24). Retrieved February 9, 2019, from https://www.pressreader. com/usa/the-commercial-appeal/20120624/281505043304123
3. Interview, Rammohan Malasani, August 19, 2016 (Recounting details used throughout this chapter on the origin and strategy of Securifi)
4. Olson, P. (2014, April 23). Exclusive: The Rags-To-Riches Tale of How Jan Koum Built WhatsApp Into Facebook's New $19 Billion Baby. Retrieved August 13, 2018, from https://www.forbes.com/sites/parmyolson/2014/02/19/exclusive-inside-story -how-jan-koum-built-whatsapp-into-facebooks-new-19-billion-baby/
5. WhatsApp: Number of users 2013-2017. (n.d.). Retrieved February 9, 2019, from https:// www.statista.com/statistics/260819/number-of-monthly-active-whatsapp-users/
6. Hulick, S. (n.d.). How WhatsApp Onboards New Users|/User Onboarding. Retrieved August 13, 2018, from https://www.useronboard.com/how-whatsapp-onboards-new -users/

## Chapter 9

1. Monahan, T. (2016, January 28). The Hard Evidence: Business Is Slowing Down. Retrieved August 26, 2018, from http://fortune.com/2016/01/28/business-decision-making-project-management/
2. Ibid.
3. Ibid.
4. Dickens, C. (1869). *David Copperfield.* New York: Hurd and Houghton, p. 276
5. Mankins, M. (2018, June 7). Reduce Organizational Drag. Retrieved August 26, 2018, from https://hbr.org/ideacast/2017/03/globalization-myth-and-reality-2.html
6. Kraines, G. (1996). Organization: Hierarchy's Bad Rap. *Journal of Business Strategy.* 17. 13-15. 10.1108/eb039789.
7. Parkinson, C. N., & Lancaster, O. (1957). *Parkinson's Law or the Pursuit of Progress.* London: John Murray Publishes, p. 2
8. Ibid.
9. Ibid. p. 7
10. This and much of the subsequent discussion is based on an interview with Tom Peters on June 7, 2019. A portion of that conversation can be found here: Dooley, R. (2018, June 21). Tom Peters's Excellent Way to Survive the AI-pocalypse. Retrieved February 9, 2019, from https://www.rogerdooley.com/tom-peters-excellence-dividend
11. Kleiner, A. (2001, April 1). *Strategy+Business,* https://www.strategy-business.com/article/17079
12. Fast Company Staff. (2012, July 30). Still Angry After All These Years. Retrieved August 26, 2018, from https://www.fastcompany.com/47166/still-angry-after-all-these-years
13. Peters, T. (2007, July 24). Liberation! The Situation Is Hopeless! Hooray! Blog post retrieved August 26, 2018, from http://tompeters.com/2007/07/liberationthe-situation-is-hopelesshooray/
14. Ibid.
15. Ibid.
16. Ibid.
17. Peters, T. (n.d.). Add Zest to Bureaucracy Bashing. Retrieved August 26, 2018, from http://tompeters.com/columns/add-zest-to-bureaucracy-bashing/
18. Ibid.
19. Smith, H. (2013). *Who Stole the American Dream?* New York: Random House Trade Paperbacks. P. 58
20. Colvin, G. (1999, November 22). Manager of the Century. Retrieved February 9, 2019, from http://archive.fortune.com/magazines/fortune/fortune_archive/1999/11/22/269126/index.htm
21. Thompson, M. C. (2011, December 14). Blowing Up The Factory. Retrieved August 26, 2018, from https://www.youtube.com/watch?v=YImfo7t8Wec
22. Slater, R. (1999). *Jack Welch and the GE Way.* New York: McGraw Hill 1999, p. 114
23. Lueck, T. J. (1985, May 5). Why Jack Welch Is Changing G.E. Retrieved August 26, 2018, from https://www.nytimes.com/1985/05/05/business/why-jack-welch-is-changing-ge.html

24. Byrne, J. A., Welch, J. (2003). *Jack: Straight from the Gut*. New York: Grand Central Publishing.
25. What Welch has Wrought at GE. (1986, July 7). Retrieved August 26, 2018, from http://archive.fortune.com/magazines/fortune/fortune_archive/1986/07/07/67821/index.htm
26. Lowe, J. (2008). *Jack Welch Speaks—Wit and Wisdom from the World's Greatest Business Leader.* Hoboken, NJ: Wiley.
27. Jack Welch, Speech, GE Annual Meeting, Waukesha, WI, April 2, 1988
28. Jack Welch, Speech, GE Annual Meeting, Decatur, AL, April 24, 1991
29. Slater, R. (1999). *Jack Welch and the GE Way*. New York: McGraw Hill 1999, p. 159
30. Ibid., p. 160
31. Jack Welch: 'I Fell In Love.' (n.d.). Retrieved August 26, 2018, from https://www.cbsnews.com/news/jack-welch-i-fell-in-love/
32. Lowe, J., p. 104
33. Colvin, G. (2018, May 24). What the Hell Happened at General Electric? Retrieved August 26, 2018, from http://fortune.com/longform/ge-decline-what-the-hell-happened/
34. The anecdotes used throughout this chapter are based on Michael Abrashoff's own words, as found in his inspiring 2012 book: *It's Your Ship: Management Techniques from the Best Damn Ship in the Navy.* New York: Business Plus.
35. Abrashoff, M. (2012). *It's Your Ship: Management Techniques from the Best Damn Ship in the Navy.* New York: Business Plus.
36. Ibid.
37. Suits, D. (2017). Oh, the meetings you'll go to!: A parody. New York: Portfolio/Penguin.
38. Perlow, L. A., Hadley, C. N., & Eun, E. (2017, June 26). Stop the Meeting Madness. Retrieved August 26, 2018, from https://hbr.org/2017/07/stop-the-meeting-madness
39. Harter, J. (n.d.). Dismal Employee Engagement Is a Sign of Global Mismanagement. Retrieved February 9, 2019, from https://www.gallup.com/workplace/231668/dismal-employee-engagement-sign-global-mismanagement.aspx
40. Zetlin, M. (2016, January 20). It's Official: Half Your Meetings Are a Waste of Time? Retrieved February 9, 2019, from https://www.inc.com/minda-zetlin/its-official-half-your-meetings-are-a-waste-of-time-.html
41. Udemy. (2018, March 20). Majority of U.S. Workers Feel Distracted at Work. Retrieved February 9, 2019, from https://www.prnewswire.com/news-releases/majority-of-us-workers-feel-distracted-at-work-blame-technology-and-lack-of-training-for-lower-morale-and-productivity-udemy-report-finds-300616305.html
42. Mankins, M. (2014, November 2). This Weekly Meeting Took Up 300,000 Hours a Year. Retrieved August 26, 2018, from https://hbr.org/2014/04/how-a-weekly-meeting-took-up-300000-hours-a-year
43. Saunders, E. G. (2017, December 6). Do You Really Need to Hold That Meeting? Retrieved August 26, 2018, from https://hbr.org/2015/03/do-you-really-need-to-hold-that-meeting

44. Titlow, J. P. (2010, October 26). Survey: Businesses Waste 4.8 Hours Per Week Scheduling Meetings. Retrieved August 26, 2018, from https://readwrite.com/2010/10/26/businesses-waste-time-scheduling-meetings/
45. Mankins, M. (2017, October 25). Is Technology Really Helping Us Get More Done? Retrieved August 26, 2018, from https://hbr.org/2016/02/is-technology-really-helping-us-get-more-done
46. Morieux, Y. (2015, July). Transcript of "How too many rules at work keep you from getting things done". Retrieved July 22, 2018, from https://www.ted.com/talks/yves_morieux_how_too_many_rules_at_work_keep_you_from_getting_things_done/transcript
47. Moskovitz, D. (2017, March 06). No Meeting Wednesdays at Asana. Retrieved August 26, 2018, from https://blog.asana.com/2013/02/no-meeting-wednesdays/
48. Kruse, K. (2016, May 10). Why This Company Only Holds Meetings on Mondays. Retrieved August 26, 2018, from https://www.forbes.com/sites/kevinkruse/2016/05/09/why-this-company-only-holds-meetings-on-mondays/
49. Peters, T. (2011, September 18). Models of Extremism: Tom Peters on Excellence. Retrieved August 26, 2018, from https://www.independent.co.uk/news/business/models-of-extremism-tom-peters-on-excellence-1376407.html
50. Mankins, M. (2018, August 14). Is Technology Really Helping Us Get More Done? Retrieved February 12, 2019, from https://www.bain.com/insights/is-technology-really-helping-us-get-more-done-hbr/
51. Ferrari: Less e-mail and more dialogue between co-workers. (2014, January 13). Retrieved August 26, 2018, from https://auto.ferrari.com/en_EN/news-events/news/ferrari-less-e-mail-and-more-dialogue-between-co-workers/
52. Plunkett, J. (2013, January 17). BBC urges staff to 'give red tape the red card' as part of simplicity campaign. Retrieved August 26, 2018, from https://www.theguardian.com/media/2013/jan/17/bbc-give-red-tape-red-card
53. Wells, M. (2002, February 08). Dyke rallies BBC with cut the crap yellow card. Retrieved August 26, 2018, from https://www.theguardian.com/media/2002/feb/08/broadcasting.bbc
54. Gibson, O. (2002, February 8). BBC divided over Dyke's yellow card. Retrieved August 26, 2018, from https://www.theguardian.com/media/2002/feb/08/broadcasting.bbc2
55. UK | Politics | BBC apologises as Dyke quits. (2004, January 29). Retrieved August 26, 2018, from http://news.bbc.co.uk/2/hi/uk_news/politics/3441181.stm
56. Plunkett, J. (2013, January 17). BBC urges staff to 'give red tape the red card' as part of simplicity campaign. Retrieved February 9, 2019, from https://www.theguardian.com/media/2013/jan/17/bbc-give-red-tape-red-card
57. BBC Annual Report and Accounts 2016/17. (n.d.). Retrieved August 26, 2018, from http://downloads.bbc.co.uk/aboutthebbc/insidethebbc/reports/pdf/bbc-annual report-201617.pdf
58. Ibid.
59. Bodell, L. (2016). Why Simple Wins: Escape the Complexity Trap and Get to Work That Matters, Kindle Edition. United Kingdom: Taylor and Francis, p. 125
60. Ibid.

## Chapter 10

1. Esther Jacobs's story draws from her website, https://estherjacobs.info/, an interview on July 24, 2016, and e-mail correspondence. Much of our 2016 conversation appears here: Dooley, R. (2016, August 03). Ep #122: Could You Become a Digital Nomad? With Esther Jacobs. Retrieved February 10, 2019, from https://www.rogerdooley.com/ep-122-become-digital-nomad-esther-jacobs
2. Jacobs, E. (n.d.). Coins for Care. Retrieved February 10, 2019, from https://estherjacobs.info/en/coins-for-care/
3. Ibid.
4. Ajay Prasad's story is based on an interview conducted on August 16, 2016, and subsequent e-mail correspondence.
5. Decades later, Ajay Prasad told me that he finally achieved his personal goal of creating jobs in Patna. He opened a digital marketing office there which, by the end of 2018, employed 80 people.
6. Crabtree, J. (2016, March 21). India's red tape causes trouble for exporting cats. Retrieved August 26, 2018, from https://www.ft.com/content/d38489fa-ecf4-11e5-888e-2eadd5fbc4a4
7. James Crabtree and I discussed the cat incident he wrote about and other aspects of India's bureaucracy in a December 12, 2018 interview and subsequent e-mail correspondence.
8. Crabtree, J. (2016, March 21). India's red tape causes trouble for exporting cats. Retrieved July 11, 2018, from https://www.ft.com/content/d38489fa-ecf4-11e5-888e-2eadd5fbc4a4
9. Hirst, T. (2015, July 30). A brief history of China's economic growth. Retrieved August 14, 2018, from https://www.weforum.org/agenda/2015/07/brief-history-of-china-economic-growth/
10. Doing Business in 2004. (n.d.). Retrieved August 14, 2018, from http://www.doingbusiness.org/~/media/WBG/DoingBusiness/Documents/Annual-Reports/English/DB04-FullReport.pdf
11. India has a hole where its middle class should be. (2018, January 13). Retrieved February 10, 2019, from https://www.economist.com/leaders/2018/01/13/india-has-a-hole-where-its-middle-class-should-be
12. Ibid.
13. Ease of Doing Business in China | 2008-2018. (n.d.). Retrieved August 14, 2018, from https://tradingeconomics.com/china/ease-of-doing-business
14. Ibid.
15. Doing Business in 2018. (n.d.). Retrieved August 14, 2018, from https://openknowledge.worldbank.org/bitstream/handle/10986/28608/9781464811463.pdf?sequence=6&isAllowed=y

## Chapter 11

1. Carrington, D. (2016, October 11). In Yinchuan, China, your face is your credit card. Retrieved February 10, 2019, from https://www.cnn.com/2016/10/10/asia/yinchuan-smart-city-future/index.html

2. The Yinchuan story is based on a visit to the city, its city hall and other technology infrastructure, and an in-person interview with Vice Mayor Guo Baichun, September 19–21, 2017.
3. Indiana Code Title 7.1. Alcohol and Tobacco § 7.1-3-10-5. (n.d.). Retrieved August 22, 2018, from http://codes.findlaw.com/in/title-7-1-alcohol-and-tobacco/in-code-sect-7-1-3-10-5.html
4. §20-2-5. Unlawful methods of hunting and fishing and other unlawful acts. (n.d.). Retrieved March 13, 2019, from http://www.wvlegislature.gov/legisdocs/code/20/WVC%2020%20%20-%20%202%20%20-%20%20%205%20%20.htm
5. Statistics and Historical Comparison. (n.d.). Retrieved August 22, 2018, from https://www.govtrack.us/congress/bills/statistics
6. Grossman, A. L. (2014, April 14). How Long Is the Tax Code? Don't Ask the *New York Times*. Retrieved August 22, 2018, from http://www.slate.com/articles/news_and_politics/politics/2014/04/how_long_is_the_tax_code_it_is_far_shorter_than_70_000_pages.html
7. Schechter-Steinberg, Z. (2016, July). Red Tape Commission: 60 Ways to Cut Red Tape and Help Small Businesses. Retrieved August 26, 2018, from https://comptroller.nyc.gov/wp-content/uploads/2016/07/RedTapeReport.pdf
8. Ibid.
9. de Jong, J. (2016). *Dealing with Dysfunction: Innovative Problem Solving in the Public Sector.* Washington, DC: Brookings Institution Press, p. 197
10. Arre Zuurmond's story is based primarily on an interview conducted on September 28, 2016
11. Martin. (2018, May 02). The Management Theory of Max Weber. Retrieved February 11, 2019, from https://www.cleverism.com/management-theory-of-max-weber/
12. Interview, Arre Zuurmond and Roger Dooley, September 28, 2016
13. Ibid.
14. de Jong, J. (2016). *Dealing with Dysfunction: Innovative Problem Solving in the Public Sector.* Washington, DC: Brookings Institution Press, p. 226
15. Interview, Arre Zuurmond and Roger Dooley, September 28, 2016
16. Bloomberg Philanthropies and Harvard University Launch Bloomberg Harvard City Leadership Initiative. (2016, August 26). Retrieved February 12, 2019, from https://ash.harvard.edu/news/bloomberg-philanthropies-and-harvard-university-launch-bloomberg-harvard-city-leadership
17. de Jong, J. (2016). *Dealing with Dysfunction: Innovative Problem Solving in the Public Sector.* Washington DC: Brookings Institution Press.
18. Interview, Arre Zuurmond & Roger Dooley, September 28, 2016
19. Doing Business in 2018. (n.d.). Retrieved August 14, 2018, from https://openknowledge.worldbank.org/bitstream/handle/10986/28608/9781464811463.pdf?sequence=6&isAllowed=y
20. Ibid.
21. Lopez Claros, A. (2014, November 5). Doing Business 2015—Going Beyond Efficiency. Retrieved February 12, 2019, from http://www.worldbank.org/content/dam/Worldbank/document/WEurope/events/2014/Doing-Business-2015-WTO-Geneva-November-5-presentation.pdf

## Chapter 12

1. Cooper, M. (2002, July 01). Cigarettes Up To $7 a Pack with New Tax. Retrieved February 12, 2019, from https://www.nytimes.com/2002/07/01/nyregion/cigarettes-up-to-7-a-pack-with-new-tax.html
2. Curbing the Epidemic: Governments and the Economics of Tobacco Control. (1999, May). Retrieved August 15, 2018, from http://www.cghr.org/wordpress/wp-content/uploads/Curbing-the-Epidemic-Tobacco-Control-World-Bank-1999-Prabhat-Jha.pdf
3. Raising the Excise Tax on Cigarettes: Effects on Health and the Federal Budget(Rep.). (2012, June). Retrieved February 12, 2019, from http://www.cbo.gov/sites/default/files/cbofiles/attachments/06-13-Smoking_Reduction.pdf
4. Ibid.
5. Effects of Gasoline Prices on Driving Behavior and Vehicle Markets. (2008, January). Retrieved August 15, 2018, from https://www.cbo.gov/sites/default/files/110th-congress-2007-2008/reports/01-14-gasolineprices.pdf
6. Ibid.
7. Cautero, R. M. (2019, February 7). What is the Federal Gasoline Excise Tax Rate? Retrieved February 12, 2019, from https://www.thebalance.com/what-is-the-federal-gasoline-excise-tax-rate-4585178
8. Pomerleau, K. (2017, January 16). How High Are Other Nations' Gas Taxes? Retrieved August 15, 2018, from https://taxfoundation.org/how-high-are-other-nations-gas-taxes
9. Gas prices around the world 2018. (2018, April). Retrieved February 12, 2019, from https://www.statista.com/statistics/221368/gas-prices-around-the-world/
10. Drivers' Annual Mileage Rates Drop to New Low. (2014, July 29). Retrieved August 15, 2018, from https://www.bbc.com/news/uk-england-28546589
11. Average Annual Miles per Driver by Age Group. (2018, March 29). Retrieved August 15, 2018, from https://www.fhwa.dot.gov/ohim/onh00/bar8.htm
12. FAQs about road transport and the environment. (n.d.). Retrieved February 12, 2019, from https://www.racfoundation.org/motoring-faqs/environment
13. Shepardson, D. (2018, January 11). U.S. vehicle fuel economy rises to record 24.7 mpg: EPA. Retrieved February 12, 2019, from https://www.reuters.com/article/us-autos-emissions/u-s-vehicle-fuel-economy-rises-to-record-24-7-mpg-epa-idUSKBN1F02BX
14. The Most Unique Job in Each State, in One Map. (2015, March 2). Retrieved August 15, 2018, from http://www.pewtrusts.org/en/research-and-analysis/blogs/stateline/2015/3/02/the-most-unique-job-in-each-state-in-one-map
15. Staff, M. (2012, April 26). Residents cost Washington millions buying sales-tax-free Oregon, online products. Retrieved February 12, 2019, from http://mynorthwest.com/35849/residents-cost-washington-millions-buying-sales-tax-free-oregon-online-products/
16. Townsend, M., & Meisler, L. (2017, November 2). These Are the Biggest Overseas Cash Hoards Congress Wants to Tax. Retrieved February 12, 2019, from https://www.bloomberg.com/graphics/2017-overseas-profits-tax/

17. Malm, L., & Scarboro, M. (2017, December 7). Map: State and Local General Sales Tax Collections Per Capita. Retrieved August 15, 2018, from https://taxfoundation.org/map-state-and-local-general-sales-tax-collections-capita
18. Greenberg, S. (2017, January 24). Federal Tax Laws and Regulations Are Now Over 10 Million Words Long. Retrieved August 15, 2018, from https://taxfoundation.org/federal-tax-laws-and-regulations-are-now-over-10-million-words-long
19. Sepp, P., & Brady, D. (2016, April 18). Tax Code Burden on Taxpayers Continues to Mount in Foundation Findings. Retrieved February 12, 2019, from https://www.ntu.org/foundation/detail/tax-code-burden-on-taxpayers-continues-to-mount-in-foundation-findings
20. Brady, D. (2016, April 6). Tax Complexity 2016: The Increasing Compliance Burdens of the Tax Code. Retrieved August 15, 2018, from https://www.ntu.org/foundation/detail/tax-complexity-2016-the-increasing-compliance-burdens-of-the-tax-code
21. Saxenian, A. (1996). *Regional Advantage: Culture and Competition in Silicon Valley and Route 128.* Cambridge, MA: Harvard University Press.
22. Ibid., p. 30
23. Ibid., p. 41
24. Guide to the Digital Equipment Corporation records. (n.d.). Retrieved February 12, 2019, from https://oac.cdlib.org/findaid/ark:/13030/c8t72p80/entire_text/
25. The RX50 FAQ. (n.d.). Retrieved July 20, 2018, from http://users.bart.nl/users/pb0aia/vax/rx50.html
26. Saxenian, A. (1996). *Regional Advantage: Culture and Competition in Silicon Valley and Route 128.* Cambridge, MA: Harvard University Press.
27. Explaining Silicon Valley's Success. (2018, June 7). Retrieved July 21, 2018, from https://hbr.org/ideacast/2014/12/explaining-silicon-valleys-success.html

## Chapter 13

1. Leslie, I. (2016, October 20). The scientists who make apps addictive. Retrieved February 13, 2019, from https://www.1843magazine.com/features/the-scientists-who-make-apps-addictive
2. Private e-mail communication with BJ Fogg, December 12, 2018
3. Fogg, BJ, Cypher, A., Druin, A., Friedman, B., & Strommen, E. (1999). Is ActiMates Barney ethical?: the potential good, bad, and ugly of interactive plush toys. In CHI '99 Extended Abstracts on Human Factors in Computing Systems (CHI EA '99), New York: ACM, pp. 91–92. DOI: https://doi.org/10.1145/632716.632772
4. Communications of the ACM. (1999, May 1). Retrieved December 11, 2018, from https://cacm.acm.org/magazines/1999/5
5. Fogg, BJ. (2015, January 21). Persuasion & Technology. Retrieved December 11, 2018, from https://vimeo.com/117427520
6. Private e-mail communication with BJ Fogg, December 12, 2018
7. Helft, M. (2011, May 07). The "Facebook Class" Built Apps, and Fortunes. Retrieved August 23, 2018, from https://www.nytimes.com/2011/05/08/technology/08class.html
8. Ibid.

9. Fogg, B. (n.d.). BJ Fogg's Behavior Model. Retrieved February 13, 2019, from https://www.behaviormodel.org/
10. Private e-mail communication with BJ Fogg, December 12, 2018
11. Fogg, B. (n.d.). BJ Fogg | Tiny Habits. Retrieved February 13, 2019, from https://www.tinyhabits.com/
12. Ibid.
13. Fogg, BJ. (2012, October 27). Tweet: My Tiny Habit. Retrieved July 22, 2018, from https://twitter.com/bjfogg/status/262244976694546432
14. Fogg, BJ. (n.d.). Tiny Habits. Retrieved July 22, 2018, from https://www.tinyhabits.com/welcome
15. Why Do We Love Kitten Videos? Have Trouble Spotting a Liar? Co-Author of "Brain Briefs" Explains It All | Dr. Phil. (2016, December 19). Retrieved July 23, 2018, from https://www.drphil.com/videos/why-do-we-love-kitten-videos-have-trouble-spotting-a-liar-author-of-brain-briefs-explains-it-all/
16. Dooley, R. (2014, September 3). Smart Thinking, Smart Change with Art Markman. Retrieved July 23, 2018, from http://www.rogerdooley.com/ep-21-smart-thinking-smart-change-art-markman
17. Olsen, H. B. (2015, January 08). 3 Goal-Setting Tips to Help You Keep Your New Year's Resolutions. Retrieved February 13, 2019, from https://www.creativelive.com/blog/effective-goal-setting-tips/
18. Markman, A. (2015). *Smart Change: Five Tools to Create New and Sustainable Habits in Yourself and Others.* New York: Perigee, p. 232
19. Ibid., p. 233
20. Clear, J. (2017). *Atomic Habits.* New York: Penguin Random House.
21. E-mail communication with James Clear, December 8, 2018
22. Clear's methods as described in this chapter come from his *Atomic Habits* book as well as an interview on June 25, 2018. A portion of that interview may be found at https://www.rogerdooley.com/james-clear-atomic-habits.
23. Clear, J. (2017). *Atomic Habits.* New York: Penguin Random House.
24. Dooley, R. (2015, July 27). Neurons That Fire Together Wire Together. Retrieved February 13, 2019, from https://www.neurosciencemarketing.com/blog/articles/neurons-fire-together.htm
25. Clear, J. (2017). *Atomic Habits.* New York: Penguin Random House. p. 156
26. Fogg, BJ. (2013, June 18) "By designing for laziness, you can stop or reduce a behavior." [tweet], https://twitter.com/bjfogg/status/347056224363220992?lang=en

### Chapter 14

1. Kessler D. Fat, Salt and Sugar Alter Brain Chemistry, Make Us Eat Junk Food. Retrieved July 27, 2018, from http://www.washingtonpost.com/wp-dyn/content/article/2009/04/26/AR2009042602711.html
2. Shapiro, E. (1992, May 08). The Media Business: Advertising; Crisper Chips, Fresh Slogans. Retrieved February 13, 2019, from https://www.nytimes.com/1992/05/08/business/the-media-business-advertising-crisper-chips-fresh-slogans.html

3. Meiselman, H. L., Hedderley, D., Staddon, S. L., Pierson, B. J., & Symonds, C. R. (1994). Effect of effort on meal selection and meal acceptability in a student cafeteria. *Appetite*, 23(1), 43-55.
4. Wansink, B., Painter, J. E., & Lee, Y. (2006, January 17). The office candy dish: Proximity's influence on estimated and actual consumption. Retrieved July 27, 2018, from https://www.nature.com/articles/0803217
5. Hunter, J. A., Hollands, G. J., Couturier, D. L., & Marteau, T. M. (2018). Effect of snack-food proximity on intake in general population samples with higher and lower cognitive resource. *Appetite*, 121, 337-347.
6. Rozin, P., Scott, S., Dingley, M., Urbanek, J. K., Jiang, H., & Kaltenbach, M. (2011). Nudge to Nobesity I: Minor Changes in Accessibility Decrease Food Intake. *Judgment and Decision Making*, 6 (4), 323-332.
7. Google's "Project M&Ms" improved employee's snacking habits, lives. (2013, September 4). Retrieved July 28, 2018, from https://nypost.com/2013/09/03/googles-project-mms-improved-employees-snacking-habits-lives/
8. Survey Reveals Employee Productivity Averages 2 Hours and 23 Minutes a Day. (n.d.). Retrieved July 29, 2018, from https://www.vouchercloud.com/resources/office-worker-productivity
9. Chance, Z., Dhar, R., Hatzis, M., & Bakker, M. (2016, March 4). How Google Optimized Healthy Office Snacks. Retrieved July 28, 2018, from https://hbr.org/2016/03/how-google-uses-behavioral-economics-to-make-its-employees-healthier
10. Kang, C. (2013, September 1). Google crunches data on munching in office. Retrieved July 28, 2018, from https://www.washingtonpost.com/business/technology/google-crunches-data-on-munching-in-office/2013/09/01/3902b444-0e83-11e3-85b6-d27422650fd5_story.html
11. Hempel, J. (2017, September 8). For Nextdoor, Eliminating Racism Is No Quick Fix | Backchannel. Retrieved November 17, 2018, from https://www.wired.com/2017/02/for-nextdoor-eliminating-racism-is-no-quick-fix/
12. Thompson, C. (2018, August 24). We Need Software to Help Us Slow Down, Not Speed Up. Retrieved November 17, 2018, from https://www.wired.com/story/software-to-help-us-slow-down-not-speed-up/
13. Adam, H., & Galinsky, A. (2012, February 21). Enclothed cognition. Retrieved August 26, 2018, from https://www.sciencedirect.com/science/article/pii/S0022103112000200
14. Dooley, R. (2014, July 16). Ep #14: Conversion Science with Brian Massey. Retrieved August 23, 2018, from http://www.rogerdooley.com/ep-14-brian-massey-conversion-scientist

## Chapter 15

1. Strauss, K. (2017, October 17). The 10 Universities with the Most Nobel Prize-Winning Work from 2000 to 2017. Retrieved February 13, 2019, from https://www.forbes.com/sites/karstenstrauss/2017/10/16/the-10-universities-with-the-most-nobel-prize-winning-work-from-2000-to-2017/

2. Walker, A. (2017, June 19). Chicago, Where Fun Comes to Die. Retrieved August 26, 2018, from https://www.newyorker.com/books/page-turner/chicago-where-fun-comes-to-die
3. Morse, J. (2007, August 16). Class of 2011 "reflects rich diversity of our nation." Retrieved February 13, 2019, from http://chronicle.uchicago.edu/070816/diversity.shtml
4. Class of 2022 Profile. (n.d.). Retrieved February 13, 2019, from https://collegeadmissions.uchicago.edu/apply/class-2022-profile
5. Levy, J. (2013, October 19). Getting In. Retrieved February 13, 2019, from http://www.personalcollegeadmissions.com/getting-in/the-great-success-of-the-university-of-chicago
6. Class of 2022 Profile. (n.d.). Retrieved February 13, 2019, from https://collegeadmissions.uchicago.edu/apply/class-2022-profile
7. The Best Colleges in America, Ranked. (n.d.). Retrieved February 13, 2019, from https://www.usnews.com/best-colleges /
8. Chris Foley's remarks and information about Indiana University's recruitment process comes from a phone conversation on May 2, 2018, and subsequent e-mail correspondence.
9. Ibid.

## Chapter 16

1. Angwin, J. (2006, November 13). Buttonless elevators have their ups and downs. Retrieved February 13, 2019, from https://www.post-gazette.com/business/tech-news/2006/11/14/Buttonless-elevators-have-their-ups-and-downs/stories/200611140144
2. Ibid.
3. Bernoff, J. (2016). *Writing Without Bullshit: Boost Your Career by Saying What You Mean*. New York: Harper Business.
4. Bernoff, J. (2018, May 22). Adobe acquires Magento to become "shoppable"—and maximally buzzword-compliant. Retrieved February 13, 2019, from https://withoutbullshit.com/blog/adobe-acquires-magento-to-become-shoppable-and-maximally-buzzword-compliantBernoff, Josh. Adobe acquires Magento to become "shoppable"—and maximally buzzword-compliant. Retrieved May 22, 2018, from https://withoutbullshit.com/blog/adobe-acquires-magento-to-become-shoppable-and-maximally-buzzword-compliant
5. Coffee, P. (2014, July 17). Study: Journalists Spend Less Than One Minute Reading Each Press Release. Retrieved February 13, 2019, from https://www.adweek.com/digital/study-journalists-spend-less-than-one-minute-reading-each-press-release/
6. Sugarman, J. (1999). *Triggers: 30 Ways to Control the Mind of Your Prospect to Motivate, Influence and Persuade*. Las Vegas, NV: DelStar, p. 9
7. Sugarman, J. (2012). *The Adweek Copywriting Handbook: The Ultimate Guide to Writing Powerful Advertising and Marketing Copy from One of America's Top Copywriters*. Hoboken, NJ: Wiley.

8. Zak, P. (2018, March 09). Dogs (and Cats) Can Love. Retrieved February 13, 2019, from https://www.theatlantic.com/health/archive/2014/04/does-your-dog-or-cat-actually-love-you/360784/
9. Zak, P. J. (2017). Trust Factor: The Science of Creating High-Performance Companies. United States of America: AMACOM, p. 4
10. Zak, P. J. (2016, December 19). The Neuroscience of Trust. Retrieved July 15, 2018, from https://hbr.org/2017/01/the-neuroscience-of-trust
11. Zak, P. J. (2017). Trust Factor: The Science of Creating High-Performance Companies. United States of America: AMACOM
12. Interview, Arre Zuurmond & Roger Dooley, September 28, 2016
13. Burkeman, O. (2012, July 15). Meet "Dr Love," the scientist exploring what makes people good or evil. Retrieved February 13, 2019, from https://www.theguardian.com/science/2012/jul/15/interview-dr-love-paul-zak
14. Ibid.
15. Rosembaum, L., & Shrank, W. H. (2013, August 22). Taking Our Medicine—Improving Adherence in the Accountability Era. Retrieved August 26, 2018, from https://www.nejm.org/doi/pdf/10.1056/NEJMp1307084
16. Patzer, R. E., et al. (2016, October 1). Medication understanding, non-adherence, and clinical outcomes among adult kidney transplant recipients. Retrieved August 26, 2018, from https://www.scholars.northwestern.edu/en/publications/medication-understanding-non-adherence-and-clinical-outcomes-amon-2
17. Nieuwlaat, R., et al. (2014, November). Interventions for enhancing medication adherence (Review). Retrieved August 26, 2018, from https://www.researchgate.net/publication/268513077_Interventions_for_enhancing_medication_adherence_Review
18. Manley, A. J., Lavender, T., & Smith, D. M. (2015, March). Processing fluency effects: Can the content and presentation of participant information sheets influence recruitment and participation for an antenatal intervention? Retrieved August 26, 2018, from https://www.pec-journal.com/article/S0738-3991(14)00478-9/abstract?rss=yes&code=pec-site
19. Dooley, R. (2014, August 13). Convince with Simple Fonts. Retrieved February 13, 2019, from https://www.neurosciencemarketing.com/blog/articles/simple-fonts.htm
20. Song, H., & Schwarz, N. (2010, February). If it's easy to read, it's easy to do, pretty, good, and true. Retrieved August 26, 2018, from http://www.rcgd.isr.umich.edu/news/schwarz_psychologist.Feb.2010.pdf
21. Ibid.
22. Song, H., & Schwarz, N. (2009). If It's Difficult to Pronounce, It Must Be Risky: Fluency, Familiarity, and Risk Perception. *Psychological Science*. 20. 135-8. 10.1111/j.1467-9280.2009.02267.x.
23. Alter, A. L., & Oppenheimer, D. M. (2006, June 13). Predicting short-term stock fluctuations by using processing fluency. Retrieved August 26, 2018, from http://www.pnas.org/content/103/24/9369/

## Conclusion

1. Gates, B., Myhrvold, N., & Rinearson, P. (1995). *The Road Ahead.* London: Viking.
2. Chapman, G. (1996, January 11). "Friction-Free" Economy Rhetoric Holds a Time Bomb. Retrieved July 16, 2018, from http://articles.latimes.com/1996-01-11/business/fi-23355_1_time-bomb
3. Lewis, T. G. (1998). *The Friction-Free Economy: Strategies for Success in a Wired World.* New York: HarperBusiness.
4. Ibid., p. 5
5. Koulopoulos, T. M., & Achillias, G. (2018). *Revealing the Invisible: How Our Hidden Behaviors Are Becoming the Most Valuable Commodity of the 21st Century.* New York: Post Hill Press.
6. Ibid.
7. Travis, N. (2018). *The Challenge Culture: Why the Most Successful Organizations Run on Pushback.* New York: PublicAffairs Books.

## Appendix

1. Fogg, B. (n.d.). BJ Fogg's Behavior Model. Retrieved February 13, 2019, from https://www.behaviormodel.org/
2. Dooley, R. (2016). *The Persuasion Slide—A New Way to Market to Your Customer's Conscious Needs and Unconscious Mind.* Austin, TX: Dooley Direct LLC.

# Index

# About the Author

**Roger Dooley** is an author and international keynote speaker known for practical business strategies based on science. He is the author of *Brainfluence* and creator of the popular blog *Neuromarketing*, the go-to blog of marketing professionals the world over. He hosts the *Brainfluence Podcast* and is a contributor at *Forbes*.

Dooley cofounded College Confidential, the leading website for college-bound students and parents. That business was acquired by Hobsons, a unit of United Kingdom–based DMGT, where Dooley served as Vice President, Digital Marketing. He spent years in direct marketing as the cofounder of a successful catalog firm. Before his entrepreneurial adventures, he was director of strategic planning for a Fortune 1000 company. Dooley earned an engineering degree at Carnegie Mellon University and an MBA at the University of Tennessee. He lives with his wife in Austin, Texas, where he's a big fan of breakfast tacos and Texas BBQ.